ROUTLEDGE LIBRARY EDITIONS:
WW2

Volume 12

HITLER'S FALL

HITLER'S FALL
The Newsreel Witness

Edited by
K.R.M. SHORT AND STEPHAN DOLEZEL

LONDON AND NEW YORK

First published in 1988 by Croom Helm Ltd

This edition first published in 2022
by Routledge
2 Park Square, Milton Park, Abingdon, Oxon OX14 4RN

and by Routledge
605 Third Avenue, New York, NY 10158

Routledge is an imprint of the Taylor & Francis Group, an informa business

© 1988 K.R.M. Short and S. Dolezel

All rights reserved. No part of this book may be reprinted or reproduced or utilised in any form or by any electronic, mechanical, or other means, now known or hereafter invented, including photocopying and recording, or in any information storage or retrieval system, without permission in writing from the publishers.

Trademark notice: Product or corporate names may be trademarks or registered trademarks, and are used only for identification and explanation without intent to infringe.

British Library Cataloguing in Publication Data
A catalogue record for this book is available from the British Library

ISBN: 978-1-03-201217-9 (Set)
ISBN: 978-1-00-319367-8 (Set) (ebk)
ISBN: 978-1-03-207615-7 (Volume 12) (hbk)
ISBN: 978-1-03-207621-8 (Volume 12) (pbk)
ISBN: 978-1-00-320794-8 (Volume 12) (ebk)

DOI: 10.4324/9781003207948

Publisher's Note
The publisher has gone to great lengths to ensure the quality of this reprint but points out that some imperfections in the original copies may be apparent.

Disclaimer
The publisher has made every effort to trace copyright holders and would welcome correspondence from those they have been unable to trace.

HITLER'S FALL
THE NEWSREEL WITNESS

Edited by
K.R.M. Short and Stephan Dolezel

CROOM HELM
London • New York • Sydney

© 1988 K.R.M. Short and S. Dolezel
Croom Helm Ltd, Provident House,
Burrell Row, Beckenham, Kent, BR3 1AT

Croom Helm Australia, 44–50 Waterloo Road,
North Ryde, 2113, New South Wales

Published in the USA by
Croom Helm
in association with Methuen, Inc.
29 West 35th Street,
New York, NY 10001

British Library Cataloguing in Publication Data

Hitler's fall: the newsreel witness.
 1. Newsreels — History 2. World War,
 1939–1945 — Campaigns — Western 3. World
 War, 1939–1945 — Campaigns — Eastern
 I. Short, K.R.M. II. Dolezel, S.
 791.43'53   D743.23
 ISBN 0–7099–4439–X

Library of Congress Cataloging-in-Publication Data
Hitler's fall.
   Published in the U.S. In association with Methuen, Inc.,
New York, N.Y.
   Includes index.
   1. World War, 1939-1945 — Germany. 2. Newsreels.
I. Short, K.R.M. (Kenneth R.M.) II. Dolezel, Stephen.
D757.H54   1988   943.086   87-20026
ISBN 0-7099-4439-X

Typeset by Photoprint, Torquay, Devon
Printed and bound in Great Britain
by Billings & Sons Limited, Worcester.

Dedicated to the founding members of the International Association for Audio-Visual Media in Historical Research and Education, Tutzing, Federal Republic of Germany, 1977.

Contents

Preface		ix
1.	American Newsreels and the Collapse of Nazi Germany *K.R.M. Short*	1
2.	Defeated Germany in British Newsreels: 1944–45 *Nicholas Pronay*	28
3.	Soviet Film Chronicles and the Fall of Nazi Germany *Sergei Drobashenko*	50
4.	The Red Army Beflags the Reichstag: Film as Historical Fantasy *Richard C. Raack*	57
5.	The Polish Newsreel in 1945: The Bitter Victory *Stanislaw Ozimek*	70
6.	Goebbels, Götterdämmerung, and the Deutsche Wochenschauen *David Welch*	80
7.	Swiss Newsreel — 1945 *Peter Gerdes*	100
8.	*Welt im Film*: Origins and Message *Heinrich Bodensieck*	119
9.	*Welt im Film* 1945 and the Re-education of Occupied Germany *Stephan Dolezel*	148
10.	The Problem of 'Authenticity' in the German Wartime Newsreels *Karl Stamm*	158
11.	Film as a Source of Historical Authenticity *Peter Bucher*	169
Notes on Contributors		184
Index		185

Preface

Over the past twenty or so years, international television has brought the events of the period 1930 to 1945 to the small screen again and again, as it will apparently continue to do in the future, clearly reflecting as well as nurturing the fascination of both producers and audiences with the origins, conduct and aftermath of the Second World War. Historical documentaries on television have evolved into a format which is a mix of participant interviews, event reconstruction, docudrama and newsreel material. However programme-makers would be seriously hampered if they were deprived of the material originally shot for contemporary newsreels. Traditionally that contemporary footage has provided television's visual impact for those events which now lie 40 or 50 years in the past and the advent of docudrama has only marginally diminished the importance of newsreel material. What television audiences seldom hear are the commentaries that their parents or grandparents heard at the time of the events, nor are they exposed to the complete newsreels which explicitly and implicitly testify to the concerns, prejudices and hopes of their forebears; television naïvely and effectively uses and misuses newsreel footage as an illustration for our own contemporary concerns and interpretation.

The Second World War in Europe had been recorded on film by military and commercial film cameramen from all of the belligerents but particularly by the United States of America, Great Britain and the Soviet Union and, naturally, Nazi Germany (needless to say, the last two did not have commercial cameramen). This enormously rich store of film material was shot at great personal risk by these cameramen, many of whom died in action along with the men whose battle lives they were recording. Their material was used for newsreels and documentary films, distinguished from one another by the comparative brevity and immediacy of the former and the length and interpretation of the latter. All of the material, regardless of country of origin, was subject to strict military and governmental censorship and was released to the respective home fronts to provide information on the course of the war; it was also intended to stiffen the resolve of the civilians, increase production, and calm anxiety concerning the future. Thus the film material was

Preface

subjected to a careful ideological reshaping which reflected not only the current military situation facing Germany or the Soviet Union, but also the propaganda line adopted by the government *vis à vis* current and future policy. The cameramen recorded on film the pathos and agony of war, some of which was never shown because it was considered to be dangerous to the cinema's primary role of maintaining high morale: thus death in its agony and horror, although recorded, was seldom shown in either newsreel or documentary unless it was that of the enemy, and even that was muted. Atrocities against friendly civilians were more likely to stiffen morale and thus were more frequently used.

This book provides a comparative approach for looking at the filmic witness of the final days of the Third Reich and the opening of that period often referred to as *Stunde Null*, Zero Hour; that moment in time when out of catastrophic destruction emerges a new Germany. Although historians today are more likely to stress continuity in German history, the moment of Nazi defeat was a watershed in European history. Brought together in this volume are articles by a group of international scholars, each dealing with the message of German defeat and chastened rebirth as it was presented to the peoples of the Soviet Union, the United States, Britain, Poland, Switzerland and Germany itself. However historians may argue about various nations' individual or corporate responsibility for the outbreak of war in Europe at the beginning of September 1939, there was not the slightest doubt in the minds of those Allied cameramen and newsreel editors who documented that conflict, or their audiences, that the war was in fact Hitler's war and the title of this book reflects that contemporary reality. On the other hand it must be recognised that major changes had taken place in the German perception of the war when the continuous triumphs following Warsaw turned to tragedy after Stalingrad.

It must be understood that access to the newsreel material of the United States, Britain or Nazi Germany is almost unrestricted in comparison to that of the Soviet Union. Whereas we are able to present critical analyses based on comprehensive study of the key themes presented in the newsreels of the Western Allied and Axis nations, we do not have that sort of access to Moscow's view of the end of the Great Patriotic War, and it is not possible to present a detailed record of Soviet newsreel reporting in the last weeks of the war. Our research therefore has to depend on the less satisfactory reconstruction of Soviet attitudes through the use

Preface

of their contemporary documentary treatment of those events; one article has been written by a Western scholar and the other, very impressionistic in comparison, by a Soviet academic. The lack of access to Soviet end-of-war newsreels is less a problem than it might seem at first, since the very nature of the Soviet propaganda machinery ensured that the message of the newsreels would be compatible with that of the war documentaries which accompanied them in the theatre programmes. Soviet newsreels had been available to their Western Allies from mid-1941 up to the beginning of 1945 and then the Soviet government, apparently confident that the war was now won and Western 'approval' was now unnecessary, decided to end the shipments of material which had been crucial for the Western newsreel interpretation of the war on the Eastern front. Thus the important collection of London's Imperial War Museum cannot help us to document the treatment of the war in March, April and May 1945 from the Soviet perspective. Hopefully, continued development of *glasnost'* on a scholarly level will bring about the opportunity to overcome this restriction.

We have one essay each dealing with the newsreels of the United States, Britain and Nazi Germany, with an additional paper investigating the important issue of authenticity in the *Deutsche Wochenschau* (German newsreel). These articles do not simply discuss the important end-of-war newsreels but set them in the context of the national newsreel's operation and impact throughout the conflict, which explains the brevity of this introduction. Furthermore there is an essay on the newsreels of Switzerland, whose neutrality had to be as carefully guarded as its domestic and foreign policy. Adding to this comprehensiveness is an article on the badly broken history of the Polish newsreels, a history that had only a brief moment at the beginning of the war and reappeared again as the battle lines rolled westwards. The book's title, *Hitler's Fall: The Newsreel Witness*, should not be so narrowly understood as to suggest that the book ends with Hitler's death and that of his entourage in Berlin, for our definition takes the study further. From the German perspective it is important to identify the key themes and the important usage of the Allied Occupation force's newsreel *Welt im Film* in the process of reinterpreting the war's reality for the German people. Thus there is an essay on the newsreel's origins and policy and a further essay on its implementation. Finally, a leading German archivist examines the importance of

Preface

film as a source of historical authenticity as seen from the perspective of contemporary German scholarship.

All of the essays in this collection, with the exception of David Welch's study of 'Goebbels, Götterdämmerung, and the Deutsche Wochenschauen', were either given as papers or derived from presentations given at the Institut für Wissenschaftlichen und Film (IWF), Göttingen, in August 1985. It had been hoped that this volume would have appeared sooner but unexpected complications over rewriting and translation produced some regrettable delays in production of this final manuscript. The occasion for the presentation of these papers was the bi-annual Congress of the International Association for Audio-Visual Media in Historical Research and Education (IAMHIST). The editors wish to thank the officers of the Association and the IWF organisers, particularly the staff of Dr Stephan Dolezel, for the exceptional opportunity to study the problems of *Stunde Null* in such a stimulating atmosphere. It is also essential to record the financial support of the Association and of the Deutsche Forschungsgemeinschaft which made the Congress possible. Furthermore appreciation is due to the Goethe-Institut, London, and its Film and Press Officer, Frau Helga Rulf, for the sponsorship of three lectures on the newsreel documentation of the fall of the Third Reich on the occasion of its 50th Anniversary; the papers given by Dr Short, Mr Pronay, and Dr Dolezel benefited from that initial opportunity of presenting their findings. Hannelore Spinner provided the translation of some sections of the German text, while Dr Sarah Street contributed towards the creation of a more readable English text, oversaw proof-correction and prepared the index. Finally, the editors would like to thank Professor Raymond Fielding, Director of the School of Communications of the University of Houston, for his encouragement and critical advice regarding this volume. Needless to say, he is not responsible for our errors.

K.R.M. Short
Oxford

1
American Newsreels and the Collapse of Nazi Germany

K.R.M. Short

Americans kept up with the news of the Second World War by listening to the news programmes and nightly news commentators on the radio, supplemented by reading the daily newspapers and the weekly magazines. The movies also made an important contribution to war information through the war reporting of the five major newsreel companies, Fox Movietone, Pathe News, News of the Day, Paramount News and Universal Newsreels. Four of them were part of the entertainment industry as a subsidiary of a major Hollywood studio, such as RKO which controlled Pathe. The fifth newsreel, News of the Day, although released by MGM, was owned principally by the Hearst Corporation, a major force in newspapers and syndicated news.

Although the newsreels maintained coverage of events through their twice-weekly releases (Tuesday and Thursday, except News of the Day which went out on Wednesday and Friday) the political reporting, used in its widest sense, seldom constituted more than 1.5 to 2 minutes of the 8–10 minute newsreel. This was not unexpected, for the average movie patron was thought by the newsreel companies to be more interested in sporting events, led by baseball, horse racing, and major college football games, in bathing beauties (especially the Miss America contest), major fires, train wrecks, plane crashes and, of course, in animals and babies, preferably together. Additionally, there were filmed reports which took the moviegoer to faraway and exotic places; entertainment was what the newsreels were primarily concerned with and as a supplement to the featured film on the cinema programme.[1]

As war broke out the informational and propaganda potentials of the United States' newsreels were recognised and plans were developed by the newly created (1942) Office of War Information (OWI) to exploit the potential. During the next four years, the New York-based newsreels faced serious limitations due to the American government's prior censorship of film material relating to the conflict. Virtually all of the foreign film footage came through US military censorship, except for important material sent by the British Ministry of Information through the OWI. British sources were particularly important in the early months of the war. War footage was shot by cameramen of the War Department (Army) and the Navy Department, in addition to cameramen provided by the newsreel companies themselves.

Each newsreel company contributed two cameramen for a pool to be operated in the European and Pacific theatres of operations. Fox Movietone, The March of Time (a monthly film 'magazine'), and The News of the Day also set up schools for the training of the military combat cameramen. The film material shot by the military and the 'pool' cameramen was priority airlifted, along with their dope sheets or log books identifying the events photographed, to the processing and censorship divisions of the army and navy. The material was then edited, commentary or script provided, and then distributed to the newsreel companies for their use. The film material was only released for newsreel use after military intelligence had determined that it contained no information of possible use to the enemy; the assumption being that there were Axis spies in American movie theatres.

The pool cameramen maintained their corporate identity and their dope sheets were distributed on the letterhead of their company. Thus in the Universal production files in which the source material is retained from each newsreel issue one finds the dope sheets from the Paramount and News of the Day cameramen, in addition to Universal reports. The Official US Army Signal Corps releases normally had full scripts to accompany the released footage, while the Navy Department was more inclined to provide informative notes, assuming perhaps that the newsreels would rephrase anything suggested. The newsreel companies also received material from the National Film Board of Canada/Canadian Army Film and Photo Unit. It is interesting to see how the locations and units mentioned in the confidential prints from the Army Pictorial Service Laboratories were simply cut out before being released to the newsreel editors. The editors and commentary writers also made use of government and business press releases and the front pages of New York's major newspapers in deciding what news was going on the silver screen. The War and Navy Department released their material directly to the newsreel companies with the News of the Day passing the material on down an established line, and after the 36-hour limit for circulation the material would have reached the OWI, The March of Time, and ended up with NBC Television. The final destination is curious since NBC Television, WNBT in New York, was forced to end its 'experimental' broadcasting in response to wartime needs, along with other stations, during 1942.[2]

It is important to recognise that individual newsreel releases were never submitted to formal censorship; rather the control of relevant film material by military pre-censorship combined with OWI's continued 'guidance', albeit advisory, ensured the requisite conformity to the nation's defined information and morale needs. The content of the newsreels was closely monitored by the Library of Congress Film Project, a covert OWI operation funded by the Rockefeller Foundation. Had any newsreel deviated from the standards of approved reporting there is little doubt that formal censorship would have been imposed, constitutional guarantees for freedom of the press notwithstanding. Despite this process of control and distribution, the newsreels nevertheless maintained their own unmistakable identities and never approached being mere reflections of each other. It has been claimed that the newsreel cameramen photographed only 20 percent of the total combat footage. Be that as it may, it would be interesting to calculate what percentage was actually used in the newsreels themselves. The domination of the released material by military cameramen had led to complaints against the overzealous military censors. Walton Ament, editor of RKO Pathe, wrote to Elmer Davis, chief of the OWI, on 14 July 1942, asking for his help in unfreezing the military censorship. Ament pointed out that the bulk of the coverage for the global conflict came from military cameramen who produced unusable material. The only 'half-way decent pictures' came through the British Ministry of Information. This was coupled with the complaint that the commercial cameramen from the pool were kept behind the lines while the military cameramen were allowed to shoot the real war — unfortunately they failed to do so, according to Ament.[3]

The treatment by the newsreels of the collapse of Nazi Germany is a useful means of assessing the limitations of this news medium, as well as making some effort to assess its role in informing the American public about the defeat of the Nazi state. Universal Newsreels are particularly important in this research because they are in public access at the National Archives in Washington DC.

The American view of Germany in the years immediately preceding entry into the war was conditioned largely by the newsreels' depiction of Nazi Germany and its leadership, using material either derived from the Nazi Propaganda Ministry or from their own cameramen operating in Germany under its stringent censorship restrictions. Either way the images of the new Germany were controlled by its masters. However, American newsreel editors were relatively unfettered because they could and did interpret for the viewer a far less laudatory view of Germany via the words and intonation of the commentary, as well as through the juxtapositioning of the 'approved' images. Perhaps even more important for the building of the moviegoer's image of the Third Reich was the role of the feature films which followed the newsreel, films which more and more provided brutal sadistic Gestapo faces such as those evident in the semi-documentary March of Time's *Inside Nazi Germany* (1938) and Warner Brothers' *Confessions of a Nazi Spy* (1939). The faces of George Sanders and that refugee from Nazi tyranny, Conrad Veit, became the suave sadistic images, rather than the earlier coarse personification of the Nazi evil genius. Relatively few good Germans were to be found in Hollywood feature films.[4]

The newsreels had earlier been faced with a major problem in December 1941 when the United States' entry into the war ended access to German material. To some extent this was compensated for by the 'mining' of sequences and images from such famous Nazi documentary films as *Triumph of the Will*, *Baptism by Fire*, and *Victory in the West*. This relative famine continued until the Allied counterattack provided a source of Nazi newsreels, as the frontline cinemas of the *Wehrmacht* and *Waffen SS* were overrun. This captured newsfilm was subjected first to decanting by military intelligence before being released to the home front newsreels for its potential propaganda value. Newsreel documentation of the collapse of Nazi Germany continued in the late autumn and early winter of 1944. At the beginning of December the newsreels' main story involved the July bomb plot against Hitler. Captured German footage was incorporated in the five newsreels showing the badly damaged bunker (Paramount Newsreel no. 29 mistakenly identified the location as Berchtesgaden, Hitler's mountain retreat). Hitler salutes and shakes hands with his left hand, keeping his injured right arm hidden under his cloak, while greeting the deposed Italian *Duce*, Mussolini. All five newsreels, although showing slightly different clips from the material released to them by the military censors, offered essentially the same interpretation, while speculating on whether Hitler was dead or insane; who was now in charge of Germany — Himmler of the SS?[5]

Nazi newsreel material was highly valued for its images, and propaganda commentary was useful for ridiculing its pretentiousness or to expose its distortions. What was required was to convert the images to American uses and this is neatly illustrated in the News of the Day issue (vol. 16, no. 228, dated 11 December 1944 — Library of Congress Project transcript). The commentary leaves little to the imagination.

Captured Films Made Behind Nazi Lines (title)

This is Fortress Germany digging in for Hitler's last stand. Men and women in labor battalions rounded up by the Gestapo, literally digging for their lives. Behind the present battle lines stretches a vast system of trenches. These captured films, officially released by our War Department, were designed to make Germans feel secure and bolster their morale.

Teenagers of the Hitler Youth reinforce labor battalions... Indoctrinated with Hitler ideology since babyhood, these youngsters boast they're fanatical Nazis.

Doctor Goebbels keeps up a ceaseless war of words, while Foreign Minister von Ribbentrop fights to keep what allies he still has left.

New recruits! Hitler may be scraping the bottom of the manpower barrel; many of these men may have since died, but there are still millions left.

German films of fighting in France... The propaganda line goes: 'Withdrawing according to prepared plan'.

Field Marshal von Kruger, one of the Junker Generals in whom the Germans are urged to put their faith, ... as they have in the rocket-gun that Goebbels advertises as the weapon to win the war.

Rockets in the night... Nazi propaganda goes all out on

this kind of weapon, showing the people everything they've got.

American prisoners in Germany . . . Picture propaganda to offset the news from the war fronts. Well, their spirit is a lot stronger than the Germans' . . . they know the Nazis fight a losing battle and they also know we have not forgotten them.

One prominent and important theme evident in the above commentary and footage is the final sequence concerning American prisoners in German hands. The direct emotional appeal of 'we have not forgotten them' is a familiar element in the newsreels as they fought to combat home front apathy. This can be seen again and again in references to the fighting man in the trenches or the wounded and dead; it was essential for Americans to produce the armaments and munitions necessary to win the war and 'bring the boys home'. The theme is carefully orchestrated and doubtless is a reflection of an Office of War Information directive.

As distinct from television coverage of the several wars fought during our 'forty years of peace in Europe', Second World War newsreels lack immediacy and the ability to portray what was actually going on along the various combat fronts. In fact, the movie audiences were going to have to wait for the official documentaries, like the British *Desert Victory* and the Anglo-American productions *Tunisian Victory* and *The True Glory*, in order to see something of the reality of the European war. The newsreels had to make do with what they were given and much of the time it was a matter of making 'bricks without straw' and stories without film footage: Christmas 1944 is an excellent example of the newsreel's problem and takes us another step closer to the collapse and defeat of the Nazi war machine.

The Battle of the Bulge or the Ardennes Offensive made it clear to the Allied military command that the defeat of the Nazi armies in the west was not 'just around the corner' as some commentators were speculating. The tremendous and totally unexpected Nazi counterattack had begun before dawn on 16 December; Eisenhower did not move his strategic reserves into the front lines until the following day. There was a total news blackout until Wednesday 20 December and then a 48-hour time lag in news came into effect, and even then the information was highly censored. On 28 December the time lag was cut to 36 hours and that was 24 hours after Model's Army Group B, exhausted in every way and under tremendous air attack, began to be forced back towards the Rhine. There was some news for the newspapers and the radio but there was no film, and the biggest story since D-Day and Arnhem had to be responded to in some fashion by the newsreels. The respective editors threw in library film and recently released Deutsche Wochenschau footage in an attempt to make up for the deficit. The material from the War Department illustrated the increased level of German mobilisation — what the News of the Day, 20–21 December headlined *Captured Nazi Films Show All Out Effort* (vol.16, no.231) — and Pathe announced that Germany had *New Measures for Total War*. Significantly the mobilisation is presented from the vantage of September (when the footage appears to have been shot) and as a genuine threat to the Allied advance. The Pathe commentary (vol.16, no.36) ran as follows:

> The night clubs close — even the Berlin State Theater. More and more German men and women are called up for war jobs. These Nazi-photographed pictures were deliberately made for their own propaganda purposes. But they can't be laughed off by Americans. German war production is still great.
> Shortage of fuel hampers German trucking. The problem is eased by hitching lines of trucks to streetcars, and making regular deliveries through Berlin. A typical example of German ingenuity under war conditions. The sign [*on the tram*] says 'Special Trip'.

The same material also appears in Universal Newsreel's (vol.17, no.357) *The Nazi Counter Offensive*; however its commentary is not quite so informative or precise in its identification of the several scenes. The five newsreels used virtually the same material for all of their stories in the first issue after Christmas. Just at the moment that the Nazi thrust had been broken, the newsreels were trying to catch up with the event of the Ardennes Offensive, one of the great Allied miscalculations of the war. It was also to be seen as a tragedy from the German perspective, as the commander of the 5th PZ (Panzer) Army, Hasso von Manteuffel, saw that it brought 'bankruptcy' for Germany, a point of view endorsed by von Rundstedt, who said it was 'Stalingrad Number Two'.[6] Had the film material been there, the newsreels would have gladly given all of their eight or so minutes to the report of the battle, but lacking film the newsreels had to use a story of US Army Air Corps planes using rockets to destroy tanks (a demonstration, not combat footage), an advertisement for volunteers to crew the US Maritime Service's merchant ships, and a seasonal story featuring the children of Washington's United Nations diplomats wishing Americans a 'Merry Christmas'. The emphasis in this story on Mexican and Cuban children was consistent with the State Department's policy of encouraging America's 'Good Neighbor Policy' relationship towards Latin America. The relative lengths of the stories gives a clear indication of the editor's (in this instance, the Universal Newsreel editor) view of their importance as entertainment and news. The Universal Newsreel devoted 55 seconds each to the stories of the rocket-firing planes and the merchant marine, 1 minute and 50 seconds to the Christmas message, and the remainder of the newsreel, almost four minutes in length, is devoted to the main story *Allies Fight Nazi Counterblow*.

Within the main story's commentary there are two interesting points of interpretation: the assertion that 'everything (in Germany) was subordinated to the grim bid for a negotiated peace', and the American desire to 'wish' Hitler away in the claim that the Ardennes counterthrust was under the direction of the German General Staff, rather than Hitler. In retrospect, it is clear that Hitler did conceive and order the offensive, along with the crippling 'no withdrawal' policy. Newsreel estimates of the German strength were on the low side with 15 divisions and 600 tanks rather than the 20 divisions and 1,000 tanks that were eventually to see action. It should not be surprising that such estimates would require later revision but it is an indication that military censorship was not going to minimise the threat of the offensive. On Thursday–Friday 28–29 December Universal Newsreel, along with the other reels (vol.18, no.360: soundtrack lost) identified General Sepp Dietrich of the 6th SS PZ Army as a key figure in the offensive, while announcing that the Nazi attack had stalled as the weather cleared and the Allied air forces went into action.

Coverage of Germany continued sporadically, mostly film shot from behind the advancing Allied armies. However, in late April the Universal Newsreel issue sheet was able to announce *Germany in Ruins!* (vol.18, no.392, 23–24 April 1945). This newsreel issue was a slightly extended edition with the main story of the

European war broken into three sections with a running time of 7 minutes and 16 seconds. The opening story of the newsreel, lasting 42 seconds, dealt with the arrival of Soviet Foreign Minister Molotov in Washington 'at the direct invitation of President Truman'. Molotov was shown with Anthony Eden of Great Britain and the newly appointed US Secretary of State, Edward Stettinius. This diplomatic story was followed by a typical pair of *Aviation in the News* items, one of which was a curious story about testing a gigantic aeroplane tyre which could not have been fitted to any aircraft in service, as the comparison with a B-17 tyre indicated. The second half of the story concerned the last B-17 Flying Fortress bomber to come off the Boeing assembly line in Seattle, Washington, before an audience of 30,000 employees who were now to devote their efforts fully to the building of the B-29 Superfortress, an example of which stood on the tarmac in the background. The story (both items) ran 1 minute and 35 seconds. The main story ran behind the title *In the Wake of War in Germany* and documented the devastation of Duisburg, Limbourg, Osnabruck and Munster (identified on the issue sheet). The issue sheet advertised that:

> The streets are filled with hills of broken buildings and wreckage. Mayors try to rally their citizens. The pathetic Volksturm (sic) — the Home Guard — surrenders, to join the thousands of combat troops previously captured. Frantic, hungry civilians break into ruined stores and stalled trains to steal food and clothing.

One of the sequences slowly tracks along a devastated street following the boots of an American soldier as he moves along a pavement strewn with German dead. Then the newsreel reported that as the Yanks arrived, the German civilians gathered 'to wonder at the fate which awaits a conquered nation'. It is interesting to speculate where the American troops were when 'German morale' breaks down and the shots of looting were taken by Signal Corps cameramen. Pointing out the contribution made by the commercial newsreel companies, the commentary reported that the pictures showing the drive on Berlin were shot by newsreel cameramen. Typical of the sort of human interest shots that the newsreels specialised in was a wrecked train carrying scrap metal. The cameraman recruited two teenage girls to collect men's and women's hats from the train's wreckage, while mugging for the camera.[7] From this briefly lighthearted episode the second section of the war report moved on to graveyards holding the remains of 30,000 Russian prisoners, followed by additional evidence of German atrocities. Slave labourers, men and women, are shown on release from the concentration camps. Much of the material was clearly staged, suggesting that the cameramen were not with the advancing units which liberated the camps. The story also illustrated the suffering of a group of female slave munition workers, showing in close-up the tattooed numbers on their arms, and their smashed and mutilated fingers. The story then cut to the pathos of carefully composed shots of French women expecting the return of their loved ones. Emotional scenes at the railway stations are shown while the commentary noted that these 'pitiful family meetings' were 'reminders of the devastation and horror visited upon the world by the Axis'.

In a typical development, the newsreel had moved from the news in Washington to aviation items and then on to the devastation and suffering of Germany, a Germany which held both Germans and captives alike. In order to achieve an uplifting effect before the featured movie came on the screen the editor closed this deeply depressing section of the newsreel with a promise of the world to come. The opening section of this part of the German defeat story dealt with Heidelberg University. The castle at Heidelberg is shown, visited by smiling American troops, but a 'modernistic building' of the university is singled out to illustrate the importance of pre-Nazi German culture. Heidelberg University had been a centre of learning of international reputation attracting both American scholars and financial support. It may have been that one of the war correspondents had studied there before the war and thus knew that the building had been built with American donations. The newsreel cameraman shot footage of the recently uncovered dedication plaque which had been removed from the building by the Nazis. Where it had been hidden and why it had not been destroyed is left to your imagination. Heidelberg is described by the commentary as 'once a great centre of German culture. The university attracted the patronage of wealthy Americans who contributed this building, captioned "to the German Spirit" by the Nazis.[8] American reporters uncovered the plaque which the Nazis had removed listing the donors, names familiar to all Americans.' The names on the plaque included such famous philanthropists as

John D. Rockefeller Jr, as well as many Jewish figures including Nicholas M. Schenck of MGM and H.M. Warner of Warner Brothers. The lasting image was that of the close-up of the name of Adolph Zukor, former president of Paramount Pictures. The motion picture industry could never resist self-promotion and it is quite likely that the footage was shot by a Paramount cameraman. The commentary continued: 'It was progressive Americans who helped maintain Heidelberg, just to have Nazi Supermen grind culture under their heels.' The war correspondents found the opportunity to make a statement about German culture, a culture that could be revived at Heidelberg and elsewhere so long as the Allied Occupation destroyed militarism.

Finally, the mood was manipulated most effectively with scenes of the smashed bridges of the Rhine at Koblenz; American troops maintained a 'Watch on the Rhine' which was going to extend this time to policing Germany until 'militarism was stamped out'. The occupation of Germany was given forceful images by the filming of General Omar Bradley and General George Patton attending flag-raising ceremonies at Ehrenbreitstein Castle. Americans were promised that the mistakes of the First World War would not be repeated: Germany would be Occupied until militarism was eradicated from the German soul, reflecting the widely held view that, Nazism apart, Prussianism or Junkerism was a fatal flaw in the German character. The commentary ended with: 'The Stars and Stripes fly in victory over conquered German soil'.

Within a matter of two weeks the war in Europe would have ended and the assurance that the 'Watch on the Rhine' would be maintained became a matter of secondary interest for the newsreels. What dominated the bi-weekly issues which followed in mid-May was naturally the war in the Pacific and the eventual surrender of Japan. The preoccupation with the Pacific theatre had been established very early on, with footage of fighting in that theatre featuring American forces long before the invasion of North Africa, much less the opening of the Second Front with Operation Torch on D-Day. However the Universal Newsreel of 26 April (vol.18, no.393) featured, along with the opening of the San Francisco Conference of the 46 United Nations, the horrifying footage of the liberated concentration camps. Under the title of *Nazi Atrocities*, theatre managers were told by the issue sheet that the newsreel would (and did) contain 'Real-life horror pictures revealing the unbelievable atrocities committed by the

Nazis in their murder camps'. Footage from Nordhausen, Buchenwald, Camp Ohrdur, Hadamar and Grasleben provided the evidence of Nazi brutality ranging from the 21,000 prisoners that survived — in manner of speaking — Buchenwald, in addition to maltreated 'Yanks' captured in the Battle of the Bulge.

Universal's release for 8 May (vol.18, no.396), *War Ends in Europe — President Proclaims V-E Day*, took the opportunity to recount rapidly the march of 'militant Germany' from Austria to Moscow, in the skies over London, and then America's entry into the war via Lend-Lease. Then came the attack on Pearl Harbour which 'precipitates America into the global conflicts. From that time [Lend-Lease] on, German power spirals downward.' The reel ended as 'New York millions celebrate in the canyons of Wall Street' and 'the playground of the world — Times Square'. Two days later, on 10 May, Universal (vol.18, no.397) showed *Germany in Ruins*, with aerial views of Leipzig and footage vividly illustrating the extent of the destruction of Magdeburg and Nuremberg: the latter city, 'once the seat of Nazi culture, is now a dead city'. It was, as the newsreel suggested, 'The Funeral Pyre of Nazidom'. The commentary proclaimed:

> Germany's cities lie in ruins, the hopes of the Nazis lie in the dust. The gutted buildings of the Reich reveal the irresistible power behind the Allied drive; a power that all the vaunted Wehrmacht could not stop. Bismark's statue frowns down upon the shattered wreckage of a Krupp munitions plant, one of the many furnishing tools of war for the Blitzkrieg, Hitler's fast-paced warfare that was stopped cold and flung back in his face as were these tanks that never left the assembly line.
>
> Nuremberg in southern Germany, the heart-fed shrine city of Nazidom was overrun by the victorious Yanks. Of all the enemy's leveled cities, none reflects greater destruction than Nuremberg, where the Allied attack poured its full fury upon the spawning grounds of the Nazis.
>
> [*Cut to Nazi eagle*] The haughty German Eagle looks down on German dead lying still in defeat. Over the vast stadium Old Glory overshadows one of the world's most hated symbols. Here, where once thousands of Swastikas flew above the goose-stepping troops parading for the strutting

Führer and where he ranted to the assembled thousands, the troops Hitler once laughed at take over. The Swastika will no longer flaunt its crooked arms above the Nazi shrine. [*An enormous US flag was raised to cover the giant Swastika behind the speaker's stand at the Nuremberg stadium — later, with the flag removed, the Swastika was blown up.*]

With the situation well in hand, the Yanks stage a review. Newsreel and Signal Corps cameramen made this record of the last days of Hitler's Germany. The cleansing fires of war have purged Germany of Nazi power. Let's be sure it never again rises from her ashes.

The Universal commentary concealed the price paid for the newsreel footage of the battle for Nuremberg, a price revealed on the Paramount News caption sheet contained in the production file. Paramount cameraman Lewis S. Cass noted that he saw MGM News of the Day cameraman Gaston Madru dead in the ruins after the attack on the Volkerschlacht Denkmal. Madru was not the first newsreel cameraman to die in Europe but he was probably the last. Perhaps what best signalled the victory in Europe was that the US Capitol's dome in Washington DC was once again illuminated, as was the Statue of Liberty in New York harbour. Furthermore the lights went on in Times Square and on Broadway: 'B'way is the "White Way" again' announced the newsreel.[9] American interest was now focused on the war with Japan and the current attack on Okinawa: a B-29 from the Boeing Seattle plant is marked with 'On to Tokyo'.

The Universal issue of 17 May (vol.18, no.399) carried the pictures of the formal surrender of Germany, as well as pictures of the gutted cities of Hamburg and Berlin. American troops are shown with the Reichsbank cache discovered in the salt mines at Merkers. There was also a story on the release of famous prisoners found at a 'villa in the Alps', which included Baroness Schussning, Fritz Thyssen, and Martin Niemoeller. Successive newsreels in June carried stories of the capture of Goering, von Runstedt, Kesselring, and the continued search for Hitler. All of the newsreels reported on the setting up of the Allied Four Power Control Commission in Berlin and of thousands of vacationing GIs swarming over Berchtesgaden. It is not until 2 August (Universal vol.18, no.421) that American audiences would see the ruins of Hitler's Chancellery and the burnt-out bunker where Hitler's 'charred corpse is supposed to have been found, together with that of Eva Braun, his legalised wife', as the issue sheet put it.

On 9 August came the newsreels' coverage of the atomic bomb, and there must have been a rush to the movie theatres to see that unbelievable event since, lacking television, people had no other means of witnessing it. The coverage of Germany throughout the remainder of 1945 is extremely limited, as a listing of Universal Newsreel stories indicates:

16 August (vol.18, no.425):
Berlin Frolics. GIs do a land office business in selling scarce commodities to Russian soldiers and Berliners. And when fraternisation is permitted, they really do fraternise with the lonely frauleins.

4 October (vol.18, no.439):
The Belsen Horror Trial. The Beasts of Belsen — the men and women who tortured and killed thousands of helpless prisoners in their horror camp, are brought to trial by the British in Luneberg, Germany. They calmly sit in their trial stalls, awaiting their inevitable fate.

11 October (vol.18, no.441):
Nazi Criminal Trial, Nuremberg. Those arch-criminals among Nazi war-lords (Goering, von Ribbentrop, Doenitz, Seiss-Inquart, von Papen, Streicher, etc.) prepare to face an Allied court to answer for their war crimes.

By October you could see that the newsreels of America were back in the entertainment business, having left the war information responsibility behind. The issue which reported the Nuremberg Trial was headlined by the victory of the Detroit Tigers in baseball's World Series. Additionally, audiences saw President Truman dedicating a new TVA (Tennessee Valley Authority) dam, the Cowboy Rodeo at Madison Square Garden, New York, New York's ticker-tape reception of the Pacific's naval commander Admiral Chester Nimitz, dancing in the streets of Manhattan, and finally the story of an ex-Army flier who was the only male student at New England's Smith College — he loved it!

Another trial story, this time at Dachau, appeared in 22 October's issue but it was not until 8 November (Universal Newsreel vol.18, no.449) that at least one of the newsreels briefly reported on what the German population would face that winter.

Universal's issue sheet warned:

> Berlin Prepares for Winter. The capital of Germany presents a desolate sight as the people clean up debris the best they can and lay in firewood for what is expected to be a cold and hungry winter.

The commentary expanded on this:

> Berlin, the ghost of a once great city, bears its gaping wounds to the sky. A city upon which has fallen the full force of retribution, and from the rubble and debris a beaten people digs its way out like frantic moles. In the struggle for survival, every hand is turned to the task of salvage. But the most crying need in gas-less and coal-less Berlin is fuel as the spectre of winter looms. Every available stick of wood is garnered against the bitter months ahead. Charcoal burners go full blast to supply cooking fuel. The small supply of bricket coal is strictly rationed to women with children.
>
> But life goes on. [*At this point a man is filmed riding an enormous penny-farthing-style three wheel bicycle, pulling a small trailer bearing an advertisement.*] A Sandwich man still has a job, and kids rush from an underground school as usual. But dark days face the children of the master race.

The newsreel does not credit the source of the material for this Berlin report; however the production file indicates that most of the film had come from the British Government's Information Service in New York, distributed through the Hamilton Wright Organization at Rockefeller Center. The continuity and commentary shows that the footage was shot within the British sector of West Berlin and suggests the concern that the British were feeling for the enormous responsibility of caring for the German population now surrounded by the Russian Occupation zone. Aerial views of the devastated city by Georges Mejat of Movietone News suggests that the newsreel pool arrangements were still in operation.

On 15 November, Universal (vol.18, no.451) featured a GI chorus singing on a Rhine cruise, as well as sounding the first and only humanitarian note with a story about thousands of German children, faced with 'near starvation this coming winter', being transported by the British to winter homes in the country where they could be 'better sheltered and fed'. The 29 November Universal issue (vol.18, no.455) reported on the Nuremberg War Crimes Trial, the execution of German spies and the hanging of five Germans convicted of murdering six American flyers who had crashed near Bruchsal. The year's final item relating to Germany appeared on 6 December with a special report on news coverage of the Nuremberg Trial, as well as the systematic destruction of the I.G. Farben nitroglycerine plant at Ebenhausen: 'This is part of a systematic Allied Campaign to destroy every vestige of factories used for war.' (Issue sheet, Universal vol.18, no.457.)

To the extent that Universal Newsreels were typical, it can be seen that American cinema audiences, which totalled a weekly 95 million admissions in 1944 with an audience of perhaps 20–25 millions, gained little appreciation of the desperate situation in Germany up to the end of 1945. The American newsreels were not going to seek sympathy for the defeated enemy, it was not going to be another human interest story; rather the newsreels stressed the war crimes committed by the Nazis and the destruction of the German armaments industry: the images are destruction and retribution. Judged on the two items with British sources it may be that the British newsreels were far more sympathetic to the problems of defeated Germany's civilian population than their American counterparts. Certainly in American newsreels there was neither talk nor implication of a re-educated Germany, apart from that exceptional issue of 22 April featuring Heidelberg University. Even in this instance pre-Nazi German culture was paired with the American soldier keeping 'Watch on the Rhine' until Prussian militarism was destroyed. By the end of 1945 the newsreels had gone back to entertainment, just as the nation had returned to peace. For almost four years the five newsreels had responded as best they could to the needs of the American war effort, chafing continually under the enormous restrictions imposed by military censorship, restrictions which, for example, would deny them footage to cover the Battle of the Bulge. Newsreel credibility must have suffered as the terrible weather conditions of the Ardennes reported in the newspapers and on the radio were contrasted with the weather which formed the background to the newsreels' library and German material.

In the final analysis the American newsreels did the very best that they could in informing the American people about the progress of the war, while continually stressing the importance of home front commitment and morale in achieving victory. It would have been easier to be complacent in 1942–5 if you did not go to the movies, for the newsreels provided the visual impact of the war's horrors, even with the highly censored material which excluded American dead. Here was a view of the world conveyed with an impact unavailable to home front America in the rest of the media, even in the great photo-journal magazines *Life* and *Look*. Perhaps this was indeed the newsreel's finest hour.

Notes

1. As Raymond Fielding points out in a personal observation to the author, there was no attempt by the newsreel editors to determine exactly what the theatre patrons desired to see in the newsreels. However, the theatre managers were convinced that as the grass roots representatives of the movie industry they were pre-eminently qualified to tell Hollywood what it took to fill their seats. I know of no documented complaints about newsreel contents; if there was dissatisfaction, either the managers felt that the newsreel was an unimportant part of their programme or their patrons did not complain. It goes without saying that the newsreel's contents were what the editors (all of them) assumed would keep the patrons happy; the probability that they were right is very high. The extraordinary circumstances of the outbreak of war in Europe not only gave birth to a new era in radio news, it also brought high levels of war reporting, by definition 'political', to the newsreels. It is significant that the metropolitan newsreel theatres which thrived in this news-hungry atmosphere declined rapidly after peace. Post-war newsreel resumed the characteristic balance of entertainment over news.
2. In May of 1940 there were 23 stations telecasting in the United States. The OWI was responsible for exchanging material with the National Film Board of Canada and the processing for All American News which was intended solely for black audiences in their segregated theatres.
3. News censorship was a fact of wartime life: newsreel footage of the disaster at Pearl Harbour was not released until a year after the event. Total censorship had been enforced concerning fears of Japanese atrocities against American and Filipino troops captured in the fall of the Philippines. It was not until the very end of January 1944 that the press, radio and newsreel were able to disclose the horrors of the Bataan Death March and its equally brutalising aftermath. See Walton Ament to Elmer Davis, 14 July 1942, in K.R.M. Short, 'Introduction' in *World War II through the American newsreels*, microfiche (Pergamon Press, 1985). This introduction also provides a detailed account of the Library of Congress Film Project. For comparison it should be noted that radio news broadcasts were not censored, again because of the control of information by the military and the careful adherence to the OWI guidelines by

NBC, CBS and Mutual networks. This arrangement was seriously threatened in 1944 by a broadcast on atomic energy. See K.R.M. Short, 'Radio's scoop of the war: the atomic bomb, 1944!', *Historical Journal of Film, Radio and Television*, vol.5, no.1, (1985). Raymond Fielding, in a personal observation to the author, notes that the great achievement of Byron Price, Director of (voluntary) Censorship during the Second World War was in avoiding official censorship of the media such as had prevailed in the First World War.

4. For a general discussion on the Nazi image in American movies see Richard A. Oehling, 'Germans in Hollywood films' in 3 parts, *Film and History* (May 1973–May/September, 1974). *The Seventh Cross* (MGM, 1944), starring Spencer Tracey, is one contribution, albeit small, to the concept that there were anti-Nazi Germans.

5. Other stories obviously appeared on Germany and the war in the preceding months (all in Universal Newsreel's volume 18). On 26 May 1944, issue 298 — *Ruins in Berlin* (German film); 8 June, issue 301 — *Fire and Ruins in Berlin*; 29 June, issue 307 — *V-1 First Picture*; 13 July, issue 311 — *Nazi prisoners . . . led by their pompous and stiff generals*; 31 July, issue 316 — *Normandy — Defiant Nurses* — 'captured Nazi ladies who had been serving as nurses, are a study as they file by Yank cameras. Most of them are docile, but though they are destined for speedy return to their own lines, some female fists are waved in defiance'; 28 September, issue 333 — *Allies Enter Germany* — 'Roetgen, Germany, near the Eupen forest, is cool to the entry of the Yanks. Occasional families show forced smiles, and the children are trusting of the invaders . . .' The preceding descriptions are from Universal issue sheets.

6. B.H. Liddell Hart, *History of the Second World War* (London, 1970) pp.690f.

7. It is difficult to fathom how Nazi priorities could allow space for a rail shipment of women's hats during the collapse of the Third Reich. One possible explanation of where the hats had come from is that they might have been confiscated from Jewish owners, along with the rest of their belongings, at an extermination camp.

8. Professor Harry Pross recalled in a conversation with the author (*Prix Italia*, Lucca, Italy, September 1986) that the original inscription had been dedicated 'to the living Spirit', a quotation from Friedrich Gundolf. After the Nazis replaced it with the inscription 'to the German Spirit', university students caustically claimed that the 'German Spirit was no longer living'!

9. The newsreel's information on the relighting was based on a Westinghouse Corporation Press Release; see Universal production file (8 May 1945, vol.18, no.396, National Archive).

Bibliographical Note

The Universal Newsreel production records at the Motion Picture Sound and Video Branch, Special Archives Division, National Archives and Records Service, Washington DC, provide an invaluable resource for researchers seeking to understand how newsreels were produced and establishing their sources. The National Archives Universal Newsreel Library (RG 200) includes half a million index cards arranged in 13 major subject divisions, in addition to a complete run of Universal 'release' or issue sheets. The issue sheets are available on microfilm from the National Archive but one must remember that the newsreel's contents can and do vary from the issue sheet as the result of last-minute changes by the editor; this happened when a more important story emerged after the printing of the issue sheet which was intended for the theatre manager's advertising.

For an informed overview of the five major newsreels and The March of Time, see Raymond Fielding, *The American newsreel, 1911–1967* (Oklahoma, 1972) and *The March of Time, 1935–1951* (New York, 1978). A popular and laudatory survey of the American motion picture industry's contribution to the war effort, including the newsreels, was published by the editors of *Look* in *Movie lot to beachhead: The motion picture goes to war and prepares for the future*, (Garden City, New Jersey, 1945). The US Army Signal Corps' combat cameraman's wartime role is described in the three-volume history of the Signal Corps: Dulany Terret, *United States Army in World War II, The technical services, The Signal Corps: The emergency (to December 1941)* (Washington DC, Office of the Chief of Military History, Department of the Army, 1956); George Raynor Thompson, Dixie R. Harris, Pauline M. Oakes and Dulany Terret, *United States Army in World War II, The technical services, The Signal Corps: The test (December 1941 to July 1943)* (Washington DC, Office of The Chief of Military History, Department of the Army, 1957); George Raynor Thompson and Dixie R. Harris, *United States Army in World War II, The technical services, the Signal Corps: The outcome (mid–1943 through 1945)* (Washington DC, Office of the Chief of Military History, United States Army, 1966).

The most important single source for studying the paper documents relating to wartime newsreels is *World War II through the American newsreels, 1942–1945*, edited by K.R.M. Short (Oxford, 1985). This is a 229 microfiche edition of the newsreel analysis carried out by the Library of Congress Project on behalf of the Office of War Information during the period 1942–5. The files of the project (held by the Library of Congress) contain 14,000 pages of analysis, issue sheets and other material relative to the monitoring and assessing of the newsreel's reporting of the war. 'World War II through the American newsreels, 1942–1945: An introduction' by K.R.M. Short (as above) contains a description of the founding and operation of the Library of Congress Project, as well as a general statement on the wartime newsreels. As noted above, Universal Newsreels are held by the National Archives, Motion Picture, Sound and Video Branch, Special Archives Division, Washington DC 20408, USA; Movietone Newsreels are held by the Twentieth Century-Fox Movietonews Library, University of South Carolina, Columbia, South Carolina 29208, USA; Paramount Newsreels and RKO Pathe Newsreels are held by Sherman Grinberg Film Libraries, Inc., 630 Ninth Avenue, New York, NY 10036, USA; News of the Day is held by MGM-Hearst Metrotone News, Inc., 235 East 45th Street, New York, NY 10017, USA.

There are two appendices to this article: the first is a specimen issue sheet; the second is an article entitled 'Notes on Newsreels' written by Library of Congress Project researcher Liane Richter, written on 25 April 1945, which gives an informed opinion of the role of the newsreels in wartime.

American Newsreels and Germany's Collapse

Appendix 1: Specimen newsreel issue sheet — front

PRODUCED BY PATHE NEWS, INC.　　　　DISTRIBUTED BY RKO RADIO PICTURES, INC.

Vol. 14　　CONTENTS SUBJECT TO CHANGE WITHOUT NOTICE　　**No. 48**

YANKS BOMB NAPLES & SOUSSE

NORTH AFRICA — Roaring into the air, giant Liberators head for Sousse, Nazi-held Tunisian port on the Mediterranean's southern shore. The harbor is plastered with many direct hits. Other American bombers strike hard at Naples, great Italian port on the Mediterranean's northern shore. The Axis gets smacked from two sides.
(Described by Dwight Weist)

CHILE BREAKS TIES WITH AXIS

SANTIAGO, CHILE — A great public demonstration in the streets honors leaders of the United Nations as Chile breaks off diplomatic relations with the Axis. Cheering Chileans parade with posters and flags as they unanimously acclaim the action of Juan Antonio Rios, Chile's democratic president.
(Described by Radcliffe Hall)

INTER-AMERICAN ROAD SPEEDED

CENTRAL AMERICA — The Inter-American Highway, stretching from Mexico City to Panama City, is being rushed to completion in record time. U. S. Army engineers, with the aid of the various Central American republics, are literally carving the vital military road through mountains and jungles.
(Described by Radcliffe Hall)

TROOPS DRILL IN — 52° WEATHER

ALASKA — Despite sub-zero cold a regiment of U. S. Arctic soldiers holds a brisk bayonet drill. Low temperature doesn't handicap their agility and alertness. The parka-clad doughboys charge through deep, freezing snow. Among the toughest troops in the Army, theirs is a cold, cold job.
(Described by Radcliffe Hall)

MCNUTT: GET WAR JOB OR FIGHT

WASHINGTON, D. C. — Paul V. McNutt, War Manpower Commission chief, explains the reasons for the non-deferrable list. For the duration of the war, he says, we do not need luxuries. He urges all heads of families who are now in jobs not vital to the war effort to see their United States Employment Service about switching to war work.

LOST AUSSIES FIGHT ON TIMOR

TIMOR ISLAND — A small band of tough Aussies, hiding in the jungle of this Jap-held island, has kept up the fight against the enemy. Assembling a radio set from scrap stolen from the Japs, they contact Darwin. By secret means they are supplied with clothing, food and ammunition and they continue their brave, unsung battle deep in Timor.
(Described by Dwight Weist)

Edited by WALTON C. AMENT　　　　*Produced by* FREDERIC ULLMAN, JR.
Narrators: HARRY VON ZELL, DWIGHT WEIST, RED BARBER *and* RADCLIFFE HALL

American Newsreels and Germany's Collapse

Appendix 1: Specimen newsreel issue sheet — reverse

Appendix 2

Reproduction from file of the Library of Congress Project
25 April 1945

Notes on newsreels

For several years the principal newsreel subject matter has been coverage of the war fronts. The five newsreel companies have drawn on a common pool of footage, composed of shots taken by Army, Navy, Coast Guard, Marine, Allied and newsreel cameramen and captured enemy footage. Each company supplies its own commentary and editing, but the visuals pertaining to the war are substantially the same in each reel.

Occasionally, in keeping with their competitive tradition, newsreel companies still feature exclusives. These usually cover domestic events of local interest. Routine non-war newsreel stories, sometimes shared by all companies, sometimes presented by only one of them, deal with sports, fashion shows, beauty contests, multiple births among humans or animals, stars receiving prizes, technical inventions, floods and fires. Wherever possible the commentary links such stories with the war, if only by such devices as describing a hat as a 'war-time bonnet designed to boost home-front morale'.

Like the majority of fictitious films, newsreels are made for showing to audiences of all ages, many varied political, ideological and religious denominations, every conceivable national and occupational group. (A notable exception is the 'All American News', a newsreel made for presentation in Negro theaters only, which will not be covered by these notes.) The result is the same in fiction and in actuality films: In order to serve such a large and heterogeneous public and in their anxiety to offend nobody, the film makers reduce their standards to the lowest common denominator intellectually, and avoid making any controversial statement. Some attitudes discernible in the newsreels may nevertheless seem offensive to some observers, as for instance the patronizing tone sometimes adopted toward foreign countries; but there is no indication that these attitudes are displayed consciously; it seems rather that they slipped through by mistake almost, as they do in feature films, without the scriptwriter's quite realizing what he is saying.

Conspicuous by their absence are reports on such subjects as labor disputes and race riots. One newsreel issue showed some non-committal shots of a coal strike, but the visuals conveyed nothing of the conflict and the commentary favored neither labor nor management. Even when a subject so openly controversial as the fighting in Athens between ELAS and British troops was touched, the narrator managed to avoid any mention of the issues.

Subject matter. The most important newsreel subject, the war, is covered by two kinds of reportage: Reports from the home-front and reports from overseas.

The home-front reports are concerned with public figures (frequently making speeches), Bond rallies, salvage drives, conferences. There is little footage to illustrate the effect of the war on American every-day life.

The 1944 election campaign commanded a great deal of space in the newsreels. The candidates and their associates were shown traveling, at clubs and in public halls, and the public was presented with excerpts from their speeches. These films helped voters become better acquainted with the candidates. Here too, the commentaries were careful not to favor either side. Through perusal of the script and keen observation, one may have been able at times to detect where lay the commentator's sympathies; but it can be safely assumed that there was no intention to promote either candidate.

President Roosevelt's death was commemorated by the newsreel companies in a brief pictorial biography and, in another issue, a quiet dignified report of the funeral. In the same issue, President Truman was seen giving a short speech.

This year's outstanding non-combat films from overseas were those of President Roosevelt's meeting with potentates of the Near East and of the Big Three meeting at Yalta. These reels had vivid sustained shots of the principal persons in the events and conveyed some knowledge of the manner in which such conferences are conducted.

Since the beginning of the war, combat footage has taken up most newsreel space. Great strides have been made in the technical development of combat photography. The synchronization of guns and cameras has made possible unified sequences which include aiming at a target, the path of the missile and the hitting of the target. These sequences now frequently replace what used to be unrelated shots of a plane or cannon, a bomb or a bullet, a blurred aerial view or an obscured outline.

There has been some recent improvement in editing which has helped to give a more complete and clearer picture of the battle-fronts. This may be partly due to the favorable progress of the war. An increasing number of newsreels has devoted its entire footage to one event, as in the invasion of Iwo Jima, the capture of Manila, the liberation of Paris. Whenever this was done, it was possible for the spectator to identify the time and place of the events shown and to form a coherent conception of what was happening. In the films of fighting in the Pacific the tendency to combine visuals of aerial and ground battles with shots of many varied locations was less marked than it was in the European footage. The films of the war in Europe, particularly during the advance through France and Belgium, were usually composed of shots from all parts of the front, shots of planes over Germany, and many sequences of the enthusiastic reception the native population gave to American troops. There was no footage to throw light on the daily life of the liberated population; they were shown only waving, shouting, kissing soldiers, or returning to their homes mournful and bedraggled. Perhaps the most recurrent 'human-interest' shots were those of American soldiers giving candy to French or Belgian or Italian children.

The tendency to show close-ups of dead and wounded is on the increase. Particularly featured are films of the enemy's maimed and starved victims. It may be that it is the companies' policy to arouse public feeling against Japanese and German brutality. But it seems more likely that they have nothing so specific in mind. For the sensational shots may be of a Japanese soldier writhing in death agony or, as in the case of the Caruso trial, of the Fascist Carretta hanging on a wall, head down, and another of the actual execution of Caruso.

Sound. Usually no sound recording is made of the actual scene shown in the newsreels. The noise of battle is dubbed in when the film is edited, as is the background music and the commentary. The reason generally stated for this is that the dubbed-in sound is a more accurate record of what might be heard in battle than could be obtained by on-the-spot recording. It is probable, of course, that it is often technically impossible to make on-the-spot recordings because of battle conditions. However, in some cases (for instance, in the Iwo Jima reel) actual sound has been used to excellent advantage. The recording was faulty and blurred, but it had the impact of being the real thing; it included scraps of barely audible conversation which, compared to the glib tones of the narrator, were like actuality shots of service-men's faces compared to polished Hollywood performances of soldiers. Another reel showed a soldier giving a fuller-than-usual account of his experiences in a tank. The soldier's talk was obviously unrehearsed and unedited; it included hesitation, a slip of the tongue; his account, by its very spontaneity, led to an intimate knowledge of the episode he described.

Shortcomings. One major and self-inflicted handicap of the newsreel companies is their untiring ambition to present headline material. Not content to furnish the public with a subsequent pictorial illustration to the knowledge of the war which they have already gained from newspaper reports, the newsreels are forever trying for the sensational, always attempting to give 'news' value, and since they cannot compete with the speed of cables, radioed newspaper photographs or radio news, they do the hastiest possible job with their material and punctuate their screen titles with giant exclamation marks. Sometimes, after particularly spectacular events on the war fronts, the companies make up stories from library footage (showing what these events may have been like), rather than wait for the actual shots. Very often in such cases, the narrator neglects to identify the library shots as such.

Another great shortcoming of current American newsreels is that the scriptwriters don't appear to have any confidence in the impact of the visuals which are being presented to the public. The shots are rarely permitted to speak for themselves. The commentary accompanies them with a steady stream of explanations, side remarks, general observations and admonitions, spoken with enthusiastic intonation. The explanations are sometimes erroneous, since the studio receives the footage with skimpy captions only, and the scriptwriters have no other information from which to identify the shots. (The commentary of one company may, for instance, call a burning airplane an enemy plane, while another company's commentary may deplore the same burning aircraft as an American loss. A group of weary American soldiers was described by one narrator as our soldiers forced to retreat, whereas another narrator claimed that the same group was advancing.) The general observations are usually about the bravery of our troops and the cruelty of the enemy. These remarks add little to the shot content, for — unless the visuals are convincing — we are free to believe or disbelieve the commentator's opinion, but they make it very difficult to concentrate fully on the visuals. The admonitions also are usually of a vague nature: Don't think the war is over, support the war effort, look how much harder the war is on these men than it is on you. During War Loan or salvage or Red Cross drives, the admonitions become more specific: Buy Bonds, collect waste paper, give your blood. The commentaries, since it is their policy not to commit themselves to any but the most general and widely acceptable opinion, and since they appear unwilling to interrupt their stream of words, are in most cases little but empty (though distracting) sound.

In spite of their faults, the newsreels have done a valuable job in conveying knowledge about the visual aspects of the war. Much of their war footage could be made available to the public only through the expert workmanship and unsurpassed courage of frontline cameramen, who have made an important contribution to our knowledge and permanent record of the war.

Liane Richter

2
Defeated Germany in British Newsreels: 1944 – 45

Nicholas Pronay

Germany began to be presented in the newsreels, the press and in official publications in terms of a defeated nation only from the end of September 1944. Despite the brave face put on it, the invasion of France was recognised to be a very unsure undertaking; not the least because of the worry about what 'wonder-weapons' the Germans might pull out of the hat, which their propaganda had threatened to do and which, or at least the existence of large-scale preparations for which, Allied intelligence had confirmed. A change of tone from the grim resolution with which the hard-slogging in June and July was reported, in the newsreels as well as in Parliament and the Cabinet, first came to be perceptible at end of August following the three weeks of good big news, the first such period for Britain since the start of the war, which started with the successful second landing in the South of France on 15 August. It was followed by the liberation of Paris, Toulon and Marseilles, the collapse of German rule in the Midi to the Maquisards, and then the Canadians swept up the Channel ports in which the Germans had for so long been facing England directly. On 1 September Montgomery was made a Field Marshal and by 4 September, Verdun, Brussels and Antwerp were also retaken. All these symbolised to British eyes the end at last of the German threat: the real 'end of the beginning'. The decision to go for a hazardous airborne thrust to reach Germany ahead of the planned slow 'broad front' strategy reflected the assumption that the Wehrmacht was ready for the knockout, and so it was at first presented. This turned out to be over-optimistic. Nevertheless, with the evident destruction of the great army, with its famous panzer divisions, which Hitler had kept in France for throwing the Allies into the Channel and so forcing England and the United States to make a negotiated peace, and evidence that Britain could cope with the 'Doodlebug', it became clear that Germany had at last shot her bolt. With the massive sweeps forward by the Red Army at the same time, defeat or even compromise was not now on the cards. The public was ready for taking a step forward in its thinking, from the certainty of having avoided defeat, to total victory.

By the end of September, when sadness for the gallant paratroopers who tried to make a rush for it had subsided, Britain was beginning to be ready to look beyond the end of the war for the first time. Victory might be a little further away than it was hoped at the end of the wonderful period in August when what was left of the Army of the West was streaming disorganised back towards their own frontier or into Allied POW camps in tens of thousands, and the smouldering wrecks of some of Hitler's most dreaded panzer divisions provided miles of film footage like balm for sore eyes at home, nevertheless it was certain. The one remaining question was how long it would take to get to Berlin and by what kind of warfare. That hinged on what might be the actual strength of the 'West Wall', or as it was known in England the 'Siegfried Line', guarding the German frontier itself: could it still force on the Allies a long and bloody version of the trench warfare of the last war, the memory of which was so firmly lodged in the people's pantheon of horrors? So, when in the last week of September the Allies proceeded to set foot on German soil and to break into the Siegfried Line, in however small a corner of it, this could be used most effectively as the perceptual trigger needed for beginning to shift the public mind towards thinking in terms of 'defeated Germany' — what shall we do with them after the war? In this case, as in most cases by this time in Britain, propaganda followed policy closely and skilfully. On 18 September the Cabinet formally confirmed the policy of 're-education' and ordered its first phase to be put into operation. The so-called 'Prisoner of War Programme' was designed to provide information about the attitudes of Germans and to begin to de-indoctrinate and re-indoctrinate those amongst the POWs who showed signs of readiness, in preparation for using them in Germany. 'Re-education' was of course as yet a secret policy, although the word had been dropped about in public. Home propaganda's task thus shifted to preparing the public for post-VE policies, the war against Japan and the post-occupation policies in Germany — a classic example of carrying into practice

Ludendorff's dictum that 'propaganda must act as the pacemaker to policy'. The capture of Roetgen, just inside the Siegfried Line a few days later provided the perfect newspeg for starting the campaign for shifting attitudes towards thinking of victory within measurable time and therefore about how to deal with the Germans in Germany. It was to be a tough policy: the German people, civilians and prisoners of war alike, were not to be treated as if they themselves had been the victims, or even the dupes, of Hitler or the Nazis or some 'ruling class'. Instead, they were to be treated as the race which needed its spirit of 'militarism' broken once and for all. As always in the British scheme of propaganda, the newsreels played the role of the bludgeon:

> Here are the most eagerly awaited pictures of the war, showing Allied troops crossing into Germany itself. At last the Reich feels the tread of conquering armies. [*Music*] Captured outpost of the vaunted Siegfried Line. A notice says Adolf Hitler personally inspected this. Fat lot of good that seems to have done. And so on into Roetgen; the first wholly German town to fall to the Allies. [*Women and children smiling, little girl talking to a GI*] The 'Heil Hitlerites' with obsequious smiles try to make friends. But Europe's backward race will have more lessons to learn before we take those smiles on their face value. Lessons such as the people of Wallendorf learned, where the Americans set fire to the whole village because of persistent sniping after surrender. [Pathe 44/77]

This remained in essence the line pushed with complete consistency through the period when the Allies were moving into areas of Germany itself. In different ways the message was pushed that the Germans were a guilty people with an inborn compulsion to war; it was they who were responsible for Hitler, just as they had been responsible for the Kaiser, and not the other way around. The German government merely represented the character and the aspirations of the German people: unless these were changed the Germans would start another war as soon as they felt strong enough. Different facets of this overall perception were stressed as suitable newspegs came up, varied too in the style of the particular newsreel. In contrast to Pathe's more jaunty tone, Movietone (MT) pressed the same line in their 'serious journalism' style, as for example in this example on the occasion of the capture of Munster:

> Most reports told of the submissive attitude of civilians, many of whom brought out the old old story of how they really hated the Nazis and never had wanted a war. Certainly they can never have wanted *this* kind of war. Today *their* homeland is being occupied and they watch *their* soldiers being marched away as prisoners ... [MT 826a]

On the occasion of the capture of Bad Godesberg most of the newsreels took the opportunity to refer back to Chamberlain's visit and rerun some of the footage of the smiling crowds there, which greatly annoyed Hitler at the time. The line taken for using this newspeg was summed up in Movietone's version: 'They exude goodwill, but this time nobody in his right senses will believe them.' (MT 825) The occupation of Cologne was also used for long flashback sequences referring to the 'stab in the back' theory of 1918 as well as to the lessons of 1929 and 1936 with the message that this time it will be made 'absolutely clear' that the Wehrmacht was 'absolutely defeated'. Those newsreels such as Gaumont British (GB) and Pathe which had made play at the time with the 'Watch on the Rhine' theme, now used their footage and commentary to revitalise the associations which that phrase had, going back to the First World War as a result of the first 'hate campaign' run then, stressing that hereafter Germany will never again resume the 'Watch on the Rhine'. (Pathe 45/21, GB 1165)

The elaboration of this theme and the completion of the stereotype of a people outside the human race, leading up to the policy of non-fraternisation, was completed by the way the immense human misery suffered by the people, women, children and the old, was portrayed. This was presented within a very skilful perspective for stifling any feelings of empathy with them as fellow human beings: 'looting'. German civilians were shown being desperate, but in the context of despicably bearing up under their misfortune. There can be little doubt that this was intentional, a matter of policy. All footage was shot under the 'rota' system and the abundance of different versions of 'looting' footage in the newsreels, and above all the clearly pre-arranged presence of cameras at points where looting took place, for example a point where a train containing food or clothing made an unexpected stop which allowed civilians to rush it before the military police could arrive to stop it, provides clear evidence of a well-thought-out and effectively carried out policy. A few examples from this depressingly hard-nosed campaign, running from the middle of March to that of April, will suffice from the two companies which, unlike Gaumont British and Paramount (Par.), went in least for the truly emotive style:

> A train load of clothing scheduled to move into central Germany is mobbed by men and women in whose gestures can be read the whole story of the disintegration of German morale. [*Long sequence, with suitable music, of women and old men clambering into wagons and getting out piles of clothing. Camera changes position during sequence*] Looting goes on unchecked. A glaring illustration of the state of Germany as she goes down. Soldiers and civilians alike throw overboard all sense of discipline and the last traces of a co-ordinated plan to resist. The Third Reich is crumbling to its dishonourable grave. [Pathe 45/31]
>
> ... The Germans are accustomed to getting orders and obeying them; well now they *are* getting them. [*British military police in action*] And here is what happens when they are not given orders. [*Looting sequence*] Of course when there is nothing left to loot the German people will have to go back to working for a living, not to mention reparations. [MT 828]
>
> ... Finally, looting at Wertheim. Here it was food of all kinds, sacks of grain, crates of *leberwurst* and other things dear to the stomach of the Hun; they were pitching it out of barges moored along the canal. [*Women with small children scrambling and slithering up and down a steep and muddy bank, hauling sacks*] Well, the Germans have boasted that they have been 'swimming in fat' and I suppose they mean to go on as long as they possibly can. [*Long line of women with young children dragging home-made carts*] But stocks like these won't last for ever. Even now they are beginning to fight over their loot. [*Two women, right in front of the cameras, i.e. a group of British military personnel in uniform, start a tug of war over some items. The scene runs on for a time*] Just a couple of werewolves. That's what *they* are. [Pathe 45/29]

This outlook on Germany, 'the backward race of Europe', was

already fully formed and projected *before* the Allies reached Belsen and the full presentation of its horrors to the British public on 30 April. To understand the reasons for the projection and, according to all the evidence we have, ready acceptance of this outlook by the British public by the time the camps were discovered, we need to look at the perception of Germany before and during the Second World War. By the end of the First World War there was a substantial though possibly a minority view amongst the public, and a significant but a definitely minority view at the official level, which already regarded the political nation in Germany as infected with an ultimately criminal set of attitudes and beliefs. These were thought to be deep-seated attitudes which lay behind the approach to politics adopted by the German governing class; they were seen in German popular culture, and were thought to be liable to be demonstrated in inhuman actions by Germans against the peoples of other nations whenever they came under their power. Above all, it was believed, they were bound to lead Germany, under whatever government, to seek the conquest of her European neighbours by war. Lord Balfour, one of the most aristocratic figures even by British standards, as well as the most intellectual, to hold the office of Foreign Secretary in this century, put it thus in Parliament in November 1917 when contrasting past wars which ended with a genuine peace with the belligerents quickly forgetting their differences:

> That is not the case in this war. You must consider the psychology of the German people, and it really is not prejudice to say that the German people have an entirely different view of international morality and of the rights and duties of a powerful state from any other community in the world.[1]

Behind this measured expression lay more than twenty years of a growing debate about the nature and dynamics of Germany's political culture, and of the cultural or even deeper factors which might explain it. Nor was it a debate confined to the mandarins of the Foreign Office. In the first piece of 'in-depth investigative journalism' in the first mass-circulation newspaper in Britain, G.W. Steevens, the father of the genre and one of the most brilliant political journalists of the age, devoted a series of no less than 16 consecutive articles to this issue. Under the series title

'Under the Iron Heel' its overall analysis was that 'the keynote of modern Germany was militarism . . . and the inherent brutality of the German character'. From this it concluded that it was inevitable that Germany would launch a war as soon as she felt ready. Northcliffe went to Germany to check for himself and came back with the conclusion that the Germans are 'being led definitely and irrevocably to war', not by a clique around the Kaiser or some such, but by the inner dynamic of their political culture and the ruling groups which it produced.[2] He determined that it was the duty of his papers to bring this fact home to the British, as yet labouring under ignorance of a phenomenon the existence of which was outside their own experience and perceptions. The upshot of that, in turn, may be measured by the impact which it gradually had on the younger generation growing up in British politics. For example, J.C.C. Davidson, Baldwin's confidant and later Chairman of the Conservative Party, recalled in his memoirs how, as a young Private Secretary to Lord Harcourt, a fine example of the old generation of Liberals to whom such notions were inconceivable, he watched his chief worn out physically and mentally by the 'profound shock' of a great country, Germany, actually going to war. Davidson, by contrast, was not in the least surprised, nor perceived any moral dilemma in contemplating a vast war in the heart of Europe for it would be against what Germany represented: 'I, who had been brought up on the *Daily Mail*, . . . was very worried lest we should abandon our French allies'.[3] This perception of Germany, through identifying a dominant type and projecting it as a stereotype, underlay, indeed alone helps to explain, the success of the propaganda machine during the First World War in instilling far and wide the 'beastly Hun', not as a caricature but as shorthand for an integrated and apparently proven psycho-political concept, a fact of international life. Balfour's measured expression of it was projected by the popular media in the most direct terms for most of the war and perhaps the best encapsulation of it at the end of the war can be found in the last official film released by the Ministry of Information during the First World War, entitled *Once a German . . .*:

> *Picture*: Two drunken German soldiers, one carrying a flaming torch, stagger in the middle of the street in a burning village, brutalising a young mother with a baby. Caption following:

Once a German Always a German.

Same two men in well-cut civilian clothes looking most respectable and innocuous, one wearing a pince-nez, stand politely at the bar of an archetypal English village pub. Caption following:

And when all this is over the men who will enter our peaceful English villages with German goods to sell...

The men walk down a street and one of them knocks on a door and enters with a saucepan in his hands which he shows to a man and his wife. Caption following:

Will be the same beasts then as they are now. The leopard cannot change his spots.

Wife looks at the bottom of the saucepan which shows label 'Made in Germany', and recoils in horror. Caption following:

How shall we treat them then?

English policeman enters and marches the two cringing men away.

By the end of the 1920s, however, this Manichaean view of Germany had become dormant amongst the public, partly as a result of the revulsion against the disclosures concerning the untruth of many of the atrocity stories peddled by, or not stopped by, the official propaganda agencies. No other popular stereotype was however developed for Germany or the Germans — it was simply that people did not want to think about Germany any more, least of all puzzle over their political or personal characteristics. As far as the political elite was concerned, who did have to form policies relating to Germany and therefore did have to think about the likely developments within Germany, a sharp division came into being between those who held to it as the key to understanding the ultimate drift of German foreign policy, such as Vansittart, and those who rejected this view as simplistic, wrong and even objectionable, such as Alexander Cadogan and Neville Chamberlain, and insisted that policy must be conducted on the assumption that no nation or people can be so utterly different. This split bedevilled the course of British foreign policy towards Nazi Germany.[4]

The phrase which, for the *British*, stood for this complex of ideas about German political and ethical culture or, as they called it, 'the character of the German nation', was 'Prussian militarism' before 1918, and simply 'German militarism' for the wartime generation. In the post-1918 period, the touchstone by which the British public judged events in Germany — and the criterion therefore whereby the British popular press and the newsreels judged whether an event *in Germany* was or was not newsworthy — was whether or not it indicated a revival of 'militarism' in Germany. If it did not, then it was not of concern, not 'news'. Interest in what was happening in Germany therefore began to revive from about 1929 because of the increase in signs of militarism detected by the British media (and also by those in the Foreign Office who held to that view) in the growth of movements such as the Stahlhelm, increasing references by Weimar politicians to the desire to increase the German armed forces, and the increasing prominence of military figures in German politics. The appointment of General Schleicher as Chancellor and his demand for the right to armaments had a particularly important symbolic impact, especially as it was brought to the public at large by the newly arrived sound newsreel. The coming to power of the Nazi party with the appointment of Hitler as Chancellor within a very short time thereafter, was seen through this perspective and it explains the curious course of British reaction to Hitler's assumption of power. At first, the coming to power of the Nazi party as the biggest party in terms of votes and as a mass movement (in place of the governments of General Schleicher and von Papen, both ruling by favour of Marshal Hindenburg) had initially been perceived as a promising sign, precisely because Hitler was not, nor were his chief lieutenants, of the military caste, because they came from outside the tainted German political tradition. In the medium of the newsreel, Schleicher had been presented in full uniform, surrounded by Hindenburg and others in that famous spiked helmet, attending a huge rally of veterans. In Movietone's version: 'To celebrate the occasion a review of the flags of the Imperial Army is held which is followed by a speech from Chancellor von Schleicher in which he states Germany's determination to obtain equality of armaments, with conscription as her ultimate goal.' Whereas Hitler's Chancellorship was presented in a directly contrasting manner. In Pathe's version: 'Adolf Hitler assumes the mantle of Bismarck. As Germany's Chancellor — once a lance-corporal — he is now master of his adopted country's destiny.' (Pathe 33/10) Paramount talked about 'this unflinching patriot whose burning zeal fires the imagination of his countrymen', and concluded: 'And so Adolf Hitler, one time labourer, becomes Chancellor, facing the gigantic task of guiding Germany back to peaceful prosperity.' (Par. 16568) 'Bismarck' represented the 'normal' or even 'good' Germany of old, Hanoverian, Prince Albert times, in English parlance. It was so memorably encapsulated in the famous *Punch* cartoon, 'Dropping the Pilot', when he was dismissed at last, expressing British fears of what is happening in Germany with the accession of Kaiser Wilhelm II.

Later on however, the same simple yardstick applied to all German events — was it a sign of Germany becoming 'militarist' again? — came to fit Hitler's Germany, Hitler himself and the German people under Hitler, into the old, well-established set of stereotypes and concerns. After some little while of wondering where it was all going, Hitler's regime in Germany came to be perceived not as something new but rather as something all too familiar; not as the government of a particular party with a particular political philosophy but simply as the sort of government which, like the Kaiser's before, expressed and personified the fundamental political and ethical attitude of the Germans — militarism. This was so particularly in the newsreels, the only genuine mass medium in the 1930s, in which this message was consistently and unambiguously pushed with all the peculiar force which film has when it comes to portraying faraway events. A few examples will suffice:

Withdrawal from the League of Nations:

Adolf Hitler, the founder of the Nazi legions which now parade before him, reviews his followers. Militarism, long dead in Germany, is re-kindled by the dynamic Hitler. . . . Nightmare visions of warring armies rise up before our eyes. Only wise statesmanship can guide the nations to peace in this hour of crisis. [Par. 2210]

Announcement of the reintroduction of conscription

Germany Asserts Right to Rearm

This is Germany's official day for mourning for her war dead. In the Berlin State Opera, General von Blomberg delivers the speech of commemoration. Then the banners are dipped while the song known as 'the air of the good comrade' is played. There follows 'Deutschland Über Alles' sung by the massed assembly with General Goering, Marshal von Mackensen and Adolf Hitler in the box of honour.

The old national anthem has the same significance today. For Hitler has just proclaimed Germany's intention to openly rearm.

The Reichswehr, the national army, now to be extended to half a million men, parades in the Berlin Lustgarten. Crosses of honour are attached by the Führer to regimental banners of the old Imperial Army. Then Hitler, Mackensen and Goering and von Blomberg proceed to the monument of fallen heroes to place the nation's wreaths.

As the present rulers of Germany emerge from the monument, the ex-Crown-Prince Wilhelm steps forward and salutes the successor to the Hohenzollern.

The Army, back to its old pride, goose-steps past its leader who was once a corporal in its rank.

So, Germany proclaims her intention to rearm, to conscript men into her armed forces. The world may well watch and mark this formidable demonstration of German armed discipline — and hope that Germany's aims are as pacific as her leader's utterances declare them to be. [MT 302/a]

Re-occupation of the Rhineland

Scraps of Paper. German Troops Enter Rhineland

European statesmen have been staggered by dictator Adolf Hitler's latest move in denouncing the Treaties of Versailles and Locarno and turning those safeguards of European peace into nothing more than 'scraps of paper'. [*The picture shown against this re-invocation of the emotive phrase 'scraps of paper', which was lodged in British memory as standing for everything about the militarist Hun, was a montage showing cheering crowds of uniformed men fronted by two German bishops wearing Iron Crosses and raising their arms in salute — a shot which came from the library and had belonged to a film about the 1933 Harvest Festival!*] At Versailles it was laid down, at Locarno it was confirmed, that Germany was forbidden to take any armed force into the Rhineland zone, and for eighteen years the fortresses of Frankfurt, Koblenz and the other garrison cities on the Rhine have been empty. But under dictator Hitler, Germany has been asserting her independence of treaty obligations. First she left the League of Nations, then she set about rebuilding her Army, Navy and Airforce, until today when her forces play at mimic battle, Germany is once again one of the great armed camps of Europe.

Pathe ran another story on it in which full advantage was taken of the possibilities offered by a shot of a steel-helmeted sentry on the Hohenzollern Bridge, including music based on 'The Watch on the Rhine'; whereas Gaumont went in for a most effective re-evocation of the whole set of associated images with a specially composed music track, ending with 'Cheers amidst echoes of the past'. (GB 230)

Even Hitler's actual Party-parades were presented in this light of the Germans reverting to their national characteristics, with what the party might stand for being irrelevant:

A Night in Nuremberg

At night in Nuremberg the jubilations of a day of heroics are continued. Nazism has held its great convention. Masses of uniformed men, stupefying and incredible to the imagination, have stood in spellbound audience to the Führer. Rank after rank of disciplined Germans marched multitude upon multitude past the author of their reviving might: Hitler. An amazing spectacle of profound significance to the world, which however you regard National Socialism must provoke reflections impossible to be ignored. [MT 332]

Pathe's version of the 1935 Nuremberg Rally encapsulated this approach of Germans just being back at their favourite pastime, never mind the politics of it, when it simply showed some of the German propaganda footage so artistically shot, while confining its comment to one masterly sentence: 'This year, they say, there will be 800,000 pairs of boots standing heel-to-heel waiting for the Führer who shouts: "My life's fight has not been in vain".' (Pathe 35/75)

By the time war had actually come, in the autumn of 1939, the once dormant perception which had in 1918 provided a coherent explanation of why the Germans did what they did and what they were likely to do again, had re-emerged. This perception of 'the Hun' inside the German, call it now Nazi if you will, was now all the stronger and clearer and less liable to discussion because of the consciousness of having tried so hard during the period of appeasement to look at the Germans in another way, despite one's doubts. There was a peculiar bitterness now attaching to this view because of the consciousness of the disastrous situation into which that effort landed Britain — and it gave people such as Vansittart the same special aura of authority which had elevated Northcliffe in 1914 as the men who had perceived and told the truth and were vilified for it. So Vansittart's famous series of talks, 'Black Record', fell on immensely receptive ears, and for all their lurid detail and curious history, they became seminal indeed. For they seemed merely to provide chapter and verse for beliefs which were already intuitively held. In the medium of the newsreel the best re-statement of this view, which was to be held deep down by the greatest number of Britons during the war, came from Gaumont British, not for the first time, on the occasion when Hitler attacked Russia. It was against the pictures coming in from the Eastern front, including German footage obtained via Lisbon as well as Russian footage:

> ... Nazi barbarians standing in field of ripening corn. In their path always death, destruction, misery. Once again the Luftwaffe has been engaged on fearful destruction. This is the German mentality. This is the race we have been fighting for over two years. These pictures were shown to Germans and neutrals as a glorious example of German handiwork. This is what Germany is proud of. This is another feat of German arms, short-range shelling of little farm buildings; somebody's office, the joy and comfort, the livelihood of decent men, smashed to fragments by the juggernaut of Prussian lust. We have GOT to win this war.
>
> [*Switching to Russian footage*] ... These are the first of the German prisoners taken on Soviet soil. It does your heart good to see the swaggering Nazi with some of the swank knocked out of him. [*Over shot of young German soldiers*] Listen Fritz, what were you doing on the Eastern front, anyway? Hitler made a pact of friendship with Stalin less than two years ago. Nothing between Germany and the Soviet Union has altered since, so why are you suddenly fighting the Red

Army? That's what Moscow radio wanted to know. That's what we want to know. One day, Fritz, that's what you'll want to know. Hitler gave you a nice victory in Poland, and then you had to fight Britain and France, and then you had a victory in Norway and France and Belgium and Holland, and then you were sent to fight against Greece and Yugoslavia, and you won again. And then you were sent to fight against Russia. And if you beat Russia, where would Adolf Hitler send you to fight next time, little man . . .? More prisoners are coming in. But quite a few of the Nazis who embarked on this invasion did not have the good fortune to be taken prisoner, and even those who were look none too happy. [*Over shots of wounded Germans being roughly handled by Russians and in obvious pain*] This is the other side of war, a side the Nazis don't know much about — YET. Even for Germany war isn't always one grand sweep of murdering and loot. War isn't always a goose-step on the victory march into a newly conquered capital. Aye — you are just beginning to find out Fritz, war is HELL. [GB 769]

German atrocities during the war therefore were simply not 'news' — it was what the Germans were expected to do once they were on the loose again with weapons in their hands. There was no point in making a show of such pictures which came to be had of them: it was not news, it was simply distressing to look at particular examples of it. Footage did in fact come trickling in from the Eastern front from the spring of 1942 of German atrocities in the retaken territories right up to footage of actual concentration camps in Poland. Similarly, there was a growing quantity of footage from France and Holland of Gestapo establishments, and of massacres such as at Oradour. Only a small part, without the sensational scenes and with only the most matter-of-fact commentary, was shown of this material before Belsen. For the same reasons there was thought to be no point whatsoever during the war of basing, or even introducing into, British wartime domestic propaganda any repetition of the 'beastly Hun' image or of atrocity propaganda in general. A brief sally in that direction under direct orders from the Cabinet, and against the advice of the public-opinion experts, was embarked on in 1940, the 'Anger Campaign', but was dropped as soon as possible. The wartime monitoring of public opinion demonstrated time after time that the British people as a whole, the vast majority of ordinary people certainly, held that view already, and with a depth of conviction.

Any lingering doubts about the thesis of the collective guilt of a whole nation were then crushed at the end of April by the footage from the concentration camps. The elaborate filming arrangements made for them have been described many times and need not be rehearsed here, nor the lasting trauma which it left on cameramen who went about the job knowing that this was an essential element of policy where they had to do their duty, no matter what. The newsreels were told to make them up into two special issues. The second version was to be shown in the following week. The cinemas were ordered to show them after some managers refused to do so the first time round, one with the memorable comment that he was running a cinema and not a chamber of horrors. Each newsreel used different devices for bringing home the authenticity of the footage. Pathe for example used Mrs Mavis Tate MP as commentator, who also appears in the film; Movietone used Clare Booth Luce in the first, as well as Lord Vansittart for the second issue in a similar way. [Pathe 45/33 and 45/34] Paramount used footage showing Eisenhower in the camp. [Par. 14465] Perhaps inevitably it was Gaumont who rose to the job the most magnificently. Its issue entitled *Horror in our Time* is masterly, with a music track once again specially composed and flawlessly recorded by a full studio orchestra, and with E.V. Emmett back to his pre-war best as both the writer and the speaker of the words, now with the added authenticity of an older voice. (GB 1181) As with some other Gaumont specials it is a timeless example of the genre. It still packs an emotional and cinematic punch with today's audience.

The message was the same in every single essential in all the reels. What happened in the camps was the work of the Germans. As Pathe put it 'The responsibility for these terrible crimes falls squarely on the German people'; or, in Gaumont's words, the camps were a 'perpetual monument to a dark age in the history of the German race; a race which does not know the meaning of the word humanity'. The conclusion to Movietone's version, once again the least dramatic in tone, sums up what was so powerfully and effectively conveyed on this, the biggest newspeg of them all:

> This is Belsen, where people from all parts of Europe were herded. Typhus and starvation killed over sixty-thousand. Here the living walked amongst the dead. Hundreds

dropped every day and lay where they dropped. Belsen had been guarded by SS men and SS women. These [*women in camera*] are some of them, and according to the prisoners they had practised many cruelties upon women and children in the camp; and the SS commandant, a thing called Kramer, you might have seen his photograph in the papers. If the Hun had invaded Britain *this* might have had power to torture and to starve any one of us. Yes. Such atrocities might have been inflicted on the people of these islands. They *were* inflicted on the people in Belsen . . . Thousands upon thousands perished. Can anyone any longer doubt the truth of German atrocities? And yet, shall we remember these things in ten, fifteen, twenty years' time? It would be wise if all of us retained a lasting memory of the horror of this place. [Movietone 830A]

The discovery of the concentration camps was therefore received in Britain not as shedding light on what the Germans had been up to — as it was in neutral European nations and also to a considerable extent in the United States — but rather in the spirit expressed in the title which British Paramount News gave its version of the Belsen footage: *Proof Positive*. What the evidence of the concentration camps, and the filmic and photographic presentation of it to which it was particularly suited, had led to in Britain was not a change in the attitude towards Germany and a conditioning factor of the post-defeat policy towards her, but rather an opportunity to rehearse again, with positive proof, the already existing and firmly established British perception of Germany, of the German people and political culture. It also gave the opportunity to rearticulate that particular solution to 'the German problem' which had been thought about in Britain since 1916 in gradually widening circles until it emerged, by 1943 at the latest, in the form of an unusually broad consensus amongst the British decision-making elite: that there would have to be a very long period of occupation (in some form or another) and a thoroughgoing 're-education' of the German people as a whole. The war on the German mind would have to be continued long after the body lay prostrate. The impact of the concentration camp material was indeed very great, and its effects lasting, as they were intended to be, the more so because it came as 'proof positive' rather than as a revelation. Its effects were increased for other and more cinematic reasons too. As the second and third run cinemas also had to show these and were widely advertised, despite some reluctance on the part of some people, the penetration of this material was enormous. Moreover, the British cinema-going public had been more than well protected by its British Board of Film Censors from ever seeing cinematic scenes of horror: even dead soldiers were very seldom shown. Nothing remotely like this could conceivably have been shown before in a British cinema — let alone shown without an 'X' certificate and thus to children of any age as well as adults. Finally, extracts as well as reminder sequences were used on every suitable occasion, such as Pathe's story headed *An End to Murder*:

> German cinema queue for a murder film. Civilians jam the pavement to see a record of the horror camps of Belsen and Buchenwald. Similar pictures were shown to the British public in a recent edition of Pathe Gazette. AMG [The Allied Military Government] have prescribed this dose of re-education. Time alone will show whether in fact Germans can be re-educated. [Pathe 45/44]

The presentation of Germany as a guilty nation and people receiving their just deserts, and the complete identification of Germans with what Hitler and his men (and women) have done, remained thereafter the sum of the presentation until the autumn of 1945. Whether it was a story about the appalling health problems threatening an epidemic (MT 837A) for which they can only blame themselves, or the footage, which would have been heart-rending if viewed within a different stereotype framework, showing the consequences of dislocation and the millions seeking food, shelter and each other, the approach remained consistent throughout the summer of 1945. Showing truly moving footage of lost women and children, Movietone commented: 'If you feel any sympathy, remember these same women applauded the Führer for his conquests. *They* showed no sympathy for the enslaved peoples of Europe.' (MT 842) It was of course a reflection, projection, of the policy in which the British (in company for once with the Russians and the French) differed from the Americans. They did not want 'de-nazification' to be more than the hunting-down of actual war criminals, in the case of the British the murderers of British commandos in particular. They had to accept 'de-nazification' as part of the price for getting the Americans to adopt their own policy for the long-term occupation of Germany and the re-education policy which rested on it — but in their own zone they did as little as they could about carrying it out. They did not believe in the basic premise which 'denazification' implied: that there were many sheep as well as goats. What they believed was that Nazism as well as the atrocities which were committed, not only in the camps but elsewhere too and not only by SS units, were just symptoms of a basic flaw in the make-up of the German people as a whole, were the products of German political culture as such.

A softening of this attitude thus came only in the later autumn of 1945, when the approach of winter brought the prospect of disease and famine — which would now be the responsibility of the Allies, having taken over the government of Germany. And when it came it also came as a part of the re-education campaign itself, in the newsreels, with a special issue covering Ellen Wilkinson's visit to schools run by the Education Branch of the British Military Government in which 'the foundations are laid for a new Germany', (Pathe 45/84). It was part of a campaign to persuade the public to see it through, even if it involved sending over food and coal badly needed at home, as the price of what the basic policy paper of 1943 described as 'stamping out the whole tradition on which the German nation has been built'.

The newsreels were still the mass medium *par excellence* in Britain during this period. They had already passed, about two years before, the peak of their popularity and begun to lose something of the trust which had been placed in them as the purveyors of truth of a higher order than the popular press — about which a healthy but indulgent scepticism had long been the dominant attitude in Britain — by virtue of the belief that 'the camera cannot lie'. Nevertheless, there was no medium at the time which had yet replaced them in terms of penetration. In fact their audience had become larger than ever in 1945–6: some 26 million per week in Britain, plus the majority of the armed forces abroad. Their credibility, weakened somewhat as it was by their wartime exploitation by the Ministry of Information, however stood in direct proportion to the distance from the events portrayed: the farther from the audience, the greater it was. Thus, in the case of Germany and the British perception of Germany, the newsreels' presentation of the view of Germany as a criminal community needing reformatory punishment could powerfully reinforce that perception, and help to fix it. However, the newsreels and their equivalents in the medium of print must not be seen in isolation, for that could easily lead to the mistaken notion that these perceptions were only those of the ignorant and uninformed sections of the public. They need to be taken together not only with the documentation at official level, but also with the evidence provided by the medium of the documentary film. It is important evidence because this was the one period when the documentary film did at last actually manage to reach its target audience, the cadres of the working class, and the intellectual and political elite of the Labour government period. Perhaps the most illuminating demonstration of the extent to which there was a basic consensus in Britain about Germany — spanning both the intellectual and the class divisions — is to be found in the remarkable fact that, for once, the right-wing populist newsreels and the austerely elitist and left-wing documentarists presented an identical perception of Germany, in all essentials, for their both socially and educationally different target audiences. The official Crown Film Unit documentary, *A Defeated People* therefore deserves extended citation. Here are its opening and closing sequences:

> [*Off-screen voices of a conversation at the end of the opening title, over a map of Germany*] 'What's it like in Germany?' 'Must be terrible.' 'Well they've asked for it, they've got it.' 'Yes, but you can't make them starve.' 'I don't know about that. I've got a son out there. As far as I can see it would be a good thing if some of them did die.'
>
> [*Pictures of ruins, etc.*] Well, a lot of Germany is dead. Our last bombing was directed against communications, against convoys, trains, road and rail bridges; against goods yards, stations, viaducts. We not only smashed up the towns, but the links between the towns. And at the finish, life in Germany just ran down, like a clock. Space and time meant nothing. Because the people, the links between the people, were smashed too. They were just left wondering, searching, looking for food, looking for their homes — looking for each other.
>
> [*People looking at a wall full of notices; male and female voices off-screen*] Ich suche meine Frau . . . Ich suche mein Mann . . . Ich suche Frieda Wintler geborene Jonuscheit . . . Ich suche meine Frau Elfrieda Schultz und Tochter Krista . . . Achtung Stalingradkämpfer! Wer kennt den Sanitäts unterofficier Heinz Kuhlman . . .
>
> [*Group of children sitting on their belongings in a street*] There are some seventy million people in Germany, and about thirty

million of them are looking for someone. Or are lost and lie looking without seeing [*Close-up of a child*] like the eyes of a dead rabbit. They are still stunned by what hit them. Stunned with the war they started. But in the search for food and the urge to get home, the life-force begins to stir again. [*Organ-grinder in front of a pile of rubble*]

[*Young family huddled around a camp-stove*] Today, our powers of destruction are terrifying. But the will to live is still stronger. That's why we can't wash our hands of the Germans. We can't afford that new life flow in any direction it wants.

[*British officer behind desk in an office*] Our military government, that is your husbands and sons, has to prod the Germans into putting their house in order. [*Group of Germans file in and are addressed by the officer*] Why? We have an interest in Germany that is purely selfish: we cannot live next to a disease-ridden neighbour. And we must prevent not only starvation and epidemics but also diseases of the mind, new brands of fascism, from springing up. What is more we have to persuade the Germans to do this themselves.

[*Closing sequence: British sentry silhouetted against bailey-bridge over Rhine, evening-time, sound of a siren*] As night falls in Germany the people must remember the curfew. Those without homes or caught on the streets disappear into air-raid shelters. [*Shots of women huddled at tables, men and children sleeping, etc.*] Then the air-raid siren wails again! To remind them that they lost the war of their own making. That it is up to them to regain their self-respect as a nation — and to learn to live in a friendly manner with their neighbours. To remind them that, much as we hate it, we shall stay in Germany until we have *real* guarantees that the next generation will grow up a sane and Christian people. A Germany of light and life and freedom; a Germany which respects truth and tolerance — and justice.

[*British officer in front of Union Jack administers oath to Germans, in judicial gowns and caps*] Now, gentlemen, you will raise your right hands and take the oath with me. I swear by Almighty God that I will at all times apply and administer the Law, and with justice and equity to all, whatever creed, race, colour or political opinion they may be, I will obey the laws of Germany, to establish equal justice under the Law to all persons. So help me God.

[*While the oath is repeated by the Germans, picture cross-cuts between them, children playing, and finally a German steel-helmet on the cross at the head of a grave against a busy square, coming back to the exterior of the building of the Military Government and the oath-taking inside. The film ends with the British officer looking on as he listens to 'So Wahr mir Gott helfe' and with a final close-up on a German judge with hand raised.*]

The presentation of defeated Germany in British newsreels — and indeed the popular press — was a classic illustration of the working of the media at its most effective. As the work of American media research, beginning with Lazarsfeld's work during the war itself and replicated many times since, has shown, the media is at its most effective where it is required to reinforce and articulate existing attitudes, when it can draw on existing stereotypes in the perceptual world of the audience, and when its job is to channel and point these attitudes towards a policy which can be presented as logically following from them. At the same time, it has also become a media-research axiom that the media is also at its most effective where the policy is novel: the greater the novelty of the policy, *given pre-existing attitudes to work on*, the greater its effectiveness for inducing the perceptual shift needed for its acceptance. 'Re-education' was about as novel a policy as could be imagined. Nothing like it has ever been undertaken by Britain in respect of another European country; nor has Britain ever contemplated occupation of a defeated European adversary for any length of time, let alone an open-ended commitment, which could most likely be for a generation or more. To persuade the general public to be prepared for such an undertaking, not to mention the soldiers and teachers and administrators longing to get back to England and get out of the terrible conditions in Germany, physical as well as spiritual, was the perfect brief for testing the skills of the media men, not only those of newsreelmen, of course. Whereas the newsreels were the media for the general conditioning of attitudes and for pointing the public towards the desired policy, the documentary was the medium for building on it in specific terms for the specific people: administrators, teachers and others who needed to be individually persuaded. It was also the medium where the issues could be put explicitly and specifically, yet would still rely on the stirring of the generalised, emotionalised attitudes built up in the audience over a long time previously.

Newsreels, the documentary, and the other media share a curious characteristic when they are used for propaganda purposes. Although they serve the policy needs of the moment, their effect, unwittingly and indeed undesired, lasts beyond the needs of the policy. They leave 'a sediment on the mind' as Sir Charles Grant Robertson called it, or have a 'hangover effect' as John Grierson termed it: others might say it can poison the mind. The way Germany was presented in her hour of defeat certainly helped with the acceptance of the policy of re-education and prolonged occupation (by one means or another) instead of seeking a normal peace arrangement, even after a number of years. However, the effects of the skilful and consistent rearticulation of the stereotype of 'the Hun' inside the German as the definition of the Nazi, the presentation of 'militarism' and Nazism alike as mere manifestations of 'the psychology of the German nation', remained. Yesterday's propaganda remains a factor to be taken into account however unwelcome. The newsreels', and other media's, presentation of Germany in total desolation therefore have an evidentiary significance not only for understanding British policy and attitudes during the *Stunde Null* period. They need to be considered also in seeking the roots of later policies and the public's attitude to them. The newsreels, documentaries (and the other media not discussed here) should be seen as one part of the evidence for understanding the history of the post-AMG period of Anglo-German relations.

Notes

1. 6 November 1917. Keith Wilson, 'Great War prologue' in N. Pronay and K. Wilson (eds), *The political re-education of Germany and her allies after World War II* (London, 1985), p.50.

2. For Northcliffe's views and the work of papers and correspondents see R. Pound and G. Harmsworth, *Northcliffe* (London, 1959).

3. R.R. James, *The memoirs of a Conservative . . . J.C.C. Davidson* (London, 1969), p.20.

4. For references to the debate about the inner dynamics of Germany during the inter-war period in Britain, and a discussion of the issues and views involved, see my 'To stamp out the whole tradition . . .' in Pronay and Wilson (eds), *The political re-education of Germany*. For a wide-ranging discussion of the whole matter of 'German militarism' see Volker R. Berghahn, *Militarism: the history of an international debate, 1861-1979* (Cambridge, 1984).

3

Soviet Film Chronicles and the Fall of Nazi Germany

Sergei Drobashenko

The film chronicles of the final stage of the war of the Allied Powers against Nazi Germany is a unique, in many ways unparallelled, phenomenon.

The uniqueness of the documentary footage filmed in the spring of 1945 can be attributed to several circumstances. The most important of these is the great significance of the event itself: the victory meant the end of a most terrible war that had cost humanity 50 million lives; it meant the destruction of German fascism. For the Soviet people this period was a crucial, historic stage in the struggle against the enemy that four years before had treacherously attacked its Motherland. For Germany, too, it marked a major turning-point in its history, with subsequent division of the country and the establishment of two German states with different social systems. All this together not only signified profound social transformations, but also influenced the individual life of every Russian, every German, every person in the liberated countries of Eastern Europe, every soldier of the Allied armies.

In this report I shall dwell on how some of these events that 'made history' in 1945 were reflected on the documentary screen.

The first large batch of film documents, grouped together by the logics of history itself, are those that show the battle of Berlin and the capture of the capital of the Third Reich.

As is known, Berlin, the citadel of German fascism, was stormed and captured by Soviet troops led by Marshal Grigorii Zhukov in the first days of May 1945. May 9, the day following the signing of Germany's unconditional surrender, has been celebrated ever since as Victory Day, a national holiday that the Soviet people regard as a very special one. The Battle of Berlin and the storming of the city were filmed by about eighty Soviet frontline cameramen, among them the future leader of the epic Soviet-American serial *The Unknown War*, Roman Karmen.

The cameramen recorded in great detail the final operations of the Soviet Army that brought about the complete destruction of Nazism. This precious footage was extensively used in numerous newsreels, in Iuli Raizman's *Berlin* and many other films. The shots of the fighting in the streets of Berlin were especially impressive, for they are not limited to artillery duels and tank movements, they let us see the fighters at close range: running from house to house in a hailstorm of shells and bullets, or standing still for a moment, gun in hand, pressed to a wall, or looking out of their shelter to locate the enemy. Soviet cameramen, breaking away from the tendency to show a battle as a confrontation between masses of anonymous troops, sought to give the spectator a close-up portrait of the soldier, the maker of victory.

A broader, symbolic meaning is easily found in the shots of artillery men loading their gun with a shell inscribed 'On the Reichstag', of Soviet soldiers crossing the square in front of the Reichstag building, storming in and putting up on its roof a red flag of victory.

Soviet cameramen showed on the screen a series of suicides by Wehrmacht officers and high-ranking commanders who thus reacted to the crushing of Nazism. Millions of people could see the ruins of Hitler's *Reichskanzlei* and a huge globe, broken, flattened, lying on the floor among the debris. The pictures of the charred bodies of Goebbels and Hitler became gruesome evidence of the final defeat of the Reich.

The documentary footage of fighting in the streets of Berlin contain shots that may be seen as a symbol of victory — hundreds, thousands of white flags hanging from all the windows. Less known is another film document, of German generals driven in an open car around the city where at some points along the route they order the remaining German troops to lay down their weapons.

German prisoners of war, thousands of them, marching on the screen: these documentary shots also contribute to the story of the defeat of fascism. We see officers and men coming out of houses and bomb-shelters, their hands up in surrender; we see them, a grey mass, trudging along the streets in an endless column. Sometimes the camera takes a closer look at their faces, the faces of broken people, tired to death, indifferent to all and everything. To a Soviet cameraman belongs a memorable shot of a German youth sitting among ruins, alone and lost, clasping his head with his hands — a striking generalised image of disillusionment and despair. Maybe we can regard it as the precursor of the 'lost generation' that in the post-war years became such a popular subject in literature, though in none of the many novels is its lot as hard and dramatic as in real life.

The burning houses, the broken machines, the dead bodies among the ruins, the long panorama of what used to be the beautiful Unter den Linden. And a finale — the endless aerial shot of Berlin, a destroyed city: house after house, street after street, heaps of brick and stone, empty windows . . .

All this material has been used in many films. A recent example is Maximilian Schell's *Marlene* in which documentary footage of Berlin in 1945 serves as an expressive counterpoint to Miss Dietrich's voice as she remembers the respectable and comfortable city of her youth.

It should be said that when showing German prisoners Soviet cameramen revealed the significant difference, noticeable in both appearance and reaction, between soldiers on the one hand, and officers, especially the top ranks in the Nazi army, on the other. The former are calm and indifferent, they submit to what they see as the inevitable outcome, though they are aware of the consequences. The latter try to conceal their anxiety and fear behind a mask of feigned arrogance. This was the beginning of a new theme in Soviet documentary film-makers' work, the emergence of a new Germany, the establishment of co-operation between the German population and the Soviet administration.

Among the prisoners, the camera singles out members of the *Volkssturm*, teenagers and old men in oversized uniforms. A Soviet general surrounded by soldiers talks with one of such boys in *Volkssturm* uniforms; there is sympathy, not hatred, in the older man's attitude — this is another development of the theme of contacts between the Soviet Army and the German people.

The outcome of the war, the end of a world tragedy — for many these are connected with the formal signing of Nazi Germany's unconditional capitulation they have seen on the screen. Here, too, the camera is not merely a registrar of a historic event, it is also an attentive witness, a psychologist, attempting to reveal the profound significance of the ceremony. We see Marshal Zhukov, with a stern face, signing the document as if putting the

Soviet Film Chronicles

last full stop to the war; we notice how Field Marshal General von Keitel's hand is shaking as he nervously tries to catch hold of his monocle falling from his eye. Behind the participants in the ceremony, their behaviour, we glimpse opposing social and moral forces, we see history being made ...

The unity and friendship of the soldiers of the Allied armies permeate the documentary episodes of the meeting on the Elbe, where Soviet and US soldiers joined hands; of the reception for Allied commanders with Marshal Zhukov raising his glass to the common victory. The well-known footage of the tripartite summit conference at Potsdam showed the difficult task of working out joint decisions on a post-war settlement.

It was natural that many of the film documents of the time feature the Soviet soldier in the days of victory. It is possible to single out several aspects of this theme: funerals of those killed in the last days, or even hours, of the war, their comrades saluting at the graves; the calm confidence of the men who can now relax after all the strain and hardship; the merry dancing to an accordion. Of the many such shots one is especially vivid: a smiling girl in an army uniform, a nurse or a telephone operator, waltzes around as an embodiment of youth, and her dance seems so out of place among the cold, grey ruins ...

The theme of great victory, of the triumph of the Soviet armed forces as reflected in documentary footage filmed in Berlin, was in many films coupled with shots taken during victory celebrations in Moscow, at other fronts, in the liberated countries of Eastern Europe.

An important topic in the documentary film material of the spring of 1945 is the fate of the German people. The usual scenes here, that we have seen in similar situations before, are civilians with suitcases and bundles returning to their homes after the end of the fighting. Many could not find their homes. And the camera recorded these moments of frustration, despondency and sorrow clearly visible in the faces of women sitting in the middle of the street, in the figure of a boy huddled on the steps of a house. So it had been in Spain, in Stalingrad, in so many other places ...

In Berlin there was no electricity, food was short, the water supply system was damaged and there were long queues for water that was brought in barrels. The city was threatened with epidemic diseases. From these shots begins the theme of the assistance given by the Soviet Army to the civilian population of Berlin.

The well-known footage: Berliners are getting hot food from Russian field kitchens, Soviet soldiers are handing out bread. And once again this is not only a reportage, with a noticeable propagandistic colouring. In these shots one cannot help feeling an attempt to study the psychology of the people, to record the gradually changing atmosphere. We see the searching, watchful eyes of both the victors and the defeated, the Germans' marked effort to preserve their independence, under no circumstances to appear servile. One little-known shot is interesting in this context: an elderly German for a long time closely watches a group of Russian soldiers passing by; that this sight gives him much food for thought is what the spectator can read in this scene.

At a time when Berlin was threatened with hunger and chaos a new word is heard in the streets of the ruined city, '*komendatura*'. That was the Russian name for the Soviet military administration.

The Soviet film chronicles recorded the work of the first commandant of Berlin, General N. Berzarin; in one shot we see him with Marshal Zhukov.

General Berzarin's first order after he took his new post deserves special attention. It read:

> The Commandants of all the districts of the city of Berlin must take measures to provide for the needs of medical institutions, including food, water and fuel. For maternity homes, hospitals and clinics, dairy cows must be provided to ensure the supply of fresh milk. All elderly and disabled people must be given housing. Food rations to civilian population to be given out for five days in advance.

This document is rarely quoted by historians who want to underline the austerity of the military administration of the time. But it exists, it can be seen on the screen in both Russian and German, and in the spring of 1945 Germans read it in the streets of Berlin.

The film chronicles give a fairly objective account of how the co-operation between the Soviet adminstration and the German population gradually developed, how both sides learned to trust each other. It is important to stress that this was a mutual confidence, otherwise it could not bear positive results.

The camera recorded examples of considerable material aid to the people of Berlin provided by the Soviet Army command: the arrival of trains with food supplies at the station, the sending of truckloads of food to the city. Here are a few figures that give an idea of the amount of that aid. In the first months of peace the German population received a hundred thousand tons of potatoes, over a hundred thousand tons of flour, several thousand head of cattle. This food was not coming from the occupied parts of Germany; it was sent to the West from the Soviet Union where the destruction and privations of the war years were still badly felt.

In the middle of May food rations were introduced in Berlin and coupons issued. There were long queues, but the Germans were surprised at the rations established by the Soviet *Komendatura* — they were getting 600 grams of bread a day. There was also real coffee and other foodstuffs.

The film documents show that these actions of the Soviet government played an important role: more and more people were coming back to Berlin; in a short time the population of the city doubled.

We can notice a distinct tendency in the work of Soviet filmmakers in Germany at that time: their attention was focused on the democratic changes in the country, on the liquidation of Nazi institutions, the abolition of the ideas and the very spirit of Nazism, on the closer relations between the Soviet administration and the Germans.

That is why the documentary film materials show in such detail the setting-up and spreading of the *Taglische Rundschau* newspaper published by the Soviet military administration in the German language; the sessions of the civilian city council jointly presided over by General Berzarin and Doctor Werner, Mayor of Berlin; the activities of the Communist Party, for instance Wilhelm Pick's speech at a rally on 11 June 1945. These film documents reflected the Soviet government's policy concerning Germany's future, clearly demonstrated the constant normalisation of life in conditions of peace, and showed the emergence of tendencies that were new to German reality.

The way to normal life was difficult, the reconstruction of the city, the removal of ruins, the clearing of streets, demanded a lot of hard work. There is a great deal of film material that shows Berliners clearing the streets of bricks and stones, restoring the tram lines, rebuilding the bridges. By the end of June 52 Underground stations were put into operation, trams reappeared on eight of the old routes, bus services were started. More than 100 cinemas functioned in the city (at some of them Soviet films attracted large audiences), there were 45 variety shows and a comedy theatre.

A correspondent for a German newspaper visited Gerhart Hauptmann at Agnetendorf. The camera preserved this interview, showed his house; later it allowed millions to attend the writer's funeral. These documentary shots are only a small portion of the footage that reflected the reviving cultural life of the German population.

In the spring and summer of 1945 Soviet cameramen filmed the work of farmers tilling their fields. In autumn they recorded the reopening of the Universities in Berlin and Jena.

The Potsdam decision, and the political actions that followed, completed the division of Germany. But this subject lies outside the theme of the present report.

In conclusion it can be said with good reason that the film chronicles of the fall of Nazi Germany and the first months of peace, thanks to the work of Soviet cameramen, reflected the major events of those days and was both detailed and convincing. In line with the Soviet government policies (and it could not be otherwise) this documentary film material showed first of all the democratic changes in Germany, the overcoming of psychological barriers and the development of co-operation between the Soviet Army and later the military administration on the one hand, and the German people on the other hand.

This documentary material was of great importance at that time. Used in many films in the first post-war years and at later stages, it played an important propagandistic role and contributed to the solution of large-scale political tasks. This documentary footage can serve as a good example of what the documentary film-maker can do in showing such complicated critical historical periods as the spring of 1945, forty years ago. This film material and the description of the shots still remain an interesting and valuable source for historians.

4
The Red Army Beflags the Reichstag: Film as Historical Fantasy

Richard C. Raack

To tell the story of the Battle of Berlin demands special effort to penetrate the historical darkness which derives largely from the nature of the original reportage as well as from the recollections and historical retrospectives which have followed. Deliberate, politically inspired, obfuscation has played its role. Rediscovering from a variety of historical sources what actually transpired at one historical moment in the battle and comparing that description with a famous film representation of the same event will reveal a part of the story, suggest the dimensions of the problem as a whole, and help epitomise the problems of relying on film as historical evidence and of finding the locally unwanted truths about the history of the Soviet Union.

For the Soviet Union the focus of the Battle of Berlin was the Reichstag. This pile of stone, steel and glass, built as the meeting-place of the democratic house of the German imperial legislature at the end of the nineteenth century, stood out with its massive cupola above the trees of the eastern part of the Tiergarten, higher than the Brandenburg Gate. Its cupola was, like those of the former royal castle of the House of Hohenzollern and of the nearby cathedral, one of the readily identifiable masses of the Berlin skyline.[1]

For some reason — a number are given by Soviet authors, film-makers and participants, who ceaselessly recount the episodes of the victory over Germany in 1945 — the Russians had pegged the Reichstag as the symbol of conquest of the city. For some time Stalin had been saying, 'Put the flag of victory above Berlin.' Whether or not he actually said, 'And put it on the Reichstag,' is ambiguous in the Russian text. But as the Reichstag is joined in the text to the command 'hoist the red banner of victory', and this is presented as the main symbol of success in the battle, the Reichstag's conquest became the victory symbol. Soviet authors of the time spoke constantly of carrying out the will of Marshal Stalin, whose motives in making the attack on the city were essentially political and symbolic, and there appears to have been no ambiguity in the minds of the Soviets at the time as to how that was to be accomplished.[2]

This choice, of course, was utterly bizarre, but not at all untypical of Soviet wartime behaviour. Not only was the Reichstag properly the symbol of democracy — for which the Soviets claimed to be fighting — under the Hohenzollerns, it was also carried over as the seat of genuine democracy under the German republic which followed the Hohenzollerns in 1918. Moreover, it had been the place of the famous Reichstag fire of 27 February 1933, the fire which the Nazis blamed on German Communist incendiaries. Using the fire as a pretext to suggest the threat to civil order, the Nazis suspended many of the Communists' election privileges, invaded and seized their headquarters, and arrested their leaders, virtually on the eve of a hard-fought election campaign whose goal was to secure Adolf Hitler's place in the Chancellery to which he had only recently been appointed. The Nazis then arrested and publicly tried some of the Communist leaders for their alleged role in starting the fire.

This was, no doubt, one of the bits of history known to Comrade, now Marshal, Stalin. He was not a cosmopolitan or well-travelled man. He certainly knew of the Reichstag fire and its perhaps incorrect but, for the Nazis, propagandistically effective connection with the German Communists and the Communist International as a whole. He knew that these events directly preceded the final Nazi takeover. Hence his likely juxtaposition of the Reichstag with 'fascism', rather than with democracy, however differently from his contemporary Western Allies he might have defined the latter term.

Most of the Red Army men made not even that connection. They were merely carrying out orders. That they had, even ambiguously, been given out by Stalin, was sufficient. Perhaps the fact that 'Reichstag' was erroneously translated into Russian as the 'imperial building' connected it even more solidly with the 'imperialists' whom the Soviet propagandists, forgetting, towards the end of the war, their earlier temporary deference to their imperial British ally, had once again begun to combat. In any case, the desire to take the Reichstag generated enormous

Film as Historical Fantasy

competition among the Red Army men to do the job.[3]

Soviet authors writing later, though not at the time, recognised the need to work out even further justifications for the concentration on the storming of the Reichstag. After all, the symbol had cost hundreds, perhaps thousands, of soldiers' lives.[4] So for Soviet historians Vorob'ev and Telpuchovski it became a 'main defence point'. For General Chuikov it was 'convenient for defence'. Yet for pro-Soviet Polish historian Ozmańczyk, it was only a *symbol* of pre-war German imperialism.[5] Later, after the purge of the memory of Stalin at the time of Nikita S. Khrushchev's attack on the 'cult of personality' in 1956, the orders for the assault were recalled as coming only from the 'supreme command' — 'High Supreme Commander' and Marshal Stalin had been moved, albeit temporarily as we now know, from central focus and responsibility into historical obscurity. Nonetheless, the importance of the Reichstag in the Berlin story, and its beflagging, remained central for Soviet writers and others who followed their motifs.[6]

In any case, Stalin had given the order. It had to be carried out. And the drama of the symbolic conquest and the fall of Berlin, which all of the Russians hoped to arrange in time for the Soviet May Day celebration of 1945, had to be recorded for all time.[7] And once the drama had been recorded, had become 'history', it was not to be changed. What was past was done, and the guild of history writers in the Soviet Union later must cover it up, rescore it more heroically or just plain ratify it by merging it into the current interpretive line.

The storming of the Reichstag had become a part of the legend of Russian and Soviet arms, one of the triumphs of the Soviet common man over evil — like the storming of the Winter Palace in 1917. In order not to change that history, the myth of the symbolic importance of the Reichstag even today still has to remain unchallenged.

As the Red Army command prepared the assault on Berlin in April 1945, the Central Red Banner Documentary Film Studio brought together a film crew of directors and cameramen around the military units to record the 'final storm'.[8] Like the revolt aboard the *Potemkin* in 1905 and the taking of the Winter Palace, both of which became eternal history on celluloid under the direction of Eisenstein in the 1920s, the film version of the Battle of Berlin was to become the preponderant account of the battle, and of the storming of the Reichstag itself.

Film as Historical Fantasy

When the Red Army assault on Berlin was launched from positions near the Oder River on 16 April, the camera crews under the direction of Soviet feature-film director Iuli Raizman went along. Following the slogan, 'put the flag of victory above Berlin', Soviet units competed with one another to carry out Stalin's charge; and Soviet cameramen competed to film the deed.[9] The Russians had often proved in earlier stages of the campaign how important to them were the symbols of victory. For example, instead of simply by-passing German armies which remained trapped at Hitler's insane orders in the eastern cities far behind the rapidly moving front, they systematically undertook to reduce each urban fortress the Nazis defended. In these places, the Germans might have been left to sit and starve until a final surrender — the strategy American General Douglas MacArthur used under not entirely dissimilar circumstances against the Japanese in the Pacific. But the Red Army bombarded each city or town fortress into rubble before it was stormed, though ironically most of them (like Tarnopol, Danzig, Königsberg and Breslau), according to the Soviet schedule of territorial changes and annexations for German and Polish lands in the east, were to become new Soviet cities or towns, or to be turned over by Stalin to their Allies, the crypto-communist temporary Polish Government of National Unity, for colonisation once the German population had been expelled. The Red Army, expending enormous numbers of troops, carried out the sieges and took the rubble. For the tops of the rubble, each unit was issued its quota of red banners.[10] A number of those, and not just one, as it turned out, were to go above the Reichstag as well.

Thirteen days after the assault on the Oder River line, the Red Army was before the Reichstag, deep in central Berlin, and only a couple of hundred metres from the bunker from which Hitler was still directing the senseless defence of what remained of the city.

There are elaborate descriptions of the assault of the Soviet troops on the Reichstag building, which had been well fortified by the desperate remaining German and other German-allied troops inside. The attack began on 30 April. Though no one knew it at the time, Hitler was, at the very time of the first attack, dead, a recent suicide in his bunker.

With the same reckless zeal with which the Russians had assaulted the city — they would later proudly (and naively) cite the number of their casualties in the final campaigns as proof positive of the dimension and sincerity of their engagement —

Film as Historical Fantasy

they attacked the well-defended building.[11] They thereby diverted countless troops from the campaign to occupy the centre of the city and Hitler's bunker, after which mopping-up operations might have been conducted. In fact, when the city surrendered on 2 May, the majority of the remaining enemy troops hiding in redoubts, bunkers and cellars — places like the gutted Reichstag — emerged peacefully.

The assault seems to have carried the first Soviet echelons into the building at about 2 p.m., on 30 April, but the Germans and their allies fought on, floor by floor, and even out of the basement, into which many of them retreated, until the next morning. By then, according to Soviet accounts — and there are literally hundreds of them as the story of glory is told and retold for every possible occasion — there were numbers of flags on the Reichstag.

Only one account of the first beflagging of the Reichstag is regularly told, that of Lieutenant Egorov and Sergeant Kantaria who, depending on the account read, put the flag somewhere on the Reichstag sometime between 2.25 p.m. and later, after dark, the same evening. But many other accounts credit different flag-bearers for the first hoisting. The competition for the honour, like the competition among the units of the Red Army to be the first into Berlin, was severe. One can only imagine the number of extra casualties that the effort required. The Soviet Commander, Marshal Georgii Zhukov, recalled hearing at *3 p.m.* on 30 April that the flag of victory was on the Reichstag. But if this was true, the story of the filming of the storm of the Reichstag, pictures of which appear with virtually every account, has to be false.[12]

Naturally this great event itself was the cardinal moment to be recorded for the victory film. But it was not: because, as most of the Soviet accounts by the film-makers tell us, the flag was put in place *after* darkness fell; that, in Berlin at the end of April, would have been after 8 p.m. Central European time. Therefore the account given to Zhukov and manifoldly repeated has to be false. But by the morning of 1 May, there were any number of red banners in place. Whoever put up 'the flag', which of the flags and wherever, whether Egorov and Kantaria at 2.30 or 10.50 p.m. (Moscow, or Central European, time?), or Lieutenant Sorokin along with Riadov and Bulatov, or Captain Samsonov, or one or two others among the numberless Soviet heroes 'not seeking any fame' (as one of the famous Soviet cinematographers, Roman Karmen, who wasn't there, reported), we'll obviously never know.[13] There is a flag, said to have been put up by Egorov and Kantaria, on display in the Soviet Army Museum in Moscow. Contemporary actor Burt Lancaster solemnly repeated its story, as if it were all true and the only one in town, when he introduced the segment of the Roman-Karmen-instigated Moscow-produced television series, *The Unknown War*, to American audiences, under a significantly different title to Western audiences in Germany and the Netherlands, and under other titles to Eastern Bloc audiences in East Germany and Poland, among others, just a few years ago. A great many of Lancaster's historical recountings in that series are, regrettably, just as inaccurate as that one.[14]

The Stalin-Prize-winning director of the famous film account of the fall of Berlin, which was purveyed under several titles in several editions in strikingly different versions since 1945, told of the filming.[15] According to Iuli Raizman it was done on the morning of 1 May. But like so many of the tales that make up the Reichstag story, and this one is characteristic of the historiography of heroism and deception by which the events of the past are either magnified or denied, Raizman told only a bare detail of what occurred that morning: the filming of the flag-raising. He does not tell us that, at that time or perhaps another, the entire storming of the Reichstag, including the dramatic charge up the main steps, was restaged and shot, as was the fixing of the flag on the statue of Germania.[16] He does not tell us that he and his colleagues even turned the chronology of historical events around to suit Stalin's imaginings about Berlin's political centre. In the first episode of the film, the narrator tells us (over a tilt-down shot of the Reich Chancellery taken by the Soviets on 2 May) that the battle for the Reichstag 'goes on'. This absurd rearrangement by Raizman and colleagues (all of whom knew better) persists into the editions of 1968 (though Stalin himself vanishes, his work lives on!) and 1979 (as in *The Unknown War* and other titles). He also fails to tell us that the cinema version endlessly repeated is no more a true recording of the actual event than were Eisenstein's restaging of the Odessa Steps sequence in *Potemkin* or the storming of the Winter Palace in *October* (also known as *Ten Days that Shook the World*) actual scenes of historical events. Nor is it any longer recalled that there are numerous published still photographs of fixing the flag in various places on the destroyed building, all of them likewise purveyed as the actual event. The famous Soviet cameraman and producer Roman Karmen

Film as Historical Fantasy

claimed for cameraman M. Shneiderov the glory of filming the planting of the flag as shown in the film. But this had to be a daylight scene even according to Karmen, perhaps taken on the morning of 1 May.[17] The flag had actually been raised during the evening and night before. In the morning, according to others, there were many. But Karmen, who, to repeat, wasn't there, was not deterred from turning Shneiderov into a bold warrior 'who stormed to the roof with an automatic' to take the 'deathless' shot, 'the hoisting of our flag of victory above the *citadel of German fascism*' (my italics). An earlier account even has Shneiderov running 'under a hail of fire' along with the first troops to put the flag above the Reichstag.[18]

This short account of the Reichstag's fall and beflagging catches the sense of so many of the stories that ought to be examined about the Second World War, about major aspects of Soviet behaviour in general, as well as about the general nature of historical reporting and verisimilitude in film. The Reichstag was a symbol of victory in a symbolic campaign for Berlin which Western leaders gladly left to the Soviet Union.[19] The symbol of victory was chosen for all the wrong reasons. Hundreds, perhaps thousands, of casualties occurred in just this one payment to the symbolic account. When the goal was achieved, it had not been cinematographically immortalised as planning would have had it. For dramatic reasons the entire scene was therefore restaged. The restaging was purveyed in 1945, and still is — by Lancaster and his Soviet colleagues — as the record of actual events. Only in Soviet professional literature about film is there even the slightest hint that the restaging was done, and even there a correct description of what happened is still elaborately circumlocuted. Probably because of the considerable rewards for heroism extended to those who beflagged the Reichstag, there is controversy in Soviet history writing about who actually did the task first, but the issue itself is never directly confronted.

The story of the recording was dramatized by one of the Soviet Union's most famous cameramen. His story obscures the truth. One of the Soviet Union's famous directors told but a fragment of the truth about the restaging of the charge, evidently to maintain the fiction he had contrived of its representation of real history.[20] American actor Burt Lancaster, years later, probably inadvertently, willingly repeats the Soviet myth about the flag of victory that his Soviet co-workers undoubtedly told him.[21] Famous men of reputation bend and are bent to the needs of those who need

Film as Historical Fantasy

supporting fables. A distinguished actor is made into an *ingénue*. As Leonid Brezhnev, probably willingly taken along in the act, not so long ago put it, referring to the banner of Egorov and Kantaria: 'This was the undying flag of October; this was the great flag of Lenin; this was the indefatigable flag of Socialism.'[22]

If a debate over the historical truth were launched, a puerile argument over pride of place, the controversy would certainly tarnish the glory of all the contenders for the honour of being first. If the staging of the scenes were directly revealed, the accepted truth would be muddied. If that, then even the wisdom underlying the storm, or even of the extravagant Soviet casualties in the Battle of Berlin itself would be questioned — not to mention those in countless bloody assaults which ended with flags in the rubble of towns which the Soviets and their Polish Communist allies had to labour to rebuild after the war.[23] And if the Reichstag assault, or the conduct of the Battle of Berlin, or the policy of taking German fortified towns behind the lines were questioned, the leader of those times and those who collaborated with him would have to be publicly recalled and their actions critically reviewed. And the *Vozhd* is still only reluctantly remembered, just now far more than at any time in the last 30 years, so that the patriotic fervor of 1941–45 can be called up in support of the state today. But only the glorious times are recalled; his murderous deeds and criminal follies have gone largely unmentioned so that recollections of his countless victims will not be aroused and so that the system which produced him and his holocausts can go on and on unchallenged.[24]

So there is as yet no Soviet historical school to systematically revise the propagandistic fantasy events of the past. Nikita S. Khrushchev, who started one, has himself been banished to the same obscurity to which he once delivered Stalin. Santayana's words about history, so often cited but rarely remembered, assure us that those who deny the past will constantly repeat it: repeat it in history so that the historical myths sustaining the apparatus of the system can go critically untested; repeat it in behaviour so that the designs of yesterday will prefigure those of today and tomorrow.

Notes

1. The Reichstag has a fascinating history ably recounted in Michael

Film as Historical Fantasy

S. Cullen, *Der Reichstag: Die Geschichte eines Monumentes* (Münsterschwarzach, 1983). There are many volumes and numberless articles on the Battle of Berlin. The best, in English or any language, is John Erickson, *The Road to Berlin* (Boulder, 1983), extraordinarily detailed and well-researched, yet unaware of the many film sources on the subject and a bit too uncritical of the Soviet evidence.

2. On the political importance of Berlin to the Soviets: Alexander Fischer, *Die sowjetische Deutschlandpolitik im Zweiten Weltkrieg* (Stuttgart, 1975), pp.135–6, cites much of the Soviet evidence. See, for example, Sergei Shtemenko, *Im Generalstab*, German edn, (Berlin, 1969), p.341; and Valentina Kutschinskaja, 'Die politische Bedeutung der Berliner Operation der Sowjetischen Armee und die Haltung der Westmächte', *Wissenschaftliche Zeitschrift der Humboldt-Universität zu Berlin* (Gesellschafts- und Sprachwissenschaftliche Reihe). XIX Jg. (1970), H.2, p.174; and Grigorii K. Zhukov, 'Die Kronung des Sieges'. *Neues Deutschland*, 25 April 1970, p.4. The Warsaw Poles (the TRJN) fielded an army on the Eastern front after 1943 and were invited by the Soviet Union in the last few days of the Berlin battle to partake in the siege and the victory. The Poles saw the invitation as political and symbolic. The invitation came from the Soviets on such grounds — another proof, if one is needed, that the Soviets saw it that way too. See Kazimierz Sobczak, *Lenino-Warszawa-Berlin: Wojenne dzieje I Dywizji im. Tadeusza Kosciuszki* (Warsaw, 1978) *passim*; Zdziskaw Stąpor, *Bitwa o Berlin: Działania 1 armii WP kwiecień-maj 1945* (Warsaw, 1973), p.288; Edmund J. Osmańczyk, *Chwalebna wyprawa na Berlin*, 2nd edn (Warsaw, 1971), p.132; and Andrzej Krajewski, *Drugi Berlinski: Z dziewów 2 berlinskiego pulku piechoty* (Warsaw, 1979), p.507. On the Reichstag as symbol and the film *Berlin* (Moscow, Central Red Banner Documentary Film Studio, 1945, several editions, and, years later, several more editions), see V. Smirnov, *Dokumental'nye fil'my Velikoi Otechestvennoi voiny* (Moscow, 1947), pp.222–4; Iulii Raizman, 'Berlin (iz bloknota kinorezhissera)' in V.I. Zeltov (ed.), *Ikh oruzhie — kinokamera* (Moscow, 1970), pp.285–6; H. Kolesnikova *et al.*, *Roman Karmen* (Moscow, 1959), p.95; Georgii Petrussow, *Begegnungen mit Berlin* (Berlin, 1970), p.7; Roman Karmen, *Geroika boriby i sozdaniia: Zametki kinodokumental'ista* (Moscow, 1967), p.38. A typical Stalinist version of the battle, which not only denigrates the role of the Western Allies in the war but even leaves unmentioned (as does the first version of the film) the role of the Poles in the Battle for Berlin, is given by N.M. Zamiatin, *Berlinskaia operatsiia* (Moscow, 1949).

3. The charge by Stalin generated enormous competition among the Red Army men and even among their senior officers to do the job. See Iulii Raizman 'Berlin (iz bloknota kinorezhissera)' in Zeltov (ed.), *Ikh oruzhie — kinokamera*, p.285; retold by Boris Medvedev, *Svidetel' obvineniia* 2nd edn (Moscow, 1971), and often elsewhere in Soviet film history literature.

4. Zentralkomitee der Kommunistischen Partei der Sowjet Union (ed.), *Geschichte der Grossen Vaterländischen Krieges der Sowjetunion*, vol. V, German edn, (Berlin, 1967), p.328.

5. F.D. Vorob'ev, I.V. Parotkin, and A.H. Shimanskii, *Poslednii shturm (Berlinskaia operatsiia 1945 g.)*, 2nd edn (Moscow, 1975), p.340, a

characteristic Soviet account: the authors describe as 'falsificatory' well-known Western writers like Cornelius Ryan, author of *The last battle* (New York, 1966), and Earl Ziemke (whose name they mispell!), the noted military historian author of *The Battle for Berlin* (London, 1969). See Boris S. Telpuchowski, *Die sowjetische Geschichte des Grossen Vaterländischen Krieges 1941–1945*, German edn by Andreas Hillgruber and Hans-Adolf Jacobsen (Frankfurt am Main, 1961), p.475; Zhukov, 'Die Kronung des Sieges'; Vasilii I. Chuikov, *Ot Stalingrada do Berlina* (Moscow, 1980), p.634; and Osmańczyk, *Chwalebna wyprawa na Berlin*, p.133. For Roman Karmen, the famous Soviet documentary film-maker, 'national artist of the USSR', winner of the State (Stalin) and Lenin Prizes, the Reichstag was the symbol of both the rise and the fall of German fascism (in Roman Karmen, *¡No pasaran!* (Moscow, 1972), p.192).

6. Even the German Communists around Walter Ulbricht in Berlin just after the war dutifully went along with the historical game: 'The Hitler Regime ended in that place in Berlin where it began — the Reichstag,' so wrote the *Deutsche Volkszeitung* (KPD), 21 July 1945, p.4. Of course Ulbricht and his *Moskali* knew exactly where their borscht was seasoned, and TASS — as an examination of the newspapers in Soviet-occupied Berlin at the time reveals — was the main source of their information.

7. Medvedev, *Svidetel' obvineniia*, p.150; Iulii Raizman, *Vchera i segodnia* (Moscow, 1969), p.41; Raizman, 'Berlin', in Zeltov (ed.), *Ikh oruzhie — kinokamera*, p.287.

8. Raizman, Berlin', in Zeltov (ed.), *Ikh oruzhie — kinokamera*, p.286–7.

9. Albert Seaton, *Stalin as military commander* (New York, 1976), p.189.

10. Klaus Scheel (ed.), *Die Befreiung Berlins* (Berlin, 1975), p.147.

11. Telpuchowski, *Die sowjetische Geschichte des Grossen Vaterländischen Krieges*, vol.V, p.335; Georgii Zhukov, *Erinnerungen und Gedanken*, German edn (Stuttgart, 1969), p.69. Less well known are the participation of the Poles recorded by Stanisław Komornicki, *Polacy w szturmie Berlina 1945* (Warsaw, 1971), and Edward Kmiecik, *Berliner Victoria, 24.IV.–2.V. 1945: Polnische Soldaten am Brandenburger Tor* (Warsaw, 1972).

12. Zhukov, *Erinnerungen und Gedanken*, p.603; Zhukov, 'Die Kronung des Sieges', p.4; Zamiatin, *Berlinskaia operatsiia*, has the flag up at 14.25 on 30 April; Telpuchowski, *Die sowjetische Geschichte des Grossen Vaterländischen Krieges*, p.475, has it on the cupola at 14.30 on 30 April. Vasili J. Subbotin, *Wir stürmten den Reichstag: Aufzeichnungen eines Front-Korrespondenten*, German edn, trans. Heinz Kübart (Berlin, 1969), p.75, reports the hoisting of the famous banner at 22.50 (Moscow or Berlin time?) on 30 April; while S. Neustroev, *Put' k Reikhstagu* (Moscow, 1961), p.73, reports it was on the roof 'on the eve' of 30 April. This is but a small selection from a voluminous literature of war stories on the subject.

13. Zentralkomittee der Kommunistischen Partei der Sowjet Union (ed.), *Geschichte des Grossen Vaterländischen Krieges*, vol.V, p.330: an uncritical summary. Roman Karmen, in *¡No Pasaran!*, pp.191–2, while offering a number of other possible stories, reported that Egorov and Kantaria put the flag on the statue of Germania (not the cupola!). Nikolai A. Vikherev, *S Kinoapparatom po zhizni* (Moscow, 1966), p.201,

tells the Egorov and Kantaria story, putting the time at 22.50 (again, what time, Moscow or Berlin?) on 30 April. Karmen, just after the beflagging, seemed to think that Sorokin and Bulatov put the flag on the façade of the building. See Roman Karmen, 'Na telegrafnuiu lentu', in Konstantin F. Telegin, *Poslednii shturm* (Moscow, 1965), p.256.

14. Karmen was the spiritual father of the series. See M.E. Zelenina, *Sovetskoe kinoiskusstvo: Rekomendatel'nyi bibliograficheskii ukazatel' v pomoshch' samoobrazovaniu molodezhi* (Moscow, 1980), p.189; Boris Vasil'ev, 'Kolokola sorok pervovo', *Literaturnaia gazeta*, 7 Mar 1979, p.8; and P. Batov in *Sovetskaia kultura*, 23 February 1979, p.3.

15. According to B. Medvedev, the film also won the grand prize for documentary films at Cannes in 1946. One must wonder what version? I have seen the Korean, British, and American versions of the 1945 editions, and part of the German version. The American version differs rather strikingly from the others. I have seen the Polish, the GDR, and a Russian-language version of the 1968 edition, from which Stalin has been wholly purged, and Zhukov mostly purged — and, when the latter appears, he goes unnamed. It may be that the original Russian-language version was longer than any of the other 1945 editions as *Pravda* cited its length as 80 minutes, and not 60, which most of those listed above approximate. See Smirnov, *Dokumental'nye fil'my Velikoi Otechestvennoi voiny*, pp.232, 238. Between Khrushchev's denunciation of the 'cult of personality' in 1956 and the 'restoration' of the film for the 1968 edition, it was presumably not shown. Its status beyond discussion in these years is suggested by the Byzantine efforts to keep it unmentioned. For example, in a large 'coffee table' volume by D.C. Pisarevskii, *Iskusstvo millionov Sovetskoe Kino 1917–1957* (Moscow, 1958), still pictures were shown from the film, but there was no mention of it in the text! As a classic, it could not go unrecognised from the famous excerpted shots by film-conscious readers. The omnipresent Karmen ('Kinokhronika Velikoi Otechestvennoi Voiny' in ibid.) refers to Iulii Raizman in the text, but one of his most famous films is not mentioned.

16. Raizman says that Shneiderov cinemated at the Reichstag for 30–40 minutes — the implication being that this was after the battle. But when? After Shneiderov arrived, ten more Soviet cameramen arrived to begin filming at the Reichstag (see Zeltov, *Ikh oruzhie — kinokamera*, p.287). Cameraman I. Panov said he arrived on the morning of 1 May, after having made some shots of the Reichstag ('last lair of the fascist beast') during the fighting to show the battle before it. But he couldn't take the storming of the Reichstag because it was too dark. He then returned the next morning to find red flags on the roof, on the façade and on the statuary groups. These he cinemated (Zeltov, ibid., pp.276–80). In the version of the storming of the Reichstag edited for the television series, *The Unknown War*, (see text below) a cameraman is clearly visible standing quite exposed to enemy fire (was there any?) on the steps of the building during the filmed charge. This shot is not in the earlier versions, and (perhaps?) shows the need on the part of the series editors to suggest at last the artificial nature of the film of the charge up the steps. Both the charge up the front steps and the beflagging of the statue of Germania in all of the versions are reshot. There are a number of soldiers, too many to

be just Egorov and Kantaria or Sorokin, Riadov, and Bulatov, in the flag sequence.

17. Fedor M. Zinchenko (who was the commanding officer of the unit which stormed the Reichstag), *Voni shturmuvali Reikhstag* (Kiev, 1978), cited Egorov and Kantaria as the crew that put up the banner, but not until the afternoon of 1 May (pp.235–6). I. Panov (see above, note 17), claimed to have filmed the flag on the morning of the same day, while O. Knorring, 'Berlinski reportazh' in Telegin, *Poslednii shturm*, p.233, said the flag had been shot off by the Germans, and wasn't there on the morning of 1 May.

18. Karmen, *Geroika*, p.38. According to E. Gerasimova, *Shturm Berlina: Vospominaniia, pis'ma, dnevniki uchastinikov boev za Berlin* (Moscow [?], 1948), p.233. Karmen, as noted, was not there when the flag was cinemated, and apparently did not arrive at the Reichstag until 2 May. See Petrussow, *Begegnungen mit Berlin*, p.20, and Karmen, 'Na telegrafnuiu lentu' in Telegn, *Poslednii shturm*, p.253.

19. Churchill was privately less glad, as many Soviets later noted, opining that their rush to take Berlin in spring of 1945 was occasioned by knowledge of Churchill's letter of 1 April 1945 to Roosevelt — which they could not have had, unless they got it from a Burgess, Maclean or Philby. See, for example, Konstantin F. Telegin, 'Na zakluchitel'nom etape voiny. Iz zapisok chlena voennogo soveta 1-go Belorusskogo fronta', *Voenno-istoricheskii zhurnal*, vol.VII (1965), no.4, p.67.

20. Even years later, with the production of the 'restored' edition, Raizman would contend that some corrections had been introduced (i.e. Stalin and Andrei Vyshinski excised, Zhukov excised where possible or unnamed (but they obviously could not remove him from the carefully set surrender scene, restaged for Soviet needs at Karlshorst, near Berlin), and that 'more objective' estimates of the historical events had been entered. See Raizman, *Vchera i segodnia*, p.47. The editors of the East German journal, *Kino DDR*, obligingly opined of this *überarbeitete* version that some of the 'contemporary pathos of the time had been eliminated', but that basically it contained the authentic character of documentation. See *Kino DDR* (1968), no.7, p.25.

21. According to Lancaster, Karmen was a battler (against fascism, against war, for peace'. Lancaster was joyful to be able to work with Karmen and to come to the USSR to do so, for the series 'may be the most important work of my life' — so reported P. Batov in *Sovetskaia kultura*, 23 February 1979, p.3. Batov noted that Karmen, who died during the production of the series, had done much of his camera work in the name of peace and for the party. Karmen had not only cinemated during the Spanish Civil War and the Great Patriotic War, but also during the Vietnamese Civil War.

22. Quoted by Zinchenko, *Voni shturmuvali Reichstag*, p.239. Undying or remade,'it' preceded, at the place of foremost honour, the largest military parade held in Red Square since 1945 on 9 May 1985, the 40th anniversary of the end of the Second World War (as reported by National Public Radio in the United States, 9 May 1985). Soviet scholars and long-term residents of the USSR can confirm that the Soviet media indulge unremittingly in dramatic reconstructions of the heroic events of

the 'Great War for the Homeland'. See, for example, *Die Welt*, 22 February 1982, p.5, and most recently (1985), for the cinema, a new version in two parts of *The Battle for Moscow*.

23. See, for example, F.A. Voight who, among others, knew and reported these facts, now generally known, to historical literature and to the east central European *Volksmund*, just after the events, in *The Nineteenth Century and After*, CXXXVIII (1945), pp.195–7.

24. But perhaps the times of *glasnost'* mean revision is on the way. Certainly the revelations about the events of those days reported by Elena Rzhevskaia, the Soviet writer who was present at the investigation of Hitler's remains in 1945, augur a major change (see 'V tot den', posdnei osen'iu,' *Znamia*, no.12 (1986), pp.157–77). She tells important facts from a discussion held with Marshal Georgii K. Zhukov shortly before his heart attack in 1965.

5

The Polish Newsreel in 1945: The Bitter Victory

Stanislaw Ozimek

> Oh God, have mercy on the Germans! ... those who are torn with rage and terror, on the innocent and their families.
>
> fragment of a poem printed in
> *The Warsaw Daily*, 3 September 1939,
> by Kazimiera Iłłakowicz (1892–1983)

The organisational structure and political orientations of the Polish Newsreel, Polska Kronika Filmowa (PKF), were established in the Army Front Unit (Czołówka Filmowa WP) of I Polish Army Corps under General Zygmunt Berling in the Soviet Union in 1943. The idea, however, of putting out a regular newsreel intended for army and civilian audiences, serving not only propaganda purposes but also acting as an eye-witness record of war events and history, dates back to September 1939.

Background

On 3 September 1939, the day when the prophetic 'Prayer for the Enemy' (printed above) appeared, cameramen from the official Polish Newsreel — Polska Agencja Telegraficzna (PAT) — had shot scenes of the 'new type of war', directed against both military objects and Poland's civilian population and its cultural heritage. The only foreign cameraman who remained in the besieged Warsaw, the American Julien Bryan, noted:

> Is a Catholic hospital a military objective? Are tenement houses, in the poor quarters of a city, military objectives?

Polish Newsreel in 1945

Are the tombs of the dead military objectives? The human eye may deceive an observer. The human tongue may hide the truth. But the camera lens is as ruthless in the depiction of actuality as totalitarian rulers are in falsifying it.[1]

The first war issue of PAT was to include a report on spontaneous demonstrations by Warsaw inhabitants on learning that Britain and France had declared war upon Germany on 3 September. The speed of the Nazi advance and collapse of the Polish resistance meant that this project was to go unfinished; it never reached the newsreel screen and PAT was shut down. During the Nazi occupation which led to the cultural decimation of the Polish nation, among others, there was no regularly issued newsreel. Between 1940 and 1944 only 'The Sound Weekly of the General Government' had been issued in the occupied country. This was a German newsreel, issued under the strict supervision of a Hauptabteilung Propaganda of the GG 'government', in a Polish-language version for the territory and population of the General Government.[2]

During the war a kind of general newsreel of original Polish provenance was provided by spontaneously formed teams of cameramen; thus at the time of the defence of Warsaw in 1939 a team was formed named after its protector and promoter, the President of Warsaw, Stefan Starzynski, a figure comparable to the heroic Lord Mayor Max of Antwerp during the First World War.

Valuable film material, although devoted mainly to the formation of Polish military units at the side of the Allies in the East and West, and to frontline actions, was shot by Army Film Units. The first unit was the War Newsreel of the Polish Army in the Soviet Union under General W. Anders. A second unit was part of the II Polish Corps fighting, among other places, on the Italian front at Monte Cassino, Bologna and Ancona. Between 1942 and 1946 this unit produced 42 issues of newsreel and several special issues. A further important wartime source of Polish-related newsreel are three newsreel issues entitled *Warsaw Fights*, released during the Warsaw Uprising in 1944. The opening film material for this newsreel of the Home Army/ Bureau of Information and Propaganda which has survived is one of the richest sources of material concerning the activity of the Resistance movement in Europe, despite the destruction and loss of a major part of it. The understandable lack of film material recording the Resistance movement in the Second World War is testified to by the invaluable, although extremely limited, film library of Archivio della Resistenza in Turin.

History, even local history such as that of the film documents, likes paradoxes. The beginnings of the PKF were in the old Polish town in the eastern region, Lublin, in the villa of the former SS-Gruppenführer Odilo Globocnik, the last chief of SS and Police in *'dystrykt Lublin'*. Globocnik's villa became the headquarters of Film Studio Polish Army, first producer of PKF. Its chief was Colonel Alexander Ford (b.1908, Lodz, d.1980, New York), who before the war was a member of the avant-garde and leftist Polish Film Society START. Another member was Jerzy Bossak, nominated as chief editor of PKF, who after the war became a prominent documentary film-maker and member of the Board of the Heigh Film School in Lodz. The film-processing laboratory was installed in the bathroom of the former SS-Gruppenführer.

The first planned number of PKF contained footage of the first Nazi death camp to be freed in Europe by Allied troops of the Polish and Red Army. Clear evidence was presented of the inability to remove traces of their murderous activity before their westward flight. Simultaneously in Lublin Castle, which had been made into a prison, Nazis shot hundreds of prisoners as a final, irrational, bloody, cruel 'farewell'. On the outskirts of Lublin stood the death camp KZ (*Konzentrationslager*) Majdanek. Cameraman Stanislaw Wohl (1912–85) from Polish Army Film Unit entered KZ Majdanek directly after Lublin was liberated. Stanislaw Wohl records:

> We entered Majdanek a few minutes after the Nazis left. Hitler's crematoria still smouldered. Live prisoners in their state of extreme biological and psychological exhaustion, wanted to greet us. But they had no strength, either to raise their hands or cross themselves.[3]

From the materials destined for the projected Polish Newsreel, Alexander Ford, with the assistance of Jerzy Bossak, made the 1944 documentary *Majdanek, Cemetery of Europe* about this KZ camp where untold numbers of prisoners from Europe's occupied and Nazi satellite states were brutally murdered; most of those who died there were Poles and Jews — Polish citizens. The film's title proclaimed that it would take the role of an 'act of accusation' against Nazism, not only from the perspective of one country, but that of all Europe. Later fragments of Polish documentary film material found their way into the corpus of materials shown as a documentary part of prosecution's case against Nazi war criminals at the main Nuremberg Trial. Interestingly enough the source of the shocking film material, excluding Bergen-Belsen, was not identified. That day on which the materials were projected, labelled by the foreign correspondents 'Shakespeare Day', was recalled by them as the most traumatic evidence of Nazi barbarism.

Between August and November 1944 it was impossible to bring out a regular newsreel, partly because of a lack of apparatus for making sound copies. The 'Majdanek' documentary was soundtracked at the Central Newsreel Studio 'Sojuzkinokronika' in Moscow. The final musical leitmotiv of the newsreel was the old Polish patriotic hymn 'Rota'. Lacking a recording of this in Moscow, Ford and Bossak recruited a Red Army military choir which sang the hymn in Polish, finishing with the words: 'Let God help us . . .'

The first number of PKF was shown in Lublin on 1 December 1944, but it was unable to appear as a weekly newsreel until the final months of the war. From the first number (PKF1/44) until issue 'number two' there was a hiatus of 41 days. Issues appeared sporadically until the end of the war in Europe and between some issues there was a five-day gap, while between others 59 days elapsed. One double number (PKF 9–10/45) featured the Fall of Kolberg (now Kolobrzeg). 'Festung Kolberg' was captured in March 1945 by the I Polish Army in collaboration with Red Army units. Compiled by Jerzy Bossak, the newsreel constitutes a modest documentary gloss to the famous and most costly film of Third Reich cinema, directed by Veit Harlan, *Kolberg* (1945). Another Bossak PKF documentary called *The Torment of Berlin* was based on film shot by Polish cameramen, as well as Soviet colleagues, of the war's conclusion. Polish units were the only ones other than the Red Army which participated in the Battle of Berlin in 1945. Mention of this was made in the second edition full-length documentary *Berlin* by Iulii Raizman.

In *The Torment of Berlin*, finished by Bossak just after the war, it was difficult to find expressions of hatred or revenge, although questions of responsibility are raised. The brutality of the war is softened by the aesthetic of photography. For example, traces of spring are shown in contrast to shots of a column of tanks, set against the background of an accordian version of Chopin's

'Polonaise'. In the finale the commentator told Polish viewers that the Nazi prisoners of war being marched out of Berlin, in contrast to the Polish Army in 1939 and the insurgents of the Warsaw Uprising in 1944, 'did not want either for food or ammunition'.

In the year 1945 those themes connected directly to war and peace amount to 90 out of 242 subjects. The total PKF output for 1945 was 10,328 metres, with individual issues running in length from 212 to 443 metres. From January to May 1945, PKF issues are dominated by war events with comparatively little emphasis on international or political themes. Subjects of a local character were chosen to impress an audience and to express the disastrous human and cultural losses which were Poland's destiny in the Second World War. In the second half of 1945 a significant number of international stories entered PKF newsreel as a consequence of agreement for the exchange of materials with foreign newsreels, including Actualités Françaises, Gaumont British, Novosti Dnia, Svensk Film News, Tydén ve Filmu, Unio News (UNO) and Welt im Film.

The Polish Committee of National Liberation (PKWN) manifesto, issued in July 1944, defined the essential changes in the political, economic and social structure to be introduced in post-war Poland, which was to become a 'people's democracy' of a socialist nature. In the sphere of the economy these changes were to lead to nationalisation of key industries and sequestration of landed estates, and in the political sphere to the domination of the workers' party within the framework of a worker–peasant alliance. However, the PKF newsreel of 1945 is not dominated by the picture of 'revolutionary changes'. Until the Victory Day itself on 9 May 1945, prominence is given in the newsreel to reports of frontline action and the liberation of Poland, as well as — throughout the whole year — to the gigantic problem of its reconstruction and the migration of its people as they returned home.

Politically the newsreel presented an overall image of plurality as it reported on various aspects of the workers' and peasants' movement, trade unions and religious life. Emphasis was also given to Congresses of the Polish Workers Party (PPR), the Polish Socialist Party (PPS), as well as meeting the Polish Folk Party (PSL), headed by the ex-Premier of the Government of the Polish Republic in London, Stanislaw Mikolajczyk. The Polish Folk Party became the legal political opposition at that time.

Polish Newsreel in 1945

The most difficult aspect of Polish life to show on the screen was the attitude of the new government to the representatives of the so-called 'London' Polish Government in exile and the several hundred thousand members of the Home Army (AK), dissolved in January 1945, as well as the problem of the Warsaw Uprising. These problems were deeply rooted in the consciousness of Polish society as was the historical hatred of Germany, amplified by the fresh memory of the martyrdom of the nation. A liberal attitude towards the tradition of the main current of Resistance struggle and the Warsaw Uprising was displayed by the first post-war Congress of the Polish Socialist Party (PPS), which had been established in 1892. A remaining fragment of the report on the Congress presented in the PKF issue 18/45 showed a moment of homage paid to the heroes of the Warsaw Uprising of 1944 by Congress participants. On the first anniversary of the Warsaw Uprising, PKF issue 21/45 brought a sensational news of its own kind — fragments of film reels shot of the Uprising by the Polish film team, recovered from the debris of the city. In succeeding years up to 1956, this unique film was regarded as prohibited archive material.

No European capital since Carthage had suffered such a total destruction from the hands of invaders as Warsaw, and no other people suffered such cruel treatment as its inhabitants, relentlessly driven out of their homes. Hitler's order, 'Warschau wird glattrasiert', given on 1 August 1944, was carried out with total dedication. The wounds inflicted on the city, first in September 1939, and then during the crushing of the Ghetto Uprising in 1943, were multiplied during the uprisings of 1944. After capitulation, without any military justification, the work of completing the destruction of Poland's ancient capital was carried out by Nazi *Brand und Spreng Battalionen*.

Pictures of ruined Warsaw, the cruel poetry of ruins in the extant film reels, were soon replaced in the newsreels by topics of reconstruction, performed at the beginning literally with bare hands. These pictures are very similar to those made in the streets of Berlin after capitulation in May 1945. The Warsaw 'zero point' period was after the war to re-create documentary films using footage drawn from these sources. These images of the Second World War became iconic symbols of the Nazis' extraordinary threat to the values of European culture and of the dehumanising aspect of war.

The situation of former members of the Home Army, dissolved

in January 1945, was reported in the PKF issue 29/45. The story recorded their voluntary reporting to the police within the framework of amnesty granted to Home Army members by the Home National Council (KRN). This topic was combined through montage with a report on the funeral of a Communist activist who had fallen victim of a political murder committed by members of the clandestine National Armed Forces (NSZ), a splinter group of the Home Army.

Among topics referring to definite historical traditions, PKF issues of 1945 included those devoted to the liberal and democratic ideals of the Polish Constitution of 3 May 1791. This tradition of the May Constitution, which was a Polish Magna Charta, was soon regarded as a rival of the Socialist May Day and was consequently passed over in silence by the mass media between 1949 and 1954. In 1945 there was a wide acceptance of the national tradition, of the commemoration of the famous historical events, as well as the recent ones of the Second World War. There were reports on the celebrations on the 535th anniversary of the victory of Polish Arms over the Teutonic Knights at Grunwald, as well as reports on the events of the Silesian uprisings (1919–21). The events of the September 1939 campaign were dealt with several times along with ceremonies honouring the heroes of Westerplatte, remembered as 'the Polish Thermopylae'. The baptism of fire of the Polish People's Army, fighting alongside the Red Army at Lenino (1943) was recalled, and tribute was paid to the memory of the heroes of the Warsaw Uprising. However, the events connected with the war record and famous battles of Polish Forces in the West, such as Narvik, Tobruk, Polish pilots in the Battle of Britain, Monte Cassino, Arnhem, Falaise, Bologna, Ancona and other places, constitute a sphere of 'reality that was not presented', to use Marc Ferro's phrase. The soldiers of the Polish Armed Forces in the West were mentioned in PKF newsreels only in the context of demobilisation and the appeals seeking to persuade them to return home (PKF 35/45).

PKF in 1945 abounds with topics connected with religious traditions, ceremonies and celebrations. The January 1945 issue featured the celebration of Christmas Eve and Christmas by soldiers of the Polish People's Army. Commander-in-Chief General Rola-Żymierski was shown visiting the wounded soldiers in hospital at Christmas (PKF 2/1945), along with the reconstruction of ruined churches and sacred monuments. The traditional ceremonies of Corpus Christi were covered by four experienced PKF cameramen at Czestochowa and Lowicz. Like an epitome of 'the times', there was a broad panorama of guests on behalf of the government, among whom were representatives of the Folk Party and the Communist Polish Workers Party walking in solemn procession arm-in-arm with the Primate of Poland, Cardinal August Hlond! An almost symbolic mini-report showed the moment when the figure of Christ the King, knocked down after the Warsaw Uprising by the soldiers of *Spreng-Batallion*, was put upright again in front of the St Cross Church in Warsaw. Christ raises his hand in a gesture of hope. The pedestal carried the inscription 'Sursum Corda' as if dedicated to the nations healing their war wounds, and to the Poles celebrating their bitter victory of 1945.

PKF cameramen passed on from the routine recording of facts to the discovery of the atmosphere of events, their dramatic content, and sometimes their general metaphorical sense. In their more ambitious achievements they were encouraged by John Grierson's maxim of documentary being a 'creative interpretation of reality'. PKF cameramen as early as 1945 had received several reproofs from PKF management for excessive 'objectivisation' of reality, which instead of mobilising the viewers to positive action, engendered defeatism in their feelings. Hence much of the material presented the enormity of Warsaw's devastation, the exhumation of the dead who perished in the Warsaw Uprising of 1944, the devastation of industry, the conditions of health of the Warsaw population undermined by the war (among other problems the epidemic of tuberculosis), remain in the archives. The newsreel issues rarely showed the effects of the armed action by the anti-communist underground or of the so-called 'small war' waged in the eastern territories by the Ukranian nationalists grouped in UPA.

The routine of showing the social and economic reality with a rejection of over-critical and alarming material was justified by Jerzy Bossak, PKF editor-in-chief, who addressed cameramen in the following manner:

> ... cameramen should become not only mechanical chroniclers, but also co-creators of this new, better reality. Propaganda should be changed into social education and disseminate optimism, without which one cannot live and change the bad into the good, and the good into the better.[5]

This idea was co-ordinated with the propaganda directives of the new government. Priority was given to reporting the integration of the politically divided society, mobilisation of Poles for the reconstruction of their country and for restoring the economic potential of the western and northern territories within the framework of the great migration, among other places, from the east. Historians seeking to construct an image of Poland in 1945 and its social consensus on the basis of PKF materials must remember that PKF was created to serve the contemporary needs of the state and thus presents a very limited view of very complicated Polish reality.

Argumentum e silentio

Policy decisions allowing for the reporting of Western news in 1945 provided numerous sequences about the United Nations Relief and Rehabilitation Administration (UNRRA) help to Poland and a re-establishment of diplomatic relations by the National Unity Government (RJN) with the United States, Britain, France, Sweden and Italy. There was a major report on the visit of Dr Johnson, Dean of Canterbury and Professor Day of Oxford to the former concentration camp at Auschwitz. Another British story was a brief report on the British Air Marshal Sir Sholto Douglas's visit to Poland and the opening of the Royal Air Force exhibition in Warsaw. (PKF33/45) A further indication of the broadening of the news base was a story on the visit of General Dwight Eisenhower and the Commander-in-Chief of the Polish Army, General M. Rola-Żymierski, to Frankfurt-on-Main. (PKF 31/45) In an earlier issue, General Eisenhower had been seen being decorated with the Order of Grunwald, 1st Class, by the leader of the Polish Government, B. Bierut. General Eisenhower, who had witnessed the destruction of Warsaw's Old City quarter, began at one moment to cry; one short shot unintentionally recorded this. (PKF 27/45)

Significantly the PKF newsreel in 1945 was silent on major issues. The major weakness of PKF's coverage in the first half of 1945 was the lack of international information. The only exception was material drawn from the Soviet Novosti Dnia newsreels and Sojuzkinokronika. There were no stories dealing with the Yalta Conference and it was only mentioned three months later. There was also an absence of general coverage concerning the progress of the Western Allied armies in Europe and lack of information about the campaigns of Polish armed forces in the west and south, such as the II Polish Corps under General Anders in Italy. The death of President Franklin D. Roosevelt and the founding of the United Nations in San Francisco on 26 April 1945 were ignored. After the Victory in Europe, there was no information about the United States' and other Allied war activities in the Far East against Japan. Most surprising was the lack of news about the atomic bomb used against Hiroshima and Nagasaki that August.

Little information about the distribution of the PKF abroad is available, but it is known that the Polish Newsreel was distributed in the British and American zones in Germany, especially in Displaced Persons Camps which held hundreds of thousands of Poles in 1945–6. General Grosz, the Chief of the Polish Military Mission in Occupied Germany, noted that the PKF was: 'often the final argument persuading people to return home'.[6]

Notes

1. Julien Bryan, *Siege — Warsaw 1939*, preface by M. Hindus (New York, 1940), p.3.

2. About 50–60 percent of issues are extant and their analysis was presented by Professor Richard Raack at the IAHMIST Congress, Vienna, in 1982 (unpublished).

3. Stanislaw Wohl, 'w Chelmie i Lublinie', *Film* (1969), nos. 28–9. This quotation is an important piece of evidence in the controversy between Prof. R. Raack and Prof. S. Drobashenko as to who entered the former KZ Majdanek first, the Polish Army Film Unit under Alexander Ford or the Sojuzkino kronika unit under Roman Karmen.

4. PKF nos. 15, 16, 17, *The Torment of Berlin*, direction and commentary by Jerzy Bossak, ed. W. Każmierczak, 608m, pre June 1945. Archive of WFD Documentary Studio, Warsaw.

5. Bulletin of '*Film Polski*', October 1945.

6. 'Dyskusja o filmie polskim', *Kuznica* (1946) no.6.

6

Goebbels, Götterdämmerung, and the Deutsche Wochenschauen

David Welch

A popular joke current in Berlin in March 1945 compared Goebbels' Ministry for Popular Enlightenment and Propaganda to the orchestra of a sinking ship.[1] A few years ago such a negative response on the part of a section of the German population to Goebbels' propaganda outpourings would not have figured prominently in the works of Western scholars. The traditional method of analysis concentrated less on its reception and instead on Nazi propaganda techniques and their organisation.[2] Even Robert Herzstein's impressively detailed study referred to Nazi propaganda as 'the war that Hitler won'.[3] More recently, by placing the study of propaganda in relation to wider interpretative questions about the Third Reich, historians have begun to challenge previously held views about the effectiveness of Nazi propaganda.[4]

My intention here is to trace the collapse of the Third Reich as revealed through the *Deutsche Wochenschauen* (German newsreels) during the final two years of the war. Nazi newsreels provide an excellent means of illustrating the ongoing debate about the 'power' (or otherwise) of Nazi propaganda, as well as revealing the response of a nation facing imminent military defeat in war. Moreover both Goebbels and Hitler clearly believed in the importance of the newsreels and as such copies of each newsreel were sent to the Führer Headquarters and the Propaganda Ministry before distribution to the general public. During the early part of the war Goebbels would personally supervise the newsreels until he was satisfied that they were ready to be released. Nearly every entry in his diary covering the years of *Blitzkrieg* contains some reference to the current newsreel he was orchestrating.[5] However, his diary entries for 1942 and 1943 suggest that his interest in the newsreels declined as the war dragged on.[6] Hitler's influence is more obscure although Goebbels was always happy to record favourable comments made by the Führer. Writing on 16 June 1941, for example, Goebbels noted: 'The most recent newsreels have given the Führer particular pleasure. He describes them as the best means of popular education and leadership. And indeed they are.'[7]

Until the outbreak of war there were four newsreels operating in Germany, Ufa-Tonwoche, Deulig-Woche, Tobis Wochenschau (which developed in 1938 out of Bavaria-Tonwoche which in turn developed from Emelka-Woche), and Fox tönende Wochenschau which was American owned. A fifth newsreel, Ufa-Auslandswoche, distributed German home news abroad. It was the Propaganda Ministry's task to co-ordinate the content of these newsreels so that they portrayed the social 'achievements' and the increasing military strength of the regime. This was achieved by establishing a German 'news bureau' (Wochenschaureferat) under the supervision of the RMVP (Reichsministerium für Volksaufklärung und Propaganda) in an attempt to combine all newsreel reports into one 'official' version of contemporary Germany.[8]

In order to achieve the most effective final results, newsreel cameramen were given special facilities for effective filming, together with the most detailed instructions on the staging of a particular event.[9] They were assisted by the so-called 'Newsreel Law' (*Wochenschaugesetz*), which was introduced on 30 April 1936 in order to ease the problems of distribution and copyright.[10] In October 1938 further legislation reduced the number of editions from 15 to 8 and made the showing of a newsreel compulsory at every film programme.[11] Under the new law, hire charges were also simplified so that future cinema-owners paid the newsreel distributors 3 percent of the box office takings. This meant that it was no longer cheaper to hire old newsreels. These reforms ensured not only that film audiences would see the very latest newsreels (which was not the case before 1938), but also that propaganda material which was considered important in maintaining the much-vaunted Nazi consensus could be dispersed as widely as possible. Eventually new mobile film laboratories were introduced near the theatres of war, facilitating the speed with which film material could be processed for swift distribution to the public. After an inspection of these new processing laboratories Goebbels referred to them in his diary as 'a technical miracle.

We are unbeatable in this area'.[12]

Not surprisingly, a propaganda weapon as important as the newsreel was subject to strict military and governmental control before being released. Censorship was exercised by the Wochenschauzentrale (having replaced the Wochenschaureferat in 1938) which was directly subordinate to Goebbels. Its main responsibility was to liaise between the four newsreel companies, ensuring that their film reports represented the political and cultural views of the National Socialist community (*Volksgemeinschaft*). After the outbreak of war the RMVP merged the existing four newsreels into a single war newsreel. This was achieved with a minimum of disruption, owing largely to the legislative measures taken by the Ministry of Propaganda since 1936. On 21 November 1940 the Deutsche Wochenschau GmbH was founded and all other newsreel companies dissolved.[13] Goebbels ordered that in future the war newsreel should simply be referred to as Deutsche Wochenschau. By concentrating such vast resources the new company was intended not only to establish a European newsreel monopoly but also to pose a serious challenge to America's supremacy in this field.[14] Until this time the public were largely unaware that the newsreels were state-controlled, as very little was known about the Wochenschauzentrale. From Goebbels' point of view such a revelation would have reduced their effectiveness and therefore no information had been given of his Ministry's role in this field. However he confided to his diary: 'Discuss the re-organisation of the newsreels with Hippler [President of the Reich Film Chamber]. We have established a new company including Ufa, Tobis and Bavaria, I intend to keep personal control of it. After the war there will be three different newsreels again. Now, in the middle of a war, this is not a practical proposition.'[15]

War reporting was the responsibility of the Propaganda Kompanie Einheiten which was established in 1938 as a compromise between the competing interests of the Reichskriegsministerium (RKM) and the RMVP. The PK units, as they were called, were appointed by the RMVP but at the front they operated under the command of the *Oberkommando der Wehrmacht*, (OKW). However, all film shot was at the exclusive disposal of the Propaganda Ministry with the proviso that military censorship was the responsibility of the OKW. At the beginning of the war 13 propaganda companies were set up (7 for the army, 4 for the Luftwaffe and 2 for the navy), together with a few special PK units linked to prestigious divisions like the 'Felderrnhalle' and the 'Herman Göring' tank corps. Each PK unit consisted of between 120 and 150 personnel.[16] The PK man was a soldier; he was trained as a soldier and was expected to be at the heart of the battle in order to capture the immediacy of the military victories that were confidently predicted by the Nazi leadership. Although Goebbels would remain suspicious of the OKW and what he felt was their unwarranted interference in his domain, he nevertheless was pleased with the propaganda material supplied by these 'soldier-cameramen' and indeed was happy to take personal credit for them.[17] In November 1940 he was moved to record the following typical entry in his diary:

> ... I receive six cameramen from the Propaganda Companies, who have just returned from active service on all fronts. They have seen and done a lot, and are able to tell the most interesting stories. One cannot hear enough. We watch the unedited version of the newsreel together. This is their work, which they are very proud of, and rightly so ...
> A heroic saga of German war-reportage. I am very pleased.[18]

Propaganda had a relatively easy task in the first years of the war in capitalising on the blitzkrieg victories. The newsreels in particular proved an excellent vehicle for portraying the invincible might of the German armed forces, and as such served to reinforce a feeling of security and reassurance on the part of a reluctant civilian population that had shown little enthusiasm for the declaration of war. In this respect the early war newsreels were deliberately compiled to illustrate the lightning speed and devastating power of the Nazi military machine. They proved so popular with German audiences that Goebbels was prompted to set up special newsreel shows screening continuously past and present editions.[19] By October 1940 newsreels were also incorporated into the schools and Hitler Youth film programmes with considerable success.[20] The increased length and improved distribution of the newsreel was another important factor contributing to their popularity. In May 1940 it was announced that all German newsreels would last for 40 minutes and that the number of copies of each newsreel would be doubled to 2,000, the latter having the effect of reducing circulation time from eight to four weeks.[21]

According to Siegfried Kracauer these early war newsreels were distinguishable from their British and American counterparts by their much greater length, their use of sophisticated editing, the utilisation of music for emotional effect, and their preference for visual images.[22] Goebbels' diaries for this period show that his unvarying nightly task was to view and orchestrate the latest newsreel. They also reveal in unmistakable fashion the Propaganda Minister's belief that the Nazis had a greater understanding of the film medium than their adversaries and an awareness of the importance of newsreels as an effective instrument of war propaganda. Consider his entry for 12 May 1941:

> Check the newsreel . . . English and Russian newsreels that we seized in Belgrade. Absolutely no competition for us. Incomparably poor and amateurish. I am downright proud of our work in this field. We have nothing to fear . . . The English films are indescribably naive.[23]

There can be little doubt that stylistically the Deutsche Wochenschauen depicting the blitzkrieg are impressive examples of film propaganda. But as the war dragged on they suffered, as did all Nazi propaganda, through their close association with German military success. Indeed, their effectiveness depended on their ability to report the victories that German leaders had promised. However, this was all to change towards the end of 1941. The time of easy victories was over and therefore the enemies of the Reich (and what they said) had to be taken more seriously. The newsreels also had to adapt to the changed circumstances: there were no more sensational marches into enemy territory, and German audiences had to be content with the more mundane activity of warfare. The initial response of the Nazi heirarchy to the first military reverses is particularly interesting for it reveals their deep mistrust of their own much heralded 'national community' (*Volksgemeinschaft*), supposedly the cornerstone of the Nazi 'revolution'. In the knowledge that there would be no speedy end to the conflict, propaganda chose deliberately to avoid mentioning the harsh impact of the war on the civilian economy and instead continued trumpeting bravado claims that increasingly failed to square with the everyday experiences of ordinary German citizens. During this period newsreels are conspicuous for the absence of any serious depiction of material problems such as the food and fuel shortages, labour difficulties and the failure of Germany's air defences to protect civilian property. By prescribing what could and could not be shown or mentioned in the mass media, the Nazis betrayed how little they were concerned with reality.[24] Not surprisingly the credibility of the regime's propaganda began to suffer as a result.

It would appear that even before the first major setback of Stalingrad, the SD (*Sicherheitsdienst* — Security Service) reports were commenting on popular criticism of propaganda.[25] Disillusionment had set in and audiences had started to question previous assumptions and the banality and lies they were witnessing in the weekly newsreels. In March 1941, for example, the SD reported that Germans were now lingering outside the cinemas until the newsreels which preceded the feature film were over.[26] Goebbels responded by closing all cinema box offices during the showing of the newsreel, so that if patrons wanted to see the feature attraction they were forced to sit through the newsreel as well![27] The RMVP was also finding it increasingly difficult to secure new and exciting documentary footage of the various theatres of war. Goebbels put this failure down to bad organisation and interference from the OKW and the Foreign Ministry.[28]

The impact of Stalingrad on the morale of the German people cannot be overestimated. It affected their attitude towards the war and created a crisis of confidence in the regime amongst broad sections of the population. Hitherto, Nazi propaganda had always tried to give the impression that the Third Reich was waging one war with an unbending consistency. With its armies now on the defensive on three fronts it was obvious that they were in fact fighting several wars and sometimes with contradictory objectives. The capture of the German 6th Army at Stalingrad did however bring Goebbels back into the forefront of German politics and he of course did his best to give meaning to the catastrophe. A huge rally at the *Sportspalast* in Berlin on 18 February 1943 was the setting for his notorious 'total war' address. It was a masterpiece in mass propaganda, carefully orchestrated for the benefit of radio and the newsreel. The audience of reliable Party functionaries had been meticulously rehearsed beforehand and knew exactly what was expected of them. Goebbels started his speech by saying that the situation reminded him of the *Kampfzeit*, the period of struggle before 1933. He said he now demanded even more effort and sacrifices from the German people for the sake of final victory. Above the speaker's platform there hung an immense draped banner with the words 'Totaler Krieg — Kürzester Krieg' (Total War — Shortest War). It was claimed that the audience represented all sections of the community. The frenzied reactions of this 'representative' audience to Goebbels' speech were broadcast to the rest of the nation. A special newsreel also recorded the event. At the climax of the speech, the Propaganda Minister posed ten questions touted as a 'plebiscite for total war', all of which elicited the appropriate chorus of 'spontaneous' assent. The following extract is how it was presented to German cinema audiences in the Deutsche Wochenschau no. 10/651 which was released on 27 February 1943:[29]

Commentator: The mighty demonstration in the Berlin Sportspalace, Reichsminister Goebbels speaks. He declares: 'In this winter, the storm over our ancient continent has broken out with the full force which surpasses all human and historical imagination. The Wehrmacht with its allies form the only possible protective wall. [*Applause*] Not a single person in Germany today thinks of hollow compromise. The whole nation thinks only of a hard war. The danger before which we stand is gigantic. Gigantic, therefore, must be the efforts with which we meet it. [*Shouts of 'Sieg Heil'*] When my audience spontaneously declared its support for the demands I made on 30 January, the English press claimed that this was a piece of theatrical propaganda. I have therefore invited to this meeting a cross-section of the German people . . .'
Goebbels: The English claim that the German people are resisting Government measures for total war.
Crowd: Lies! Lies!
Goebbels: It doesn't want total war, say the English, but capitulation.
Crowd: Sieg Heil! Sieg Heil!
Goebbels: Do you want total war?
Crowd: Yes! [*Enthusiastic applause*]
Goebbels: Do you want it more total, more radical, than we could ever have imagined?
Crowd: Yes! Yes! [*Loud applause*]
Goebbels: Are you ready to stand with the Führer as the phalanx of the homeland behind the fighting Wehrmacht?

Are you ready to continue the struggle unshaken and with savage determination, through all the vicissitudes of fate until victory is in our hands?
Crowd: Yes!
Goebbels: I ask you: Are you determined to follow the Führer through thick and thin in the struggle for victory and to accept even the harshest personal sacrifices?
Crowd: Yes! Sieg Heil! [*A chant of 'The Führer commands, we follow'*]
Goebbels: You have shown our enemies what they need to know, so that they will no longer indulge in illusions. The mightiest ally in the world — the people themselves — have shown that they stand behind us in our determined fight for victory, regardless of the costs.
Crowd: Yes! Yes! [*Loud applause*]
Goebbels: Therefore let the slogan be from now on: 'People arise, and storm break loose!' [*Extended applause*]
Crowd: Deutschland, Deutschland über alles, über alles in der Welt . . .[30]

In his 'total war' speech Goebbels pulled out all the stops; after the 'heroic epic' of Stalingrad (which was depicted in the second part of the Deutsche Wochenschau), total sacrifices together with the complete mobilisation of the home front are required in order that Germany should become one fighting body, united under a powerful leader. Partly this was to convince foreign governments that there was a full accord between the rulers and the ruled in Germany, but it was also intended to persuade Hitler to completely mobilise the home front to facilitate a concentrated war effort. Although Hitler was deeply impressed with the newsreel recording of the rally, he would, however, never fully agree to complete mobilisation, despite repeated requests from his Propaganda Minister. Nevertheless, in the short term at least, Goebbels enjoyed considerable success with this campaign. Its immediate effect served to strengthen morale. The Secret Police report noted that the newsreel of the mass demonstration 'made a deep impression and subsequently dissipated any feelings of scepticism which have prevailed up until now'.[31] But once this intoxication had worn off, people began soberly to question the military situation and in particular the threat coming from the East. Nevertheless, Nazi propaganda continued to insist that final victory was assured however great the difficulties. In the final two years of the war Goebbels would achieve a number of minor propaganda successes, but the overriding conclusion (not surprisingly) must be of the failure of propaganda to compensate for the worsening military situation.

After 1943 a number of major themes recur in Nazi propaganda, all of which figure prominently in the Deutsche Wochenschauen. They include:

1. orderly retreat and promises of revenge;
2. anti-Bolshevism and 'strength through fear';
3. loyalty to the Führer;
4. the need for a popular uprising.

The overriding impression that one gains from the newsreels during this final period is of a 'fortress Germany' preparing for Hitler's last stand. Newsreels were now put together with a combination of fake studio material and genuine combat footage specifically to bolster the critical state of German morale.[32]

As a result of the success of the 'new realism' of Goebbels' 'total war' speech, emphasis was placed on minimising the public's expectations by stressing the orderly nature of Germany's new defensive war. This allowed the accumulating military defeats to be rationalised as 'strategic withdrawals'.[33] During the same period, the newsreels began to take on a quite discernable structural pattern. The first half would show aspects related to the total mobilisation of the home front, while the second part covered the traditional battle scenes. Thus, for the first time, women began to appear regularly in the newsreels. In line with the ideological chauvinism that pervaded all aspects of National Socialism, the newsreels had previously confined the coverage of women's activities to domestic scenes. Now, because of their new role within the home front, they were shown enthusiastically contributing to the war effort. For example, the Deutsche Wochenschau released in July 1944 starts with the traditional view of German women by showing a home built especially for war widows. The women can be seen studying and playing with their children in the kindergarten attached to the home. But this is juxtaposed with a sequence depicting the 'new' woman at work and play, Women of the Air Defence Corps exhibit their skills by manning AA guns, listening for enemy aircraft and operating the searchlights. After work they are seen enjoying a variety of sporting activities including competing in a rowing regatta.[34]

Similarly, two months later, the diversity of women's contribution to the war effort is reported in the September newsreel by means of an extended sequence celebrating their work in the armaments factories, as tram conductors and drivers, and in the police service and fire brigade.[35]

Even previously censored topics like the effects of Allied air raids were discussed. Clearly this manifestation of the enemy's superiority in the air was a topic the propagandists would have preferred to have ignored. But for some time Goebbels had been aware of the danger of remaining silent about the devastation that was affecting large sections of the urban population.[36] Accordingly, *Gaupropagandaleiter* had been given instructions to stress the 'heroic fortitude' of the people.[39] In Deutsche Wochenschau no.712, released in April 1944, a succession of air raids on the Reich are shown. The commentator proclaims that: 'the people have had to endure terrible trials during the enemy's attempts to break the German will to fight, but they have paid dearly for it — over 1,000 Flying Fortresses have been shot down!' The course of a single air raid is then followed through. The news of the attack is telexed to the fighter bases, an automatic camera is loaded into a plane for take-off. The alarm warns people to take shelter — fire wardens take up their positions in the factories and hospital patients are moved to shelters while Fighter Control guides the defence operation. There follows a spectacular sequence of the air battle filmed from the automatic camera. Enemy planes are shot down and American pilots are interrogated. Fighter squadron returns to base and an officer praises the training and performances of the young pilots. Civilians leave their shelters, and the Hitler Youth is highly commended for its excellent work during the raid.[38]

The newsreels did their best to bolster civilian morale, but clearly Nazi propaganda had been forced on to the defensive. This was confirmed by Goebbels in an address to his *Gauleiters* in February 1944 when he stressed the need to reassure the population by emphasising the merits of fighting a defensive war *within* Germany's borders.[39] The Deutsche Wochenschauen bear unwitting testimony to the changing reality of the military situation. Almost every newsreel report of this period ends by referring to the disciplined retreat and high morale of German troops. 'Digging in' became synonymous with the Deutsche Wochenschau; little wonder that they were no longer received rapturously by war-weary cinema audiences. For some time however the Nazi leadership had been alluding to some forthcoming retaliation by means of a secret 'miracle' weapon. Goebbels had launched the campaign way back in June 1943 when he assured an audience in the Berlin *Sportspalast*: 'One day the hour of revenge will come'.[40] The SD reports noted at the time that the country generally welcomed his announcement of counter-terror, particularly the inhabitants of bombed cities. But the success of 'revenge' (*Vergeltung*) depended on its realisation. Throughout the autumn and winter of 1943–4, German morale continued to deteriorate. Nazi propagandists had little in the way of assurance other than the promise of Vergeltung, which was widely seen as a panacea to all Germany's troubles. Many Germans were convinced that Vergeltung was an invention of Goebbels' Ministry to secure the fanaticism necessary to carry on a war that could not be won. When the V1 and V2 (V for Vergeltung) missiles were eventually deployed in June 1944, they failed to live up to expectations. These 'miracle weapons' made their first appearance in the Deutsche Wochenschau in early July 1944, when the V1 rocket was officially announced and shown being launched on London.[41] A few weeks later in Deutsche Wochenschau no.725, Goebbels was seen telling a rally in Breslau that 'the Reich was now answering terror with counter-terror', and claiming that Britain could no longer defend itself against these pilotless guided missiles: 'The Führer can rely on the loyalty of his people as they follow him. We deserve victory!'.

While there is evidence that Goebbels' exploitation of the Vergeltung theme did initially raise the morale of both the home front and German troops, this soon gave way to a spirit of dejection once it became apparent that the new miracle weapons would not bring England to her knees nor alter the course of the war. On the one hand, the concept of the 'orderly retreat' of German forces had been designed to minimise the public's expectations, whereas on the other hand, the whisper campaign of 'miracle' weapons had falsely raised them. Vergeltung, the promise of 'revenge', was the Nazis' last-ditch guarantee of future victory. It was a promise that could not be kept. Belief in retaliation and other propaganda clichés had been wearing thin for some time. Criticism of Nazi propaganda often expressed itself in the form of political jokes. Typical is this anecdote reported by the SD towards the end of 1943:

> Dr. Goebbels is bombed out in Berlin. He has two suitcases,

leaves them on the street and goes back into the building to rescue other things. When he re-emerges the suitcases have been stolen. Dr. Goebbels is very unhappy. He shouts and moans. Someone asks him why the suitcases were so important and he replies: 'One had the revenge weapon in it and the other final victory.'[42]

In the last year of the war, Goebbels continued his activities relentlessly. After the failure of the V1 and V2 miracle weapons to realise his promise of revenge, Goebbels achieved a short-lived revival of trust in the Führer following the failure of the 20 July plot against him. He even exploited the attempted assassination to show that the hand of providence was guiding Hitler by coining the slogan '*Hitler ist der Sieg*' (Hitler is Victory). Goebbels had already embarked upon a major campaign to intensify personal commitment to the cult of the Führer before the abortive plot on Hitler's life. In April 1944 a special Deutsche Wochenschau was released to celebrate Hitler's 55th birthday. Following the Party's congratulations to the Führer, the commentator refers to 'the German peoples' birthday gift to their leader' — a statue engraved with the words: 'Our Walls may break but our hearts do not'. This is followed by Hitler's birthday parade along the Unter den Linden. The slogan is repeated on the banners draped over the bombed ruins. Diplomats, citizens and children arrive at the Reichschancellery to sign Hitler's birthday lists. One child has written 'To dear Uncle Hitler'. In August Deutsche Wochenschau no.33/727 reported the plot on Hitler's life in the following manner:

> Introduction: Trumpet fanfare, German eagle (designed by Albert Speer).
> 1. The funeral: A state funeral for one of the victims of the plot, General Korten; Goering and Doenitz condole with relatives and Goering makes a memorial speech (with a reminder of past triumphs at Tannenburg as a backdrop) regretting that Korten should have been so cruelly taken from them 'in the middle of his great task'.
> 2. The hospital: Hitler visits the bomb plot victims in hospital — Scherk, Wortmann, Assmann, Admiral von Puttkammer and General Buhle. Outside the hospital crowds and government officials wait to congratulate the Führer on his escape — Funk, Gauleiter Sauckel, Speer,

Sauer, Lammers, Himmler, General Schörner, Goering, Goebbels, Guderian, Bormann and Jodl are all present. Major Remer who suppressed the bomb plot insurrection is promoted to Colonel and inspects a guard of honour. In his speech he thanks God that they have all become 'political soldiers following political orders, dedicated to the defence of the Fatherland and the National Socialist ideal until final victory is assured'.

3. Total war effort: A Führer decree of 25 July confirms that Goebbels has been appointed the new Reich Plenipotentiary for the Total War Effort. The civilian population of South Wurtemberg enrol in Civil Defence. Gauleiter Lauterbacker reviews the new detachments and speaks of the imperative need 'for men of all classes to do their duty for Germany'.

4. East front: Strategic withdrawals under heavy fire with refugees following the Wehrmacht. Pioneers blow up railway lines and mine key buildings to cover the retreat. Army reserves dig new trenches and fortifications. A counterattack is launched.

5. West front: Infantry battle south of Caen. SS Sturmführer Wittmann, holder of the Knight's Cross, controls the tank operations resulting in 'heavy American losses'. The commentator concludes that 'Even in this final critical phase, German soldiers behave as if the Führer has given each one a personal order to hold out to the last'.[43]

By portraying the officers' plot of 20 July as a cowardly, unpatriotic act, Goebbels attempted to diminish their status in the eyes of the people. The intelligence reports confirmed that after the initial shock there was indeed a short-lived revival of trust in Hitler.[44] But such optimism was soon dissipated by the harsh realities of the war and the failure of Hitler to address the nation. The 'Hitler-Myth' was finally on the verge of disintegration. In a desperate attempt to raise morale and to intensify the war effort, Goebbels stepped up his propaganda of hate and fear against the Bolsheviks. By invoking the *Untergangsmotif* and declaring that only the Wehrmacht stood between Germany and a 'fate worse than hell', Goebbels was once again appealing to German fears of the barbaric Bolshevik that he had employed so successfully in 1933. In the last phase of the war, fear and terror became a dominant theme of Nazi propaganda.[45] There could be

Goebbels, Götterdämmerung, Wochenshauen

no mention of surrender, for life under the bestial and primitive *Untermenschen* did not bear contemplating. Evidence of Bolshevik atrocities had figured prominently in the newsreels for months,[46] and the press regularly listed the horrors which retreating Wehrmacht officers had witnessed. The German people were left in no doubt as to what they could expect.

Goebbels now urged everyone, including women and children, to join in the struggle, and to set an example by their heroism and sacrifice. The popular rising which Goebbels had been demanding since his 'total war' speech in February 1943 culminated in the formation of the new home defence force, the Volkssturm. Every man between the ages of sixteen and sixty, regardless of class or occupation, was ordered to join the Volkssturm and defend the homeland. The announcement of the Volkssturm had been given a big build-up in the November edition of the Wochenschau, where Himmler was seen proclaiming the Führer's instructions for the new home guard.[47] At this stage Goebbels was continually looking for a sign that would persuade the people to believe in final victory. Consumed by the lure of historical parallels, Goebbels likened the adolescent and ageing Volkssturm to the *Landsturm*'s resistance to Napoleon in the previous century. The thrust of his message was that if only the German people stood firm, a miracle might yet save them.[48] 'The great hour has arrived for German propaganda', he declared in a message to his *Gaupropagandaleiter* in February 1945.[49] But there were no 'miracles' to offer in 1945, only the Volkssturm and the fear and terror of reprisals from the Werwolf organisation. In his diary Goebbels lamented: 'We need a military victory now as much as our daily bread.'[50] From the gloomy reports of defeatist behaviour coming in from all over the Reich, the people, it would seem, would gladly have settled for the bread![51] However, where they existed, the cinemas remained one of the few sources of entertainment open to the beleaguered population. As late as 21 March 1945, Goebbels was receiving encouraging statistics from the *Gaus* suggesting that the people were still regularly visiting cinemas.[52] The penultimate *Deutsche Wochenschau* was released in the same month. There can be no more poignant evidence of the extent to which the National Socialist leadership had lost touch with reality. However, it was entirely appropriate that it should contain the last appearances of Hitler and Goebbels, acting out roles that had changed little over twelve years:

Goebbels, Götterdämmerung, Wochenshauen

Deutsche Wochenschau no. 9/754, March 1945

Introduction: German Eagle, list of war reporters.

1. USA: Scenes of American industrial unrest; strikes, police fighting with strikers, strikers unceremoniously taken away in police vehicles. American prisoners of war on the Rhine. Gauleiter Grohé in conversation with German officers. Anti-tank units and infantry in a fight against enemy tanks.

2. East front: General Wlassow takes charge of groups of Russian volunteer groups. Wlassow and General Köstring review troops fighting a rearguard action. March past.

Infantrymen involved in defensive battle at Courland (on the Baltic). Shots of soldiers in dug-outs, battle scenes and firing German artillery guns. Wounded soldiers are transported home across frozen lagoons.

Marienburg — pictures of the partly destroyed fortress together with individual shots of German soldiers defending the town.

Guben — entry of German soldiers in the recaptured town and shots of street fighting.

Autobahn near Dresden — Russian prisoners including a *Komissar* and a woman soldier in uniform.

3. Lauban: The attack on the town, German soldiers enter, passing burnt-out Russian tanks. Goebbels views the town. In Lauban's market-place, Reich Minister Goebbels talking with officers and crew of an anti-tank assault unit. Lieutenant-Colonel Schoerner greets Goebbels. Goebbels talking with 16-year-old Hitler Youth Hübner who distinguished himself in the fighting. Every house is marked by evidence of Bolshevik atrocities. The commentator talks of old women being murdered and raped: 'clear reasons why the hordes from the Steppes must be resisted'.

4. Görlitz: Goebbels speaks at a mass rally: '... our soldiers now arriving on the Eastern front give no mercy and expect none in return. Those divisions which have already begun small offensives, and these are to be expanded in the coming weeks, will enter this struggle as if it were a divine service (*Gottesdienst*). When they shoulder their guns and climb into their tanks they will have only their slaughtered children and dishonoured wives before their eyes, and a cry of rage will rise from their breasts [*among the crowd, camera focuses on a nun in habit*], that will

make the enemy turn pale. [*Loud applause*] As the Führer achieved victories in the past, so he will in the future. Of this I am firmly convinced; only the other day he said to me: 'I believe so much that we will overcome this crisis. By placing our forces onto new offensives we will beat the enemy and push him back. And I believe as I have never believed in anything in my life that one day we will hoist our flags in victory.' [*Applause*] Another speaker agrees by giving the 'Seig-Heil' salute three times.

5. Hitler: Hitler visits a division command post in the East. Hitler talks with officers and is seen leaving a building. He gets into a car and drives off. Soldiers jubilantly acclaim him. *Wochenschau Eagle*.

Even this hastily composed collection of old and new film material could not shake the unreality of Goebbels' mental picture of the war. Writing in his diary on 11 March after having viewed this newsreel he enthused:

In the evening the weekly newsreel is run through for me. It includes shots of Lauban and Görlitz which are really moving. The Führer's visit to the front is also included. In short this newsreel contains pictures of which we can make really good use for propaganda purposes. Unfortunately the weekly newsreel can only appear at irregular intervals since we have neither the necessary raw materials nor facilities for distribution for regular showings. Since it only appears irregularly our efforts to make it effective must be all the greater.[53]

Just over a month after its release, the Russians had encircled Berlin, and the Propaganda Ministry, like other government departments was disbanded. Hitler and Goebbels retreated to the *Führerbunker*, abandoning the German people to their fate, accusing the nation of weakness in the 'life or death' struggle against 'Jewish-Bolshevism'. And yet it is a measure of the limited success of the Nazis' ideological programme that the civilian population held out until 1945. Although tempting, this should not however lead to exaggerated conclusions claiming proof of a Goebbels' 'propaganda victory'.[54] Propaganda before 1939 had attempted to prepare the German people psychologically for war and to convince them of their own cause and invincibility. In fact Nazi propaganda became so intrinsically linked to German military success that defeat after Stalingrad found propaganda in a difficult position. Goebbels' response, in his frantic efforts to veil the truth, was to surrender to the irrational elements of National Socialism, which failed increasingly to survive reality during the last years of the Third Reich. The Deutsche Wochenschauen in particular suffered through their close association with 'final victory'. In the early days of war they served to reinforce a feeling of security and reassurance on the part of a reluctant German audience. By 1943 following the 'heroic epic' of Stalingrad their role had undergone a radical change. In line with Goebbels' 'realism propaganda', they now attempted to counteract defeatist attitudes by whipping up the radicalism of the masses. In the last year of the war, the newsreels had almost totally substituted myth for reality. For the historian the development of the Deutsche Wochenschauen provides unwitting testimony to the gradual retreat of Nazi propaganda into myth from 1939 to 1945.[55] Myth need not necessarily be reconcilable with truth, but if such propaganda is to prove successful it must survive the battlefield. Under such adverse military circumstances, a 'propaganda success' in the spring of 1945 was hardly feasible. This need not however lead us automatically to revise our attitude to resistance to the Nazi regime, or to suppose that popular support of National Socialism was not as widespread as previously assumed. A more critical approach to the oversimplified picture of the success of Nazi propaganda is to be welcomed. Nevertheless, one is still left with the feeling that it was only the series of unrelieved military disasters in the war that undermined propaganda, not the nature of the Nazi ideological message itself.

Notes

1. Quoted in V.R. Berghahn, 'Meinungsforschung im Dritten Reich: Die Mundpropaganda-Aktionder Wehrmacht im letzten Kriegshalbjahr', *Militärgeschichtliche Mitteilungen*, vol.1 (1967), p.114.

2. See the works of E. Bramsted, *Goebbels and National Socialist propaganda 1925–1945* (Michigan, 1965); Z.A.B. Zeman, *Nazi propaganda* (Oxford, 1973); and M. Balfour, *Propaganda in war 1939–45* (London, 1979).

3. R.E. Herzstein, *The war that Hitler won* (London, 1980), pp.24–5, 415.

Goebbels, Götterdämmerung, Wochenshauen

4. Such an approach is implicit in the following studies: M. Broszat *et al* (eds), *Bayern in der NS-Zeit IV: Herrschaft und Gesellschaft im Konflikt Teil C* (Munich, 1981); I. Kershaw, *Popular opinion and political dissent in the Third Reich* (Oxford, 1983); D. Welch (ed.), *Nazi Propaganda: The power and the limitations* (London, 1983). The debate initially focused on the 'manipulation versus mobilisation' question, and this is incorporated in R. Bessel, 'The rise of the NSDAP and the myth of Nazi propaganda', *The Wiener Library Bulletin*, vol. XXXIII, nos.51–2 (1980), pp.20–9.

5. See F. Taylor (ed.), *The Goebbels diaries 1939–1941* (London, 1982).

6. See L.P. Lochner (ed.), *The Goebbels diaries* (London, 1948).

7. Taylor, *Goebbels diaries*, p.416.

8. For a more detailed discussion of these early developments see D. Welch, 'Nazi wartime newsreel propaganda' in K.R.M. Short (ed.), *Film and radio propaganda in World War II* (London, 1983), pp.201–19.

9. For an interesting example of just how detailed these instructions could be see F. Terveen, *Die Entwicklung der Wochenschau in Deutschland: Ufa-Tonwoche no. 451/1939 — Hitlers 50, Geburtstag*, (Göttingen, 1960).

10. H. Tackmann, *Filmbandbuch als ergänzbare Sammlung herausgegeben von der Reichsfilmkammer* (Berlin, 1938).

11. Tackmann, 31 October 1938.

12. Taylor, *Goebbels diaries*, p.403, entry for 10 June 1941.

13. *Bundesarchiv Koblenz* (hereafter *BA*), R55/504 (Gründung bei Deutsche Wochenschau GmbH: 1940-2).

14. *BA*, R2 (Akten des Reichsfinanzministeriums), 4809, 3 December 1940.

15. Taylor, *Goebbels diaries*, p.172, 14 November 1940.

16. By the spring of 1943 the PK units had to be reorganised as they were employing over 1,500 men. See K.W. Wippermann, *Die Entwicklung der Wochenschau in Deutschland: Die Deutsche Wochenschau no. 10/651* (Göttingen, 1970), pp.41–3.

17. See Goebbels' speech to the Reich Film Chamber, 15 February 1941. The full speech is reproduced in G. Albrecht, *Nationalsozialistische Filmpolitik, Eine soziologische Untersuchung über die Spielfilme des Dritten Reichs* (Stuttgart, 1969), pp.465–79.

18. Taylor, *Goebbels diaries*, p.186, 26 November 1940.

19. *BA*, R109I (Akten der Ufa-Film GmbH), 1034a, 1412, 16 June 1940.

20. *BA*, R58 (Akten des Reichssicherheitshauptamtes), 155, 24 October 1940.

21. *Licht-Bild-Bühne*, 23 May 1940.

22. S. Kracauer, 'The conquest of Europe on the screen: The Nazi newsreel, 1939–40', *Social Research*, vol.10, no.3 (September, 1943), p.340.

23. Taylor, *Goebbels diaries*, p.361, 12 May 1941.

24. *BA*, NS18 (Reichspropagandaleitung der NSDAP/Gruppe Filmwesen), 282, 10 July 1941.

25. H. Boberach (ed.), *Meldungen aus dem Reich* (Neuwied-Berlin, 1965), pp.82, 102.

26. *BA*, R58/158, 27 March 1941.

27. W.A. Boelcke (ed.), *Kriegspropaganda 1939–41: Geheime Ministerkonferenzen im Reichspropagandaministerium* (Stuttgart, 1966), p.652.

28. Taylor, *Goebbels diaries*, p.434, 28 June 1941.
29. *Deutsche Wochenschau* (hereafter *DW*) no.10/651. February 1943. The first figure denotes the number for the year followed by the overall number. Wherever possible I have provided the Imperial War Museum's reference and number to facilitate viewing and hiring. An extract of Goebbels 'total war' speech is available for hire, ref.: GW 392. I would like to thank Steve Perry and the staff of the Imperial War Museum for their help in making material available to me.
30. For a detailed analysis of this newsreel see Wippermann, *Die Entwicklung*, pp.17–29.
31. *BA* R58/1148, 4 March 1943. See also J. Sywottek, *Mobilmachung für den totalen Krieg: Die propagandistische Vorbereitung der deutschen Bevölkerung auf den Zweiten Weltkrieg* (Opladen, 1976).
32. For an idea of just how low morale had slumped during this period, see *BA*, R58/186, 29 July 1943; also *BA* R58/187, 2 August 1943.
33. See J.W. Baird, *The mythical world of Nazi war propaganda* (Minneapolis, 1974), pp.217–18.
34. *DW* 28/722, July 1944, GW 223/3.
35. *DW* 36/730, September 1944, GW 231.
36. For an interesting and balanced analysis of Allied bombing and Goebbels' attempts to offset its effects, see G. Kirwin, 'Allied bombing and Nazi domestic propaganda', *European History Quarterly*, vol.15 (1985), pp.341–62.
37. *BA*, NS18 (Reichspropagandaleitung der NSDAP/Reichspropagandaministerium) 1434, 24 August 1942.
38. *DW* 18/712, April 1944, GW 213.
39. See Baird, *Mythical world*, p.217.
40. The speech is reproduced in full in H. Heiber (ed.), *Goebbels Reden*, 2 vols (Düsseldorf, 1972), vol.II, pp.225–8. For a further discussion see G. Kirwin, 'Waiting for retaliation — A study in Nazi propaganda behaviour and German civilian morale', *Journal of Contemporary History*, vol.16 (1981), pp.565–83.
41. *DW* 28/722, July 1944, GW 223/2.
42. *BA*, R58/191, 27 December 1943, quoted in R. Taylor, 'Goebbels and the function of propaganda' in Welch (ed.), *Nazi propaganda*, p.42. The V2 rockets were still being shown in the Deutsche Wochenschau as late as January 1945. See *DW* 2/748, GW 245/1&2.
43. *DW* 33/727, August 1944, GW 228/1.
44. For a discussion of the 20 July plot and its short-term effects, see Bramsted, *Goebbels and National Socialist propaganda*, pp.335–57; Baird, *Mythical world*, pp.228–40. A wider discussion can be found in I. Kershaw, *Der Hitler-Mythos: Voksmeinung und Propaganda im Dritten Reich* (Stuttgart, 1980); also Marlis Steinert, *Hitlers Krieg und die Deutschen, Stimmung und Haltung der deutschen Bevölkerung im Zweiten Weltkrieg* (Düsseldorf, 1970).
45. Goebbels was happy to record Hitler's support for his propaganda tactics during this final period; see entry for 11 March 1945: 'the Führer is of the opinion that the atrocity propaganda I have initiated is entirely right and should be continued', in H. Trevor-Roper (ed.), *The Goebbels diaries: The last days* (London, 1978), p.104.

46. Representative examples can be found in *DW* 45–6/739–40, November 1944, GW 240; and especially *DW* 8/753, February 1945, GW 249.

47. For an analysis of this newsreel see Welch, 'Nazi wartime newsreel propaganda' in Short (ed.), *Film and radio propaganda*, p.214.

48. This is the sentiment of a revealing Wochenschau (*DW* 3/748–9, January 1945, GW 246/1&2), dealing almost exclusively with the Volkssturm. It is a report of a home-guard recruiting station with the banner 'Believe, Fight, Victory'. With the new recruits having registered for the Volkssturm and now wearing their new uniforms, the commentator cries: 'The Führer's call is a holy command to us.' At which point the camera focuses on a banner draped in front of a building with the words: 'The people are rising, the storm is breaking.'

49. Quoted in Baird, *Mythical world*, p.243.

50. Trevor-Roper, *Goebbels diaries*, p.91, entry for 9 March 1945.

51. See Trevor-Roper, *Goebbels diaries*, p.112, 12 March 1945; also p.315, 4 April 1945, when Goebbels actually cites bread riots in Berlin. For examples of morale and public opinion during the last stages of the war (April 1943–5), see the weekly activity reports (Tätigkeitsberichte) *BA* R55/601.

52. Trevor-Roper, *Goebbels diaries*, p.192, 21 March 1945.

53. The last Deutsche Wochenschau was released on 3 April 1945. (DW no. 10/755). An in-depth analysis can be found in R. von Thadden and D. Waterkamp, *Die Entwicklung der Wochenschau in Deutschland: 'Die Deutsche Wochenschau' no. 755/19/1945* (Gottingen, 1977).

54. Trevor-Roper, *Goebbels diaries*, p.110, 11 March 1945. For a content-analysis of this edition see, R. von Thadden and M. Friedel, *Die Entwicklung der Wochenschau in Deutschland: 'Die Deutsche Wochenschau' no. 754/9/1945* (Gottingen, 1979). Goebbels' final reference to the newsreels in his diary was entered on 26 March, p.236:

> In the evening the new Wochenschau is submitted to me. It includes some really shattering pictures from the West which we cannot possibly publish. Demolition of the Rhine bridges in Köln, for instance, makes one heavy at heart. To see our beautiful cities on the left of the Rhine now being bombarded by our own artillery is truly heart-rending.

55. See Herzstein, *The war that Hitler won*, pp.414–15.

7

Swiss Newsreel — 1945

Peter Gerdes

Any analysis of Swiss Newsreel in 1945 will have to take into account the publication by Bernard Gasser entitled *Ciné-Journal Suisse: Aperçu historique (1923–1945) et analyse de tous les numéros de 1945* published by the Cinémathèque Suisse in Lausanne in 1978. Gasser's approach shows much prejudice against Swiss Newsreel. In his view, they were *a priori* superficial, uncommitted, lacking any critical clout and conviction of one sort or another. What he does not take into account are the conditions under which this fairly unique newsreel company worked, a company which had been set up to counter the propaganda emanating particularly from German newsreels (which were freely shown in Switzerland although occasionally censored). Ciné-Journal Suisse was to be part of the 'spiritual defence' of the country and as such had to try to direct its 'propaganda' inwards rather than outwards, i.e. since Switzerland officially did not have any enemies, neither abroad nor in the country itself (such must be the view of a small neutral country even though this view was well known to be distorted), Ciné-Journal Suisse (CJS) simply had to help lift morale and act as a unifier in a monopolistic situation, namely in the audio-visual field. It is very simple for a researcher today to infer that CJS was too patriotic and harmless, giving too much prominence to the great politicians and not enough to the little people, that it took a paternalistic approach towards women (which newsreel did not at the time?) and that it made too much of the farmer toiling the field and not enough of the worker fighting for a decent living. Most of these arguments contain a grain of truth but work from the assumption that a state-subsidised media monopoly, totally under-funded and understaffed, could have worked along the lines of investigative newspapers at a time when Switzerland was totally surrounded by forces of the Axis (few people realise that a Swiss diplomat or businessman who wanted to travel to the US needed a German transit-authority to get to Lisbon, for instance).

In a previous article[1] I have suggested that the art of CJS was to keep a sense of neutrality without giving up totally a certain amount of fighting spirit. During the war years, a lot could be seen and heard between the lines and behind the pictures which must, under critical analysis, be regarded as 'sticking one's neck out'. The question now is: come 1945 and the liberation of German-occupied countries, did CJS change in any sense, did it rid itself from self-censorship and the careful attitudes it had developed since its start on 1 August 1940?

During 1945 CJS produced 48 issues, altogether a total length (according to the indications on the communiqués) of 9,530 metres (5 hours 49 minutes 26 seconds).[2] During a short summer break between mid-July and mid-August, no issues were produced. The lengths of the issues varied, the shortest being the Armistice issue (no.239) of 150 m, the two longest (300 m each) called *Borders* (no.238) and *A day in the life of the General* (no.247). Most other issues measured around the 200 m mark (7 mins 20 sec). Twenty issues were dedicated to one single topic (some of those were produced by private film-production companies), the other 28 issues contained a total of 82 stories. Because my intention here is to look more at the content in general than at the neutrality aspect, I have decided to code the content somewhat differently from the method applied in my article mentioned above. I drew to some extent from a coding system which I have developed over the past few years in connection with detailed television news analysis. Two major categories applicable in a modern-day TV news analysis did not figure at all in the newsreels of 1945: 'Crime and Law' and 'Industrial Affairs'. No stories relating to these categories can be found in CJS 1945. Under the category of 'Disasters and accidents' only a minimal amount was shown and presumably one could have recoded the two bombing stories under 'International affairs'. It must be pointed out that under 'Disasters and accidents' no natural disaster, no major accidents, no fires, floods or avalanches were reported. In short, apart from the bombings, apparently nothing really bad hit Switzerland in 1945. Little was shown under 'National affairs', where government affairs — whether on a federal or cantonal level — were practically ignored. Nothing was shown under 'Defence' as such and under 'Army' only some aspects of a soldier's life and the life of the General. 'Community affairs' covered approximately 10 percent of all issues, many devoted to one topic only. These were *Mothercraft* (no.222), *Women in our times* (no.226), *Educational radio* (no.255) and *The dangers of alcohol abuse* (no.249). 'Business affairs' got somewhat more prominence.

Under 'Primary industry' one story dealt with farmers trying to keep up with grain production, one with fish breeding and one

Table 7.1: Swiss Newsreels 1945 — subjects covered

National affairs		length in metres	
Swiss government	221	292	
Swiss army	224/2&3; 245/1; **247**; 234/3	541	833
Business affairs			
Primary industry	225/1; 244/2; 253/3	200	
Secondary industry	227/1; 229/1; **243**; 252/3; 253/4	513	
Trade	227/2; **231**; 257/3; 259/1; 263/4; 254/1	356	
Tourism and R & R	253/5; 246/2; 262/3	162	1231
Community affairs			
Education	**255**; 266/1	373	
Health and medical	**222; 249**	386	
Women	**226**	210	969
International affairs			
International relations	236/1	70	
Effects of war (international)	236/2; **238**; 240; 242/1; **251; 261**; **256**; 259/4; **250**	1509	
Effects of war (internal)	**239**; 252/4; 260/4; 265/2; **268**; 266/3	594	
Humanitarian aid	**232**; 234/2; 235/2; 242/2; 246/3&4; 260/1; 254/3&4; 263/1; 244/3	638	2811
Disasters			
Bombings	229/2; 230/2	123	123
General interest			
Customs	228/1; **233**; 248/1; 257/1	373	
Arts	245/3; 235/1; 253/1; 263/2	133	
Fashion	248/2	52	
Animals	**259**; 259/3	303	
Country & its people	260/3; 264/2; 265/3; 245/2; **237**; 224/1	575	
Films	252/1; 253/2	130	
Personalities	230/1; 245/1; 254/2; 260/2; 263/3; 264/1; 265/1; 266/2	419	
General	**267**; 262/2; 245/3	331	2315

Swiss Newsreel – 1945

Sport and sport-related			
Soccer	235/3; 241/2; 257/2; 262/1; 264/3; 225/3	465	
Skiing	225/2; 228/2; 230/3; 234/1; 223/1	504	
Ice hockey	223/2	117	
Boxing	241/1	59	
Cycling	259/2	39	
Gymnastics	244/1	39	
Tennis	252/2	25	1248
			9530

Figures in **bold type** indicate that the whole issue has been devoted to one topic only
Source: Communiqués CJS

Summary	%
National affairs	8.7
Business affairs	12.9
Community affairs	10.2
International affairs	29.4
Disasters	1.2
General interest	24.5
Sport and sport-related	13.1
	100.0

with Swiss coal-miners. Not one whole issue has been devoted to, for instance, agriculture which in previous years had featured prominently. This surely could be read as a sign that the food situation was on its way to improvement. I have listed under 'Secondary industry' reports about engine-building, new types of shelters for war victims (a story which has strong humanitarian overtones), a complete issue on watch-making, one about the delivery of locomotives to Holland and one about liquid glass: in spite of the considerable footage devoted to 'Secondary industry' one gets the impression that at this stage no effort was made as yet to speculate as to the future of Switzerland as an exporter. That the watch industry should find itself the topic of a complete issue might be seen as typical. Under 'Trade', two topics stood out: the visit of the Allied Trade Delegation (about which, more later), and the situation at the Port of Basle, the key to Swiss trade since the Rhine provides the only link with the sea. The category 'Tourism and R & R (Rest and Relaxation)' may seem strange. But then it is hard not to sense a certain amount of clever marketing when one finds stories about GI's holidaying in Switzerland and soldiers of the 8th Army crossing the country being filmed by the Swiss Tourist Office. Almost 40 percent of CJS in 1945 was devoted to classical newsreel items, 'Sport' and 'General interest'. In many of these stories a connection with the war was made, however, such as when an art exhibition was shown, organised by artists serving in the army, or when reference was made to French soccer players who had fought in the Resistance. The Christmas issue *Toys for children* (no.267) showed the making and selling of toys but made reference throughout to those children in the world unable to speculate about their Christmas gifts. Many of the personalities shown had a direct link to events during the war. Of particular relevance is the category 'Country and its people' which could be seen as the original reason for CJS: spiritual defence. A story about archaeological digs in the Heimat (*Heimatforschung*) is linked with the necessity to know about the history of one's country in order to appreciate it; the complete issue *Village on Wheels* presents the life of side-show artists and gives an indication that the lighter side of life has not yet died. The story about the 400,000th telephone subscriber is split: in the first part, the oldest lady-telephonist is actually interviewed (an extraordinary step by CJS), then the possible 400,000th subscriber is found and his life described: telephone, community and history all linked together. There is talk about the difficulties of communication with and within an Alpine valley, a celebration of citizenship and a long story about an isolated community which tries to protect its heritage by building a museum.

The most popular sport, seemingly, was soccer. Skiing got more footage, but only because a long story about the opening of a ski-lift (no.228/2) had been included here. Indeed, soccer seemed to be so important that one story (no.257/2) was shown although the footage came three months late. The game between Switzerland and England took place on 21 July but could only be shown in the issue of 12 October because the footage which had been shot in collaboration with British Paramount News had been lost 'somewhere in France'. But since the event presented 'one of the most beautiful wins of our team', delayed showing seemed to be justified.

'International affairs', under which I have coded everything connected with the Second World War (except the accidental bombings), took up approximately 30 percent of all time whereas

Swiss Newsreel – 1945

a considerably greater proportion of footage was devoted to the illustration of the situation outside Switzerland (first directly along the border, then further into France and Italy) than to any effects inside Switzerland. And, as was expected after its general attitude in previous years, CJS devoted much footage to stories about 'Humanitarian aid'.

CJS in its 1945 issues reassured the Swiss people that the political, economical and social situation was stable and on the way to improvement; it appealed for humbleness in the face of suffering; actively encouraged people to do more for humanitarian help; was uncritical of several major events taking place in the country (although they were referred to); and through this gave the impression that, in spite of the apparent chaos outside, the world within was still intact.

In short: CJS lived up to the expectations the government, distributors and exhibitors had of a minimally funded monopoly medium in a neutral and politically highly vulnerable country. It never reached the highly critical, sometimes even brave, standards of some of the print-media and on occasions radio, which in spite of censorship and political pressure continued throughout the war to analyse and criticise political, social and economic events in Switzerland. Whether the audience would have wanted the CJS to take a more critical stance, we do not know.

Table 7.2: Swiss Newsreels 1945–6 — titles and length

No.	Date	Title
	1944	
220	29 Dec	Old and new from the railways 180m
	1945	
221	5 Jan	New Year's speech by the President of the Federation 292m
222	12 Jan	Mothercraft. Some advice. (Gloria Production) 230m
223	19 Jan	1. Gritli in the skiing camp 113m
		2. Ice hockey match Lausanne–Davos 117m
224	26 Jan	1. Archeological searches in the Heimat 60m
		2. In a little town in the Jura ... 61m
		3. Les Rangiers: The General's speech (according to handwritten note on communiqué: 'commentary lost') 60m
225	2 Feb	1. About food supply 57m
		2. Demonstration of skiing in Zurich 40m
		3. Soccer: Romandie–Lyons 79m
226	9 Feb	Women in our times (Pro Film Production) 210m
227	16 Feb	1. Aerodynamics and engine-building 175m
		2. Arrival of the Allied Trade Delegation in Les

Swiss Newsreel – 1945

Table 7.2:—continued

No.	Date	Title
		Verrières 24m
228	23 Feb	1. Carnival in Basle 45m
		2. The longest ski-lift opens in Chateau-d'Oex 138m
229	2 Mar	1. Shelters for war victims 57m
		2. Stein am Rhein bombed 88m
230	9 Mar	1. Death of Mgr. Marius Besson 40m
		2. Bombing of Swiss cities 35m
		3. National Skiing Championships 130m
231	16 Mar	Declarations of the delegates to the Allied Trade Delegation in Switzerland 170m
232	23 Mar	Exchange of war casualties in Switzerland 280m
233	30 Mar	In the days before Easter . . . 200m
234	6 Apr	1. Army skiing competition Switzerland–France 83m
		2. Red Cross trucks leave for Germany 19m
		3. The General talks about the situation (not transcribed in communiqué) 56m
235	13 Apr	1. Exhibition by artists serving in the Army 40m
		2. Helping farmers in the Alsace 15m
		3. Soccer: Switzerland–France 100m
236	20 Apr	1. New French ambassador 70m
		2. The path of war. The situation in neighbouring France 154m
237	27 Apr	A village on wheels (Praesens Production) 180m
238	4 May	Borders . . . 300m
239	11 May	Armistice 150m
240	18 May	Prisoners of war 160m
241	25 May	1. Boxing 59m
		2. Soccer: Switzerland–Portugal 113m
242	1 Jun	1. Exhibition of 'Le maquis' 35m
		2. Preparing for the journey to Palestine 120m
243	8 Jun	The exact time 200m
244	15 Jun	1. Workers' youth. Gymnastics 39m
		2. Swiss miners 100m
		3. Swiss doctors at work in Yugoslavia 26m
245	22 Jun	1. Death of Councillor Vodoz 43m
		2. The 400,000th telephone subscriber 107m
		3. Visit by French journalists and writers 53m
246	29 Jun	1. Parliament thanks the General 64m
		2. Visit by American officers 20m
		3. Shelters for French children 30m
		4. Saved from Buchenwald 49m
247	6 Jul	A day in the life of the General 300m
248	13 Jul	1. Alpaufzug 20m
		2. Fashion show 52m
		3. Geneva song competition 96m
Holiday break		
249	17 Aug	The dangers of alcohol abuse (Praesens

Swiss Newsreel – 1945

Table 7.2:—*continued*

No.	Date	Title
		Production) 156m
250	24 Aug	Russian internees 240m
251	31 Aug	War has ended ... 240m
252	7 Sep	1. Two film weeks 98m
		2. Tennis match
		3. Locomotives for Holland 20m
		4. American bombers leave Switzerland 45m
253	14 Sep	1. Art from the Ticino 21m
		2. French film exhibition 32m
		3. Fishbreeding 43m
		4. Liquid glass 61m
		5. The 8th Army crosses Switzerland 30m
254	21 Sep	1. The port of Basle 33m
		2. Josephine Baker in Geneva 102m
		3. French children arrive for a holiday 27m
		4. Activities of the Red Cross 24m
255	28 Sep	Educational radio (Kern Production) 283m
256	5 Oct	Rome: Summer 1945 ... 197m
257	12 Oct	1. After the vintage 108m
		2. We receive from London ... (delayed soccer: Switzerland–England with Paramount News) 49m
258	19 Oct	The camera in the zoo 192m
259	26 Oct	1. Freight from England 14m
		2. Cycle racing 39m
		3. Horsepower 111m
		4. Help for Norway 13m
260	2 Nov	1. Red Cross meeting in Geneva 20m
		2. The camera observed. Banned sequence 32m
		3. Communications with an Alpine valley 58m
		4. The War Office for Food Supply announces ... 53m
261	9 Nov	Misery and reconstruction in the Vercors 170m
262	16 Nov	1. Soccer: Switzerland–Italy 54m
		2. Souvenirs and kitsch 35m
		3. GIs in Switzerland 112m
263	23 Nov	1. Collection for the Swiss winter charity 28m
		2. Sculptures by Hermann Hubacher 19m
		3. Swiss–French friendship 70m
		4. Our link with the sea 67m
264	30 Nov	1. Consecration of Mgr. Charriers 70m
		2. Zurich greets its young citizens 50m
		3. Soccer: Switzerland–Sweden 70m
265	7 Dec	1. The King of Siam leaves Switzerland 43m
		2. Swiss return from Eastern Germany 27m
		3. A community builds a museum (Gloria Production) 120m
266	14 Dec	1. A new telephone system 90m

Swiss Newsreel – 1945

Table 7.2:—continued

No.	Date	Title
		2. A historian meets Resistance fighters 18m
		3. Camp for Swiss returned from Eastern Germany 94m
267	21 Dec	Toys for children: 200m
268	28 Dec	After six years of war 225m
	1946	
269	8 Jan	1. In the peace of winter 47m
		2. Efforts of skiing 41m
		3. The ski-test (Dahinden Production) 150m
270	15 Jan	1. The empty League of Nations 55m
		2. First flight Zurich–Prague 21m
		3. Imports (with Pro Film Production) 170m

Source: CJS Communiqués
For length/time conversion: 10 metres = 22 seconds

More than in the four preceding years, CJS in 1945 presented a spectacle of war. Consistent with its past policy, it still did not show any footage of actual fighting and no reference was made to battles or the progress of the liberation until it became so safe that a reporter could actually travel with American troops and Italian Resistance fighters and film the execution of Mussolini. As a neutral newsreel, CJS only showed and talked about the *effects* of war. As an extension of this attitude, it appealed throughout the year to its audiences to help alleviate the suffering, most of which was taking place in France (CJS headquarters were in Geneva and in the first half of the year a strong francophile attitude can be sensed), then in Italy. No footage was filmed in Germany and reference to the suffering in Germany was made only in connection with pictures of refugees trying to cross the Swiss border. (CJS filmed in Germany only in 1946.) As in previous years, CJS made no comments about the possible identity of those responsible for the bombing attacks on Stein am Rhein, Basle and Zurich. The stories are long, slowly paced, with little comment so as to let the pictures speak and create the strongest effect possible, but in the end these events were relativised in an almost apologetic fashion: 'Stein has only been touched by war'. After summarising the damage in Zurich and Basle the commentary ended 'such drumbeats of war give us an idea as to how much the people in regions of war have to endure'. Moral: the bombings of Switzerland may have been bad but aren't we lucky not to have to suffer more of them.[3]

Very little time or space was devoted to matters of 'National affairs'. The Federal government was presented, intentionally or not, only once in the first issue for 1945, which showed the election of a new Federal Councillor, Max Petitpierre (omitting any reference to the political debate which had led to the resignation of his predecessor Pilet-Golaz), followed by a summary of Petitpierre's family background, a visit to his home, and a short synchronised statement by him concerning several major political crises. A corruption scandal involving officers, the Russian-Swiss conflict about the treatment of internees, the international attacks on Switzerland about the Swiss government's handling of trade with the Axis were mentioned, but only if the story could be shown in a positive light. For instance, approximately 9,000 Russian soldiers had been interned in Switzerland. The Russian government intervened with the Swiss government about the alleged mistreatment of the internees. Russian representatives were invited for an inspection tour and on 10 September 1945 a statement was issued that Switzerland regretted any incidents and Russia expressed its satisfaction with the treatment its internees received. On 11 August, even before the signing of the final statement, the first internees had already been sent back to Russia. Most of them were very reluctant to go, knowing that they would be treated as traitors. According to CJS however, they asked 'every morning: "When can we go home?"' Issue no.250, having shown the daily life in an internee camp for Russians, the work of the inspection delegation and the preparations for departure, ends with the words: 'Finally! The return home! This is the friendly and hopeful ending of a difficult chapter in the Swiss policy of asylum.'

No political events taking place in the cantons were covered. In previous years, open-air election assemblies were usually shown and used as symbols for the strength of democracy. Obviously in 1945 such symbols were not needed any more.

The army, too, received relatively little coverage in comparison with previous years where the readiness and the fire-power were unashamedly presented.

Obviously the direct threat of war was over, and indeed there existed, right from the beginning of 1945, a strong move within the population for demobilisation. Issue no.224 contains a story which could be interpreted as an appeal for more heart and understanding of a soldier's lot. A small township is shown, empty and quiet. This night the inhabitants have returned, but there are soldiers who 'seek warmth and friendliness'. The 'don't need meat and bread alone but respect and affection. Any citizen is given these emotions in better circumstances.' Obviously the strong citizen–soldier link which traditionally had existed among the Swiss where every citizen is also a soldier, had begun to weaken. In other issues the official resignation of General Guisan was shown, and, one week later, a whole issue was devoted to *A day in the life of the General* which, according to CJS, could not have been shown before for security reasons. That the General was described in glowing terms is not surprising since he had indeed been a much-admired person throughout the war and had almost become a legend which no one sought to fault.[4]

More prominence than to the army was given to primary and secondary industry and to trade, clear signs that the tide had turned. In this context, the coverage of the visit of an Allied Trade Delegation to Berne is of particular interest. As early as 1943 the American press in particular had begun to attack the Swiss government for its alleged secret gold deals with Germany,[5] its alleged harbouring of war criminals from Italy and Germany, for its export of goods to the Axis where some goods were used for the war-machinery, and for allowing Italian-German transits on Swiss railways. Even within Switzerland the government was strongly attacked for its secrecy in these matters, but it argued that it had to deal somehow with the Germans if Switzerland wanted to remain alive economically. Without German permission, Switzerland would have been cut off from the rest of the world for years. However, once liberation began, it became clear that Switzerland had to establish immediately excellent relations with the Allied Powers in order to get trade flowing again quickly. Therefore an Allied Trade Delegation was invited. Its arrival was mentioned in one story and, shortly afterwards, a whole issue (no.231) was devoted to synchronised statements by the delegates from France, Britain and the United States. The commentary gives no reason at all as to why this visit had taken place, and the statements themselves are very diplomatically formulated. There is even a sense of joviality: 'for nearly four years our two countries (Britain and Switzerland) were cut off from each other, but during that time we occasionally waved over to you and no doubt you yodelled back'. Only the French delegate made it clear that his country expected Switzerland to act 'in the traditional framework of neutrality' so that France could help to open up the essential trade routes. According to CJS, everybody seemed happy. In reality Switzerland had to make considerable concessions such as blocking German funds, refusing further transits and waiving repayments of a French loan. What made matters worse, at least in the eyes of some, was the fact that only two weeks previously Swiss communities had been 'accidentally' bombed by Allied air forces. Otherwise, international relations on a diplomatic level were covered only once with a story which showed the accreditation of the new French ambassador whose links with the Resistance and de Gaulle were strongly stressed and who was allowed to make a synchronised statement. (no.227/2)

The most important CJS issues of 1945 were, no doubt, those which showed to a Swiss audience the effects of war as seen through the eyes of a Swiss film-reporter. In April CJS had the opportunity once again to enter France near Geneva (CJS had been in France in 1944 and shown pictures from Lyons). No.236/2, filmed 'only 500 metres from the border' showed the difficulties with which farmers began to clear their fields of mines. The images have nothing of the general destructiveness, cruelty and madness associated with war. In spite of the ruins of farmhouses, the story could be called 'idyllic', were it not for a sense of inherent suffering. The camera pans slowly, the commentary has a strong melancholic touch. At the end a decomposing body is contrasted with a farmer ploughing his field and a mother suckling her baby. The issue about the reconstruction of Vercors, though shown much later and using by now a fairly blunt language as far as references to German atrocities are concerned, showed ultimately the same sense of 'humanity in spite of cruelty'. The Vercors issue ended with a picture showing the farmer's family sitting at the same table as the German prisoners who were employed in the reconstruction of what German troops have destroyed: 'yesterday's enemies united with the house community as brothers and sons, accepted in the warm circle of humanity which already has forgotten hatred'. (no.261)

Perhaps the most important issue was no.238, shown during early April. Entitled *Borders*, it dealt with refugees, POWs and the liberation of Northern Italy. It had an immediacy missing in most other portraits of war-ravaged places, although the comment is patronising, bombastic and uncritical as usual.

It opens with pictures of Russian soldiers crossing the Swiss border ('they are astonished that they are offered food and shelter without being forced to work . . .'). Then one of the Federal

Swiss Newsreel – 1945

Councillors is seen inspecting the border with Germany. In the background is a bridge, in the foreground, refugees being inspected by border-guards: 'Behind the barricades almost 100,000 people wait for entry — a line of 16 kilometres. The haunted huddle, lashed by cold rain. The entry into our country is their rescue from the threats and horror.' No reference is made about whether they were let in or not and in fact most were refused entry. An element of irony creeps in when a convoy of Red Cross trucks is shown driving into Germany carrying 'food for prisoners in Germany'. The next sequence was filmed at the German–Swiss border in Konstanz. First, a former Swiss officer 'who had to be degraded' is shown crossing from Germany to Switzerland. He had joined the SS but 'after the collapse, he is seeking refuge in his fatherland. He is led to prison.' At the same place, the following morning, events were filmed involving the German Army and the local populace. News had arrived that the French Army had reached the outskirts of Konstanz. The German soldiers confer with Swiss authorities and their internment is arranged. Whilst the soldiers cross the border 'women and children are pushed aside. Rules about internment give preference to troops being chased by an enemy.' A German customs officer, under suspicion of espionage, is led away to be imprisoned in Switzerland. He prefers to return to Germany. Finally the French arrive. A group photo is taken, the acquaintance with the Swiss authorities established, then the border is shut again.

The following sequences were filmed in the south of Switzerland, at Chiasso. Swiss officers are seen conducting negotiations between Italian and American officers. Then the reporter accepted the offer of Partisans to join them on their way to Milan, where he arrived in time to film the gruesome end of Mussolini. For once, in this issue, there is no room for pathos. It is fast-paced and gives the impression that things are really happening minute by minute. For once, CJS presented 'news' almost unstructured, providing a sense of immediacy. But not everybody had been pleased. As Gasser reports, a private company had also sent a team to Northern Italy in order to get exclusive footage of the liberation. Its material arrived too late and the claim to exclusivity failed. The company wanted to sue CJS but for once CJS was bravely defended by its board.

One whole issue was devoted to the life of prisoners of war in Canada and what the commentary called the 'Far East', the only reference CJS ever made about theatres of war outside Europe. The commentary makes no reference as to the source of this footage, which shows routine life in POW camps, although the POWs under Japanese rule look terribly undernourished. Further stories were devoted to an exhibition about the French 'Maquis', to impressions from Italy from the Pontine Marshes to Monte Cassino (contrasted with a celebration on 19 August of the end of active military service in Switzerland), and another entire issue given to life in Rome in summer 1945.[6]

As in previous years, there were many stories about humanitarian aid. One complete issue was devoted to the exchange of wounded from both warring sides in Switzerland. The commentary makes a strong appeal for understanding of human suffering and evokes pity. In other stories, Swiss drivers are seen driving American trucks to get food to Allied forces POWs in Germany, and a group of Swiss citizens is shown helping farmers in the Alsace to get on with their work. Unusual is story no. 244/3, filmed on 16mm by doctors from the Centrale Sanitaire Suisse in Yugoslavia which provided Yugoslav Resistance fighters with an insecticide to prevent typhoid. Different again is story no. 242/2 which shows Jewish children preparing for their departure to Palestine. The fate of their parents is bluntly described: 'murdered in the slaughter of Novissad' or 'deported and murdered'. No. 246/4 is the only story referring to the existence of concentration camps. Refugees arriving from Buchenwald, several weeks after their liberation, are described: 'their body is nourished and clothed but their soul is hurt or destroyed beyond help'. The question of asylum, this biggest of all political and humanitarian issues in Switzerland, is brought up again: 'only children are allowed to stay with us. But many adults have jumped on the train . . . should they, the homeless, be sent back? They have just heard that they can stay.' Then the fate that some of these refugees suffered is described and the group itself is put into context when the comment is made: 'how small this group of saved human beings is, compared to the pale mass of those murdered'. There is no mention of who murdered them. CJS ends with an appeal to the hearts of the Swiss: 'the gesture with which we take the innocents in our care should come as natural to us!'

Arrival of some Swiss aid in Norway, the delivery of locomotives to Holland 'to help a brave people in its reconstruction', and the above-mentioned film from Yugoslavia brought, at least once in over four years, some references to happenings in countries not directly linked with Switzerland.

Apart from the bombings, Switzerland experienced little in direct effects from the war, according to CJS. National Service had to be endured, women had to replace men (issue no.226 is entirely given to this topic), and farmers kept on toiling to keep the country in food. The Armistice issue looks very uneventful and pale, mainly because the most exciting material had been used in the previous issue (no.238 already described). In the Armistice issue, the 'German capitulation' is mentioned but otherwise no reference is made to the cause of the war and its effects. Stress is mainly on the expressions of joy expressed by the French colony celebrating outside the Consulate in Geneva, waiting for Geneviève de Gaulle to make an appearance. The last issue for the year 1945 (no.268) offers a summary of six years of war (although CJS had only started on 1 August, 1940). Main topics are the General, and humanitarian aid; the war itself is hardly touched upon. Switzerland, looking back through the eyes of CJS, rests on itself. No wonder the outlook is positive, although misery elsewhere is acknowledged:

> ... the war in the skies has hurt us, too. But how dare we compare with the horror in our neighbouring countries? For us, ruins are nothing but pictures, we look at them from a comfortable seat. There, however, people have to build something new from ruins. After six years of war, we look on a beautiful, unhurt country.

Not even in this summary can one find a reference to the many problems which faced Switzerland during the war and which created considerable and open debate during those years. In a strange twist of interpretation, once the worst was over, CJS adopted a certain admiration for some aspects of the warmachinery. Story no. 252/4 shows 'over 60 American bombers which had been interned'. They were repaired for repatriation 'and thus those warring birds are being made healthy again — in a peaceful flight they will get back to their homeland.' There is no mention that some of those 'warring birds' could well have been the cause for a lot of heartbreak and damage caused by the accidental bombings of Swiss towns. In another strange twist, three stories were shown mixing aspects of tourism with visiting or passing foreign troops. It began with no. 246/2, a visit of American officers looking for places for the rest and recreation of some 250,000 soldiers (according to CJS). 'The officers from the US should see Switzerland the way they expect it to look.' Hence a lot of folklore and a trip to the Gornergrat to view the Matterhorn. And the story ends with a clear mercantile punchline: 'The Swiss trip of the American officers is bound to bring our country many enthusiastic guests. We welcome them warmly'. In no.253/5, under the title *It's a long way . . .*, extracts from a film produced by the Swiss National Tourist Office were shown. Soldiers from the 8th Army travel across Switzerland and admire the views with 'happy faces'. A touch of respect found its way into the comment: 'These are the soldiers which have won battles on foreign soil, battles which were decisive for us too.' Their destination, England, is referred to as having been 'the hope of all suppressed' during dark days. No.262/3 is the ultimate picture-book celebration of touristy Switzerland: entitled *GIs in Switzerland*, it celebrates cheese and yodelling, and does not refrain from a joking reference to the 'Swiss navy'. But there is a more serious side to this visit: 'in their shyness they would never dare to start talking to a Swiss girl in the streets' gives an indication of the excellent manners of US soldiers. And after visits to factories and a few skiing lessons, the tours are called 'a great success . . . our American guests will take with them many good memories — memories of a beautiful country which in cruel times was lucky to stay free and undamaged.'

Much less cheerful was the impression gained from the return of Swiss expatriates from Germany. Many Swiss had worked as farm-managers and farm-hands in the eastern parts of Germany and could only return at the end of the war. 'They will need much courage and confidence to start a new life in their homeland which to many of them is a foreign land.' Interestingly enough, the viewers were not encouraged to help them in this effort. Since they were Swiss, they were presumably expected to pull themselves up by their own boot-straps. The massive category of 'General interest' stories covered the usual newsreel ground. However some of them showed links with events surrounding the war. In no. 245/3, visiting French journalist, Rene Payot, is seen being fêted in Monbeliard for his broadcasts which helped the Resistance, and in no.266/2 a professor of history, von Salis, is celebrated in a similar fashion by Resistance fighters in Austria's Vorarlberg.

The number of international sports competitions began to grow again. In April a skiing competition between a French and a

Swiss Newsreel – 1945

Swiss Army team was shown. Before that, in February, a soccer match between a Swiss selection and a French selection ('amongst the French team are players who were prisoners of war') was presented. The first official international soccer match since 1939 between France and Switzerland was important enough to be attended by the General. But in none of the sports stories can one find those underlying appeals to keep fit and healthy in order to be strong which were so frequent in previous years.

The pictorial quality of CJS in 1945 is excellent, if excellence means carefully composed and framed images, a steady hand (more often than not a tripod), and a sense for the 'high quality beautifully framed picture'. Little is left to chance; there always seems to be time for the reporter to look, choose and carefully set up his shot. Very seldom is there a feeling of pressure, improvisation, immediacy. Even the shots showing the destruction after the bombings look carefully set-up, as do most of the reports from France and Italy. It is precisely for this reason that issue no.238 stands out, where for once a lot of information is packed, to some extent crudely, into one issue and where the pictures do give the impression that events in Northern Italy have almost overtaken the reporter. It is interesting to note that no.238 starts with a careful montage of Russian soldiers crossing the border but ends in a hectic pace creating the feeling of excitement concerning the liberation of Milan.

The images certainly did not make for propagandistic effects. Neither did the comments. Language throughout was restrained, indicating the acceptance of the *status quo* and sounding rather optimistic. There was hardly any criticism and those responsible for the worst aspects of the war were never named.

The term 'SS' was used twice, once in connection with a Swiss ex-officer who had joined the SS, once in the description of the causes of misery in the Vercors ('not SS hangmen but ordinary Wehrmacht soldiers'). Germany was never referred to as the 'Third Reich'. Fascism in Italy was exemplified by Mussolini's death which was called 'the last act of a tragedy'. Mussolini (like Hitler) was never mentioned by name. Only in no.256, the issue of Rome in summer 1945, was there a reference to 'an ambitious one who wanted to make a group of hard heroes of his lovely people'. 'Fascism' was first used in connection with the Russian internees who read in their own newspaper how they were 'abused, beaten, tortured by the Gestapo, often close to death. But Fascism could not rob us of our soul . . .'[7]

Perhaps the strongest linguistic condemnation of German activities in France was used in no.254/3, a story about the arrival of French children in Geneva on their way to Swiss holidays: 'these children have grown up in misery and amongst lies, in a bitter fight against the criminal occupation forces'.

CJS in 1945 had become a medium of conciliation, an appeal for understanding and humanitarian attitudes and actions. Stories about the Red Cross and the effect of the Swiss Gift (a wartime charitable organisation) appeared regularly, and humbleness was preached where no doubt many citizens would have preferred some outspokenness. CJS presented a picture of internal peace which indeed did not exist to this extent. Only very careful scrutiny reveals that some of the more popular issues were touched upon: the sagging willingness to continue with the mobilisation, criticism of trade practices, problems with Russia about its internees, growing alcohol consumption (issue no.249 on the dangers of alcohol abuse is the only story openly showing the existence of a serious social problem in Switzerland). It would have been interesting to get General Guisan's view on the CJS. On 25 July 1940 he had assembled his highest-ranking officers on the Rutli, the birthplace of Switzerland, and in a historical statement presented them with his ideas, motivations and intentions as to how to defend Switzerland during the war. He said: 'there must be a will for resistance against any attacks from the outside and against the many dangers from the inside like slackness and defeatism'.

Very little of Guisan's spirit had penetrated the prime instrument of 'spiritual defence' in Switzerland. But then one has to admit that the Swiss government, even in 1945, was still more cautious, secretive and self-righteous than most citizens wanted it to be. And although not a direct government instrument, the CJS could ultimately only work within a framework set up by the government. And that meant nobody was allowed to rock the boat.

Notes

1. 'Ciné-Journal Suisse and neutrality, 1940–1945', *Historical Journal of Film, Radio and Television*, vol.5, no.1 (1985).

2. This paper is based on the transcripts (communiqués) of the Ciné-Journal Suisse issues kept by the Cinémathèque Suisse in Lausanne,

Swiss Newsreel – 1945

Switzerland. It is important to note here that the Ciné-Journal Suisse used very little synchronised sound, but of the few synchronised statements which had been made in 1945, some have not been transcribed. For instance, all comments made by General Guisan are missing from the transcripts.

3. Those three bombing attacks were officially termed 'accidental', although the weather situation had been fairly good. British and American Air Force pilots were responsible.

4. Switzerland has no permanent General. A General is elected by Federal Parliament for the duration of a war. With demobilisation, General Guisan had to resign.

5. These gold deals have led to renewed discussion in recent years. More than ever, Swiss bank secrecy has become a topic of critical analysis, even for historians.

6. This report from Rome in summer 1945 is the only report to show city life in a war-torn country. Otherwise, CJS only showed the effects of war on country people. Even where there was talk of humanitarian aid, a strong rural touch prevailed.

7. Note that the commentator here quoted a camp newspaper printed in Russian. CJS itself never used the term 'Gestapo'.

8
Welt im Film: Origins and Message

Heinrich Bodensieck

In 1944 the major powers of the United Nations agreed upon the basic principle of their future military rule in Germany. On the one hand Germany was to be territorially administered in four zones, yet at the same time integrated in crucial economic and political areas. Each occupying Power (the United States, Britain, France and the Soviet Union) intended to guard its exclusive right of adjudication in its zone, while at the same time remaining responsible for 'Germany as a whole' in conjunction with its Allies. An Allied Control Council was to co-ordinate the destruction of National Socialism and German militarism. The special area of 'Greater Berlin', up until then the capital of the Reich, had been assigned as the seat of this authoritative body, with sectors of the city to be occupied by the four major victorious Powers.

While the summit conference at Yalta was dealing with the above arrangements, Western specialists in psychological warfare were preparing their plans for the imposition of an information policy following total victory.[1] They also took into consideration the joint war aims of the United Nations and the national interests of their states, in particular their systems of government and social orders as well as spheres of influence and interests.

Since 1943 two facts had determined Western 'white' psychological warfare (i.e. openly and duly identified war propaganda), as well as its plans for the post-war stages: first, the primacy of the formula 'unconditional surrender';[2] and secondly, the rivalry with the 'Nationalkomitee Freies Deutschland' (NKFD), which was supported by the Soviet Union,[3] as well as the competition offered by communist or even socialist propaganda. British and American experts had worked and argued in accordance with

Welt im Film: *Origins and Message*

these basic requirements and step-by-step they had prepared a 'Western'-orientated re-education and reorientation of the German people after their defeat; their post-war thinking and their conduct were to comply with the 'democratic way of life'. In the spring of 1944 the individual 'stages'[4] were in turn geared to the destruction of the fighting morale of the German armed forces to the inducement of members of the armed forces and civilians to surrender and the preparation of them for a new political system, as well as encouraging all Germans to accept and support the absolute regime of the Allied Military Government. This was to be followed by the preparation of a few Germans to take over regional tasks of administration and to re-educate their fellow-citizens subsequent to a guarantee of 'law and order'. The Western Occupation governments would then supervise the autonomy granted to the Germans and finally delegate to a purged German government a limited degree of political sovereignty.

As far as the most modern mass media — including audio-visual media — were concerned, the United States and Britain assumed agreement by all victor nations on their use, according to the basic ideals for multipartite occupation rule. At the very beginning of the era of military rule and before the first meeting of the Allied Control Council, they would produce a joint radio programme for all Occupied zones, broadcast from the central studios and transmitter units in and around Berlin ('Deutschlandsender' on medium and long wave).[5] This was intended to at least supplement zonal broadcasts. Analogous to this, joint sound-film reporting was not deemed necessary.[6] Previously there had been a difference of opinion, particularly on the part of the United States, about the film medium. On the one hand influential Hollywood film studios had tried hard to undertake the re-education of the masses themselves, thus hoping to capture the German market.[7] On the other hand, towards the end of the anticipated military government and during the setting-up of German administrative bodies, 'Supreme Headquarters, Allied Expeditionary Force' (SHAEF) had anticipated using mass media only as a channel of communication which the Western Powers could easily direct centrally, while simply influencing the Germans as individual readers and listeners: in other words, radio and newspapers only — not cinema newsreels.[8] For their part, Department of State experts had insisted that only material of the highest quality would be broadcast by the media, and only

Welt im Film: *Origins and Message*

instruction of exemplary high standard would be made available; thus they hoped to reach the democratic elite which was to re-educate its compatriots. Wanting to exploit the need for entertainment by the defeated people, good feature films had to be coupled with objective documentaries.[9]

As far as the United States was concerned up to February 1945, differing ideas regarding the use and usefulness of films and especially cinema newsreel for information policy purposes had been championed during the stages after the unconditional surrender in May. In the case of officialdom the ideas were mostly of a negative nature. What actually did happen in the entire 'Control Area' of the Supreme Commander, Allied Expeditionary Force (SCAEF), i.e. General Dwight D. Eisenhower, after 8 May 1945 is therefore all the more remarkable. The SHAEF guidelines came into operation on 12 May 1945. From 18 May *Welt im Film* existed as the only German-language weekly newsreel in the whole *Kontrollgebiet* (Control Area) of SCAEF. Produced in London by the USA, at first only a few copies existed. As a result the impact of *Welt im Film* was considerably overshadowed by the vastly greater exposure of radio broadcasts and newspapers of, initially, the military governments and later the first German licensees. In any case newsreels were only shown in those cinemas of the two Western zones which were open to German audiences, as well as in several camps in Britain which held over 100,000 prisoners of war.[10] But even these first editions of *Welt im Film* in spring and summer 1945 brought home to the defeated Germans the hard and intimidating facts and consequences of the final collapse of the National Socialist Greater German Reich.[11] Reports about military successes and military parades of the Allied victors emphasised the strength and exemplary standards of the Western democracies. Each running of a newsreel was coupled with the showing of a documentary film.

SHAEF was dissolved on 13 July 1945. Throughout the latter half of 1945 the Allied Control Council, together with the military government, administered the four German occupation zones and the special area of 'Greater Berlin'. There was not to be a cinema newsreel for which all four Powers took responsibility, nor were there to be German editions of the various American domestic newsreels in the US zone. Instead, the governments of the United States and Britain jointly produced *Welt im Film* beginning on 30 July 1945, for their German occupation areas,[12]

Welt im Film: *Origins and Message*

as well as for their occupation zones in Austria.[13] This was done without any specific written agreements. Admittedly the United States, at the beginning of November 1945, had given notice of termination of Anglo-American co-operation in favour of a four-Power produced newsreel.[14] With the failure of this project, *Welt im Film* continued.

What were the determining factors that shaped the decision of the United States representatives in the SHAEF commands and in the Psychological Warfare Division (PWD/SHAEF) between the Yalta Conference and VE (Victory in Europe) Day? Furthermore, up to the autumn of 1945, what had been instrumental in causing the apparent contradiction between the intended demilitarisation of Germany and the cinema glorification of the Western Allied armed forces put before the German people? These questions can be answered with the help of the files of the Information Services Division (ISD) from the OMGUS (Office of Military Government for Germany of the United States) resources.[15] They contain, especially in the Motion Picture Branch (MPB) sections revealing material, related to the wartime propaganda and planning priorities from the beginning of 1944. The documentary material proves that the use of films for the purpose of demilitarisation and re-education had always been debated within the framework of the overall information policy. Already, in such early considerations, there were reflected the intrinsic problems of the Grand Alliance and, more specifically, relations with the Soviet Union and thus potentially with Communism. If one also takes into account the manuals which were produced for the occupation governments, then these documents help to differentiate between Smither's[16] description of the early London history of *Welt im Film* and the Films Division of the Office of War Information (OWI) of the US Department of State, and the initial stage in June 1945,[17] bearing in mind, of course, the characteristic pro-Western trend of all *Welt im Film* productions.

The belated US initiative for newsreels and documentary films

From early February 1945, the staff of the OWI Films Division in London knew of the existence of papers expressing doubts about the use of film, particularly newsreels, during the first phases of

Welt im Film: *Origins and Message*

the era of military government in Germany. The Films Division soon equipped itself with arguments that stressed the importance of its contribution towards 'approaching the German mind'. In support of trends in favour of founding a newsreel for Germans, its promoters utilised the ideas of the 30 January 'Draft Operational Plan for Germany' which had been more positive about the role of film in the re-education programme and the rough demarcation of short- and long-term plans.[18]

Particular kinds of film were considered to be appropriate for helping to accomplish the main tasks of these two phases. Experts backed up such reports with information designed to break down prejudices against newsreels. The following extract shows that in the initial stages it was important for Germans to obey:

> 'Control'-Propaganda is for the purpose of creating and maintaining order. Newsreel films can implement this type of propaganda by objective and impartial reporting; by the inclusion of stories which show disorder being curbed, or law and order being created or maintained. As an adjunct small [film] trailers may conceivably be extremely useful in giving the widest possible circulation to instructions which require dramatic or visual implementation. The essential need here is that an authority is speaking and requiring obedience; an attempted persuasion should be secondary, possibly implicit.

In spite of this, the long-term task of changing minds and attitudes could only be performed educationally and by encouraging reconstruction. Documentaries therefore had to be screened 'showing in incontravertible forms *what can be done*', using the United States as a model. The magnificent engineering achievement of the Tennessee Valley Authority was given as an example: 'This will foster the renaissance of hope in the audience. All the positive sides of German history and culture can be drawn upon as well as the achievements of other cultures.'[19]

When this criticism of the Draft Operational Plan was prepared the author agreed with three aspects of the draft manual's ideas as well as those of the 30 January draft:

(a) Objective reporting;
(b) The Germans were prepared to be re-educated;
(c) They should use the United States as their model.

Welt im Film: *Origins and Message*

But two different appreciations of the role of film were added:

1. It was impossible to confine US informational efforts to an elite within German audiences.
2. The Films Division's activities had to be considered from the beginning of the period of all-out occupation so that newsreels and documentaries could be screened together after VE Day.[20] This conviction of the undoubted importance of audio-visual mass media became decisive for all further discussions and decisions.

As a result of the final preparations for the Yalta Conference in 1945, there was a new trend from mid-February. The United States was interested in producing one multipartite newsreel for all zones[21] and, if possible, without zonal supplementary issues. But public opinion in the United States and among the Allies had to be convinced. First of all a policy directive would have to be passed and issued to Films Divisions[22] and Allied efforts in the initial phase of occupation considered more intensively. Priority had to be given to making the Germans realise the dimensions of their responsibility and aware of Allied power and the unity of the Alliance. These were the arguments:[23]

> We can use the newsreel as an instrument for making the Germans understand this policy as not one of revenge but of justice. It is obvious that this can best be done in the media we are discussing by showing the German people the cost in human agony and physical destruction that their aggression has cost the civilised world.
>
> Needless to say, this can often be shown by indirection, that is the pictures of rehabilitation to men and cities which processes of rehabilitation have been made necessary by the Nazi incursion on the other lands. On the negative side the directive should contain a prohibition against more than a minimum use of any world events which tend to show a joyous and prosperous world unrelated to war ... In the initial stages nothing could be more cynical in view of the immediate objectives of Allied activities in Germany than to bring to them in the form of the newsreel sequences devoted to the joys and beauties of the Democratic way of life. It would, I am sure, tend to lay us open to the charge of hypocrisy. And the American people enjoying a great

Welt im Film: *Origins and Message*

> Sunday of freedom at the ball park would set up in the average German a feeling that we at least had no right to make a claim upon them because, all in all, by the evidence of what we have decided to show them, we have done pretty well in this war and have come out almost unscathed ...
>
> During the time that these newsreels will be shown in Germany there will be in that country over eight million impressed workers and prisoners of war and the machinery for returning these men and women to their former homes will have only begun and not completed its work. I am well aware that the desire to escape will be intense in the German people, but it is not the business of Allied newsreels to pander to that desire. We can hardly hope for the Germans to be aware of the enormity of sacrifice they have thrust upon the United Nations by their attempt at world domination if these same United Nations do not make a determined attempt to bring to the Germans a full knowledge of what they have done ...

Strength and unity of the United Nations could be proved as follows:

> One of the methods which I think will best reinforce the German sense of Allied power would be the portrayal of events in the Pacific. I believe that almost every issue, if not every one, should carry a sequence displaying this power. I am well aware that the Germans will have had the best evidence of Allied war strength from the fact of their defeat, but I see no harm in keeping that fact alive and I believe the Pacific war the natural medium for doing it.
>
> Wherever possible evidence of Allied unity should be shown. Sometimes this can be done through sequences showing the activity of UNRRA [United Nations Relief and Rehabilitation Administration] and others by the works of various United Nations commissions in the fields of medical help, meetings on universal food problems and any of the other activities which the Nations will naturally undertake. Every meeting of the Foreign Secretaries of Great Britain, Russia, France and the United States should be a must. The use of the air fleets of the United Nations to distribute critically needed supplies throughout the devastated portions of Europe should be shown when possible.

Welt im Film: *Origins and Message*

George Backer, the author of the assessment, therefore wanted to use film as well as the monopoly of editorial selecting of subjects to influence the Germans with regard to all aims of war. Of course for him the United States represented the decisive military power as well as the true democracy, so he did not advocate compulsory viewing by Germans of the newsreels:

> At the argument that the Germans will refuse to enter theaters in which such subject matter will be shown to them, there are two answers: (1) I do not believe that to be the fact and (2) but if it is the fact and a portion or a majority of the Germans do not wish to see these films, they are at liberty to stay home.[24]

But did Mr. Antonow, the film representative of the Soviet Union in London,[25] or his superiors in Moscow, know of these tendencies and their preconditions or of the consequences, so that they hesitatingly followed up the project of only one multipartite newsreel of all four Powers? In any case, from mid-March 1945 it became clear to the OWI in London that only the United States and Britain would co-operate in this field, and they also guessed that although their British partners were planning, they did not envisage presenting German civilians with a newsreel immediately after VE Day. In order to encourage more British co-operation, therefore, William P. Montague, responsible for the production of films, urged that the OWI Films Division should act and that PWD/SHAEF should screen their newsreel at the very onset of military government in Germany. At the end of March, Montague referred to preparations in two fields: the production of the London edition of the United Newsreels, as well as of the Free World newsreels,[26] and second, material prepared for a German public in accordance with the last internal discussions. The latter was to include key quotations from Roosevelt and Churchill about the results of the Yalta Conference which had been distributed on leaflets all over Germany since February:

> As you know, we have prepared a two-reel special which we will ship to all accounts the day after Germany officially surrenders. This German reel looks like a long drawn out argument by the policy boys of four countries, so why shouldn't we prepare innocuous head title like 'News of the

Welt im Film: *Origins and Message*

world' (stock) and as soon as the war ends slap it on our special and on subsequent issues of United News, make a few prints with a German track and try out distribution in the few spots where theaters might be open in Germany. We won't be double-crossing the English because we would not be making the official joint reel but just a temporary one under a temporary name. It will, however, put us in the field right away and so establish our making the newsreel, that is eventually decided on. Also the fact that we are doing business will jar the combination project into action.[27]

Montague's memorandum, 'Film Program for Germany',[28] evaluated the conditions regarding timing, objectives and their feasibility, which had been known since the end of March, and arguments in favour of screening newsreels and documentaries used during the last weeks. He presumed that within the foreseeable future all the occupation powers would jointly produce in Berlin a newsreel for the Germans. In the long term this necessitated building up and controlling film production in Germany, but not for features:

> Film production is the most easily controlled of all communication media, because of the elaborate nature of production and the essential centralisation of all the many facilities required for film production. A Program such as the above would lay the ground for a desirable industrial development for Germany: easily controlled by central authority, based on reality and not on escapism, since it primarily deals with actuality films and industry that eventually should be of the greatest value to the world as a whole since Germany has always excelled in the production of news, science and educational films and the production technique that they require.[29]

Montague emphasised that two different audiences had to be considered as important addressees and would be tackled by the United States:

(a) Films for distribution within Germany to the German people.
(b) Films for the outside world, informing it as to what is

Welt im Film: *Origins and Message*

happening within Germany and thereby holding its interest on the German problem over the long occupational period.[30]

As far as the second task was concerned, Montague was anxious not to repeat mistakes made in the aftermath of the First World War.[31] The following sorts of film were considered to be important to assist short-term aims:[32]

> 1. Newsreels. These would be treated simply as a medium of communication in order to bring to the Germans a knowledge of what was happening in their country and in the outside world in relation to their country.
> 2. Trailers. These would be attached to the newsreels for distribution purposes and would be a straight message of instructions from the occupying military force to the German people stating the latest regulations for their control. The fact that they were in motion picture form would simply be an added way of clarifying an order and supplementing all other communication media when it came to blanketing the country with new instructions in the shortest possible time.
> 3. A non-theatrical newsreel. This would be a two reel, once a week affair with an outlet through the 42,000 non-theatrical projectors that did exist in Germany, schools, youth movements, factories and travelling trucks.

To achieve the long-term aims:[33]

> 1. News shorts. These would be a monthly series of two reelers, made according to March of Time formula from actuality film, each one explaining some basic phase of the long range directive, such as the first might be on the cost to the world in misery, destruction and life that Germany's war had resulted in. The second might be on Allied unity, others might be on Allied fighting might as depicted by various angles of the Pacific campaign. They would all relate the German situation to the Allied plan and policy.
> 2. Documentaries. These would be based on the workings of democracy in the outside world and be of value in long-range re-orientation work as contrasted to the above which would be more short range to meet the immediate state of German mind resulting from military occupation.

Welt im Film: *Origins and Message*

> 3. Features. These would be ordinary commercial feature pictures, selected because of their value in re-orientation.

Montague did not succeed in implementing this extensive plan as soon as he would have wished. Lack of money was a drawback, and he mentioned the production of reports from Germany for foreign countries and that all wartime arrangements with private publishing firms would expire after the end of the war, warranting a consideration of existing international financial contracts for all governmental propaganda activities. It was therefore impossible to use features as products of private producers, and during the phase following VE Day it was impossible to produce a non-commercial special edition.

In spite of these obstacles, it was decided to offer the Germans a weekly programme of four reels (60 minutes) for the initial phase of military government. 'General information' about Germany and the world was not allowed. Instead news stories from all over the world and of a high quality were to be encouraged. Reels nos. 2 and 3 had to deal with and influence the Germans. The latter obviously had to be edited accordingly:

> The four reels of news material will roughly break down into one reel of 'flat' type material of outstanding news stories from around the world. The second reel will be of outstanding material that by film editing and interpretation can be brought to focus directly along the propaganda line for Germany.
>
> The third reel will be a weekly feature to be developed through the combination of old German and American newsreel material.
>
> The fourth reel — and this should be expanded at the expense of the other categories as fast as possible since this type would be the only material that would carry a complete sense of verity from a propaganda point of view — would be various news stories conceived and shot with the only view of implementing propaganda aims. These would have that value from the nature of the subjects selected and a sense of verity from the way they were shot since the propaganda angle would not be injected by clever editing and tricks, but would be there by the nature of the story itself.[34]

As keeper of the minutes Montague recorded the following —

but he could also distance himself from it. He knew that only a few experts could produce the kind of sound-film reports necessary and that this meant the reports would be more important in the final phases. The plan also needed to be adequately supplied and maintained.

> To make this last category of material, we will need a complete network of cameramen covering Europe in order to pick up every single news story developing that illustrates our propaganda points. In other words, we would need a man in each of such countries as Denmark, Norway, Finland, Belgium, Holland, Poland, Czechoslovakia, the Balkans, three in France, possibly one in each of Spain, Portugal, Switzerland, Sweden and certainly two *in Russia and Great Britain*.[35]

Thus was conceived a new type of newsreel for the defeated Germans: it was to be fully manipulative by editing and effective use of the camera.

The interrelation between 'verity' and Western propaganda illustrated the new trend in the output of the OWI's Films Division. 'Verity' ('the fourth reel ...') was related to the 'Propaganda point of view' that was prevalent when the reports were produced. As a consequence, advocates of film as a mass medium had more than succeeded in the recognition of newsreel and documentary film along with the press and radio as an essential part of political re-education. Instead of academic standards for all factual films those keynotes of psychological warfare which were used for leaflet operations had been effected again: impressive presentation of 'selected facts', of 'hard news' as being 'the truth' — but not 'the whole' truth, of course.[36]

Developing and testing of a weekly joint newsreel for Germany

The OWI's Films Division decided to use a propagandistic newsreel in Germany because its staff was acquainted with all Allied material and captured issues of the *Deutsche Wochenschau*. They were anxious to obtain the consent of PID (the British Political Intelligence Department)/PWE for producing and distributing the newsreel as a joint operation by the United States and Britain.[37] The films were tested on different audiences of

Welt im Film: *Origins and Message*

German POWs, e.g. of selected anti-Nazis.[38] One result was that the majority of anti-Nazi POWs reacted differently from liberated Frenchmen or from 'progressive' US citizens.[39] The OWI therefore had to deliver clear messages[40] and concentrate on the documentary illustration of 'Allied power', including the equipment of the Soviet Union and 'German atrocities'.[41] As far as the first point is concerned, since March 1945 the BBC monitoring service[42] had recognised different lines of propaganda from the Moscow stations broadcasting for Germans, in spite of the Yalta Conference agreements: officially the Soviet Union agreed with her Western Allies regarding Germany, but at the same time the 'Movement of Free Germany' was allowed to operate in a nationalistic manner. Radio Berlin was on the air with similar tendencies since May, stressing Soviet relief for Germans. Many Germans became sympathetic towards the Soviet Union[43] and since mid-June licensing policies of the Soviet Military Administration in Germany for German political parties, trade unions and newspapers, as well as its film policy, placed the Western Powers in a difficult position,[44] especially after the Western sectors of Berlin changed hands. But as far as the Potsdam Conference was concerned, the United States realised that propaganda should not be affected. Continuous use of 'Allied unity' marked the 'hard' line, although it was 'realistically' accentuated on the fourth anniversary of the German attack on the Soviet Union when — in accordance with British propaganda — the importance of the Eastern theatre of war had to be played down.[45] Obviously those responsible knew that 'Allied unity and power' should be contrasted with 'collective responsibility' for 'German atrocities', in preparation for the war trials.[46] But care had to be taken,[47] and SHAEF and PID emphasised differentiating between Germans according to sex and age: women and teenagers were more prepared than men to free themselves from Nazism.[48]

After some plans had been effected,[49] Brigade-General Robert M. McClure (chief of PWD/SHAEF) had to counter criticism published because of the notorious Soviet successes in Germany. On 25 May General McClure explained his concept to the press in Paris, stressing that the governments of the United States and Britain not PWD/SHAEF were responsible for all propaganda output to Germans:

> Films will be shown to the German people. Obviously they

will be carefully selected. The main items, perhaps, will be a weekly newsreel and selected documentary films produced by OWI and MOI [Ministry of Information]. We shall also arrange for the importation and exhibition of certain Allied feature films, when it is felt that the time has come to give the German people full-scale cinema shows.

Beyond this, an hour-long film of German atrocity camps is being completed. This film will include material from most of the larger Nazi concentration camps and is being carefully and soberly documented. It will attempt to show Germans what was going on in those camps in the light of daily life in the villages nearby, and the theme is simply that the people of Germany must consider themselves responsible for the atrocities, as does the rest of the world, because they and they alone are responsible for the creation and maintenance of the system of Government which used these shocking methods as a means of control.

At the same time he mentioned additional materials:

As soon as transportation and other facilities permit, selected and specially prepared Allied publications will be imported into Germany, but manifestly, they will not be of a light or entertaining nature. They will be the beginning of the long-term task of attempting to reorient the German mind. We have just completed an illustrated booklet on German concentration camp atrocities which will be 'required reading' for Germans. It will be distributed to German troops in our hands as well as to German civilians . . .[50]

Although as early as 4 July Elmer Davies (chief of OWI) had given the President the impression that the 'OWI–Army news-team' was already providing the Germans with information, 'through newspapers, the radio, and newsreels', too,[51] McClure could not publish his next statement before the Potsdam Conference. After the dissolution of SHAEF and PWD, McClure acted as Chief of Information Control Division, USFET, and Information Control Services, US Group CC. On 2 August in Berlin, he stressed that the United States had a special interest in the reorientation of the Germans:

Welt im Film: *Origins and Message*

> We want to remove the individual German's misconception about Germany and its relationship to the world and to prepare him for ideological and political reorientation by confronting him with objective historical facts and truthful world news. Part of this reorientation will be toward correcting the German people's misconception about the United States by making them aware of the reasonableness and justice of American views, and the decency and attractiveness of American Institutions. Finally, we aim to try to help the individual German prepare himself to take his place in a democratic society. We hope to do this by making available to pro-democratic forces within Germany all possible facilities for making themselves heard, and to convince the German people, by precept and example, that the assumption by the individual of civic initiative and responsibility is the prerequisite for responsible government.[52]

The general was able to report three results:

1. The publishing of the 'KZ'-booklet;[53]
2. For the first time the publication of a licensed newspaper in the actual territory of the US zone of occupation: *Frankfurter Rundschau*, no.1, 1 August 1945;[54]
3. The opening of a few cinemas for Germans: 'Just this week, on Monday night, July 30, we began exhibition of motion pictures to German civilians in the American zone, and there were, to be sure capacity audiences at every showing. The first films shown were a newsreel, "WELT IM FILM", prepared jointly especially for Germany by the OWI and its British opposite number, the Political Intelligence Department of the Foreign Office, and a documentary. In about half of the theaters, the documentary was "TOSCANINI" and in the rest it was "TVA", both produced by OWI. Altogether, 15 theaters opened Monday night — four in Berlin, three in Frankfurt, three in the Munich area, and one each in Offenbach, Bad Homburg, Friedberg, Bad Nauheim and Wiesbaden. We expect to open five more theaters within a week, and 20 more by mid-August.... Movie exhibitors ... will be supplied with U.S. features, documentaries and shorts, both commercial and government-produced, as well as with specially-edited newsreels.'[55]

Welt im Film: *Origins and Message*

In the above statement on achievements since May, McClure did not mention an additional documentary on atrocities in KZs.[56] His motto was 'go slowly at first', so he delayed licensing publishing companies and the release of *Welt im Film*.[57] Issues were released gradually in the US zone after the testing period.[58] The town of Erlangen was chosen as a prime target area for propaganda[59] and since mid-June the first two out of a series of five test programmes were shown for a week each in two cinemas.[60] Publicity for the performances was of the normal commercial type and admission was charged for the performances. The first programme offered:

Die Welt im Film No.1 (two reels)
Jeep: Die Selbstbiographie eines Jeep (two reels)
TVA: Das Tennessee-Tal (three reels).

The newsreel included, among other items, scenes of the ruins of German cities, of German ex-prisoners of war returning home, of looting in Germany and the execution of a German spy.[61]

According to the playbill the second programme offered the following titles:

Welt im Film No.2
Pipeline
Duke Ellington's Orchestra
Cowboy

At least during the first performance the title last mentioned was replaced by '*KZ*'.[62]

Audience reactions were observed by PWD experts (especially the Intelligence Section), and questionnaires were completed. There was no refusal to comply with the experiment and the analysis of reactions to the first programme showed that 'most people believed that the programs presented the truth and not a one-sided picture. They did not in the main feel that they were being propagandized. Only 20 people stated that the films were biased.' But 'the young and educated — mainly students — were far more critical of the films than other groups ... They were more apt to find them biased.' Irrespective of this difference, the majority of the spectators had violently objected to the newsreel.

This was by far the least liked of the three films and was

Welt im Film: *Origins and Message*

also chosen overwhelmingly as the one most disliked . . . Many people merely stated that it was biased and tendencious, but others were more specific. A sizeable group found the material presented depressing and humiliating . . . It is clear that the facts of Germany's defeat are unpalatable to German nationalistic and patriotic feelings . . . Another group dislikes the newsreel simply because it deals with war at all . . . Still another group dislikes the newsreel specifically because of the scenes showing German civilians looting. They displayed great emotional resistance to the idea that the looters could be German. It is undeniable that this film did not prove entertaining; whether it is of value for other reasons is a separate problem not thoroughly probed in the present study and dependent upon policy objectives. A small number of people did like the newsreel, mainly because of the variety of material presented, including world events of which they had been unaware, and the truth of the reporting. A few liked it specifically because it showed German POWs returning home.[63]

Concerning the second programme the observer stated the reactions to the newsreel: 'The audience was respectful, but scarcely enthusiastic. During the showing of the next picture, *Pipeline*, there were expressions of admiration at the mechanical equipment shown. The picture went down very well . . .'.

The audience, therefore, had reacted to 'Allied power' (Anglo-American power) exactly as had been anticipated. The second issue of *Welt im Film* was not so predictable: 'Our newsreel is judged to be inferior to the *Wochenschau*', and the short of jazz 'evoked bewilderment'. The KZ film on atrocities did not appear to be shocking to most viewers. The experts were dissatisfied.[64]

Field Marshal Montgomery's Headquarters also criticised the films. All issues including no.6 were seen to contain no clear line on policy and the viewer pointed out that:

Some of the material seems to be selected for its interest to an audience outside rather than inside Germany (e.g. scenes of queues or of empty streets after curfew). Occasional sentences of the commentary (e.g. on the arrest of Doenitz) seem to lapse into propaganda. At the same time it is clear that mistaken selection or propagandist use of this

Welt im Film: *Origins and Message*

German material will most easily discredit us with a German audience.

The following advice was given to producers:

1. Avoid scenes which have no news value for a German audience.
2. Pictures of destruction should include a reasonable proportion of bombed factories and railway stations to bombed churches and houses. Commentary should not (as in the Frankfurt scenes) draw special attention to the destruction of cultural monuments).
3. Pictures of destruction should at this stage be relieved, if not balanced, by any available pictures of Germans engaged in or released for reconstruction work.
4. Avoid, particularly in scenes of historic interest, any 'propaganda' comment and stick to documentary treatment.

I am sure that your experts have additional points to raise, and would be grateful if you could put our views together with theirs before the London authorities.[65]

When the Chief of FTMC (Film, Theater and Music Control Section of PWD/SHAEF) had read these reports on the newsreel testings, they were sent to OWI London.[66] He probably knew that the British expert in political warfare really wanted to achieve more than simply an impression of a good Anglo-American partnership in the German mind. Why? First, the British author criticised the United States' decision to replace real documentation by propaganda. Second, the selection of what must be shown to bring home to all Germans the consequences of their consent to Nazism had to be treated carefully, making sure that the beginnings of reconstruction were not neglected. At a time when Germans were showing signs of pro-Soviet Union sympathies, the British author had reservations about the PWD's output.

On 12 July during the last meeting of PWD/SHAEF, the British experts presented General McClure and his staff with a report: 'Short term Information Control Policy in the British Zone'. This marked a degree of independence from United States policy, backed up by Montgomery's order to open 370 cinemas immediately and to show films. Whereas the Americans had

Welt im Film: *Origins and Message*

planned to begin full cinema shows at the end of September, the British order forced both Britain and the United States to agree on the fixed day of the new film policy.[67]

The joint newsreel for Germany had to be produced 'on a quadripartite basis'. The common information policy mirrored the concept of Allied Control Council for all four occupation zones. Each partner was granted the right to veto decisions which made it difficult to secure national interests, and in turn influenced the negotiations for a bipartite agreement on *Welt im Film* and co-operation on a weekly basis. To counter this problem a 'Joint OWI-PID policy instructions' manual was written and a control-structure was established, the group of production being headed by W.P. Montague. The British distinguished themselves from all OWI-edited issues of *Welt im Film* because of their criticism of the American approach:

> The newsreel at present has its limitations owing to lack of proper facilities. It is in the interest of PID and OWI to improve the quality of the newsreel in order to bring it up to a high professional standard, and to use all available means to that end.

Nothing was arranged with regard to the extent of every issue although responsible persons on 13 July had been in accordance that it would be better 'that another reel be added in order to provide more scope for handling allied informational policies in this medium in Germany', that is, to publish consequently 'a weekly newsreel three reels in length'.[68] Setting of objectives and restrictions were decisive, agreed during the negotiations before 1 August:

> PID and OWI have agreed to provide a joint newsreel for distribution in the American and British zones in Germany. This newsreel is for the emergency period during which newsreel companies cannot be licensed to service newsreels to the German public. It is clearly understood that there is no intent on either side of perpetuating governmental newsreel operation. Nothing will be done which will create a precedent that will prejudice eventual newsreel operations by private enterprise uncontrolled by government. Naturally, Allied Government supervision of newsreels in Germany will be maintained as long as judged necessary.[69]

Welt im Film: *Origins and Message*

Britain and the United States took it for granted that *Welt im Film* as an overt publication would only be produced for a short period of time. As soon as licensees were allowed to work in the same field it would have to be stopped. 'Private enterprise' was to be kept free from the influence of any German government once it was established. In practice this meant that Anglo-American companies were placed in a most favourable position. One stipulation was that they would manufacture *Welt im Film* as soon as it was produced in Germany, under the covert influence of the two Occupation Powers. But was the Soviet Union considered in any of these plans? Securing the compliance and profits of internationally active companies and eliminating German influence was contrary to Soviet Union policy. Although the British did not comply with the July agreement, they did produce *Welt im Film* with the OWI. This was a major step forward and after initial testing the way seemed to have been made clear for realising information policy plans.

US film policy after Potsdam

After Potsdam, General McClure stressed both the continuity and the success of US information policy in Germany, without mentioning that this policy had been altered because of the Soviet Union and British reactions.[70] Perhaps McClure and his staff did not yet realise that profound differences existed between the Allies. Four factors left over from the PWD/SHAEF era blinded them to these differences and to the need for a new information policy:

1. All important guides on psychological warfare had been written outside PWD/SHAEF, or by those inside PWD but who represented other institutions.[71] Even when PWD experts criticised decisions with SHAEF backing, they had often been ignored.[72]

2. Strained relations between Eisenhower and Montgomery had affected PWD's activities. Certain actions by General McClure had caused the British to be suspicious of US policy.

3. McClure was responsible for political warfare and wanted to take all the decisions without necessarily consulting the relevant experts.[73]

4. PWD/SHAEF did not produce films. All the problems of the

Welt im Film: *Origins and Message*

newsreel for Germans had been discussed at OWI, London, and all PWD did was to release and use the films without even contributing to early reports or plans.

Consequently, in Germany only a few people responsible for United States information policy realised the need for change,[74] which eventually took place in the autumn of 1945. Problems soon surfaced and newsreels were deficient in three fields, as shown by the Erlangen tests and since the beginning of the Nuremberg Trials:

1. Although all material was supposed to refer to experiences and expectations of the addressees, the first issues had been collected from reports shot and produced for non-German audiences. The long time lag between shooting and printing a newsreel had to be diminished.

2. The pro-US bias of early issues edited by OWI had to be reconciled with the need to stress Allied unity.

3. Inadequate knowledge of the Germans presented problems. It had not been taken into consideration that Nazi propaganda must have had a profound influence. It was also important to distinguish between propaganda for Austrians and propaganda for Germans.

The basic ideas behind propaganda in this period were still 'Allied unity and power' and 'German guilt/atrocities'. The two were not always compatible, and Nazism and German militarism had to be fought radically, with peacefulness and democracy now forming a positive facet of 're-education'.[75] At the beginning of the Nuremberg Trial the 'KZ' film *Todesmühlen* (*The Mills of Death*) was released. Compulsory viewing was not insisted upon, but it was first offered to the inhabitants of the 'Greater Hesse'.[76] After Mr. Robert Jackson's speech for the prosecution in Nuremberg, certain formulations of Basic Central Directive JCS 1067 had to be altered.[77] At the same time as the 'Allied unity' thesis was supposed to be shown, there were reports on strained relations in the Middle East, released for reprints in US-licensed newspapers.

At the beginning of November, the Americans had to consider different circumstances and trends:

1. On 15 December the contracts for 'United News' ended and — in spite of the new situation — OWI's London office was

Welt im Film: *Origins and Message*

disbanded.[78]

2. Central Europe had become an area of US–USSR conflict. What were the consequences with regard to political warfare in Germany, especially in the field of audio-visual propaganda? Obviously those responsible in Washington found that Soviet newsreels and documentary shorts were unexpectedly very impressive and that the Soviet Union with its Babelsberg 'Ufa' studio base could outstrip US film output from its more limited Munich 'Bavaria' studio base. Did the Soviet's control of the raw-film stock plants of AGFA-Wolfen and the central position of Babelsberg near Berlin play a part, say, compared with the shortage of film stock in the Western zones and to the 'poor communication and transport relations that Munich has with the outside world'?[79] Did the Americans see the newsreel as a form of propaganda that could disguise tensions in the 'Alliance' more than in zonal broadcasting and newspapers, or as the mass medium fit for influencing Germans in all zones of occupation in the most effective way?

In this state of affairs the Americans pressed their British partners of *Welt im Film* to choose between supporting 'a serious effort to achieve a quadripartite newsreel or the termination of the present bipartite arrangement'.[80] During negotiations (inside OWI) the Americans highlighted the need for a four-Power newsreel in order to achieve the following ends:

1. The Germans should be shown Allied unity in at least one field of informational output.[81]

2. British official consent to the bilateral agreement on *Welt im Film* was essential, but the United States wanted dropping all those conditions aggravating US information policy to follow closely any change of policy.[82]

3. Some tried to continue propagating the message of 'collective guilt' by producing a 'B' newsreel, adopting a harsher tone which would not be shown in conjunction with features.[83]

4. In the case of licensing newsreel companies 'one should bear in mind the legitimate corporate interests of the American newsreel companies' because 'before the war several of the most important companies were wholly owned subsidiaries of the American newsreel firms'.[84]

In any case the United States wanted to form their information

Welt im Film: *Origins and Message*

policy in all media according to their own interests. At least in their zone, and if possible in the British zone, too, they had to be prepared if the Soviet Union could take the initiative in licensing Germans for producing a communist newsreel at the Babelsberg studios. The answer seemed to lie in laying the foundations for a newsreel to be used in Germany as an effective weapon in the next stages of political controversy. Thus *Welt im Film* might survive those first stages of the occupation era, for which this newsreel had merely been intended.

Notes

1. The principal sources of information for this paper are to be found in files in US National Archives Record Group 260: Office of Military Government for Germany of the United States (OMGUS), Information Services Division (ISD). Microfiches of all important files are held at the Bundesarchiv, Koblenz, and at the Institut für Zeitgeschichte, Munich. See J. Hastings, 'Die Akten des Office of Military Government for Germany (US)', *Vierteljahrshefte für Zeitgeschichte* (*VZG*), vol.24 (1976), pp.75–95; H. Weiss, 'Abschlussbericht über das OMGUS-Projekt (1976–1983)', *VZG* vol.32 (1984), pp.318–26. For list of OMGUS files used for this report, see note 15 Koblenz: 245f.

2. Hans Simons, 'The conditions of unconditional surrender', paper read on 6 October 1943, printed in *Social Research* vol.X, no.4 (November 1943), pp.399–416, esp. pp.403ff; Hans Speier, 'War aims in political warfare', text of an address delivered at the New School for Social Research (Institute of World Affairs), on 4 March 1945, printed in *Social Research* vol.XII, no.2 (May 1945), pp.157–80, esp. pp.165f; Daniel Lerner, *Sykewar: Psychological warfare against Germany, D-Day to VE-Day*, Library of Policy Sciences (London, 1949), pp.18–25: 'Problems of unconditional surrender'.

3. OMGUS 5/260–2/4. Daniel Lerner, Deputy Chief of Intelligence, ICD, to PWD/SHAEF Chief Gen. McClure, 5 March 1945, 'Radio Moscow transmissions to Germany', answering questions of the Intelligence Section. See note 42.

4. First phases according to 'Standing directive for psychological warfare against members of the German armed forces [for] June 1944', by Richard Crossman, printed as Appendix D, pp.141–9, in *The Psychological Warfare Division, Supreme Headquarters Allied Expeditionary Force. Account of its operations in the Western European campaign 1944–1945*, (Bad Homburg, Germany, October 1945), hereafter *PWD Account*.

5. Planning 1944–5: Manual for the control of German information services, chapter IX, point 25c: 'Deutschlandsender', printed in *PWD Account*, p.230. Proposal PWD/SHAEF Chief Gen. McClure, 24 April 1944, for European Advisory Committee, London, *re*: quadripartite control of the Deutschlandsender; representatives of the USSR did not answer. OMGUS 10/18–1/1: Information Services Control Group,

Welt im Film: *Origins and Message*

Record . . . of an unofficial meeting, Berlin, 7 January 1946, 'Appendix G'.

6. OMGUS 10/17–3/13. W.D. Patterson, OWI, London, Director Films Division, 3 March 1945: 'We are hopeful that an arrangement can be reached with the Russian authorities so that there will be one newsreel', Appendix: Joseph Dunner (Intell.Sect.) to Patterson, 15 March 1945, p.2.

7. OMGUS 5/267–3/4. Letter from Harry Warner of 6 December 1944, mentioned in McClure's answer, 28 May 1945.

8. Manual for the control of German information services, printed in *PWD Account*, pp.177ff.

9. OMGUS 10/17–3/13. 'Draft operational plan for Germany', 30 January 1945, referring to: 'Long-range directive for Germany'; see 'Treasury memo', 19 January 1945, in FRUS, 'The conferences of Malta and Yalta 1945' (Washington, 1955), pp.175f.

10. OMGUS 10/17–3/13. Pretests from February 1945.

11. E.g. *Welt im Film* issue no.7, 29 June 1945, commentary (translated) printed in Roger Smither, 'Welt im Film: Anglo-American newsreel policy', in Nicholas Pronay and Keith Wilson (eds), *The political re-education of Germany and her allies after World War II* (London and Sydney, 1985), pp.168–70.

12. OMGUS 10/17–3/12. Draft 'German Newsreel Operation', 1 August 1945, letter from W.D. Patterson, OWI, to Cmdr. D. MacLachlan, PID.

13. OMGUS 10/17–3/12. J.R. Foss, Deputy Chief of FTMC (Film, Theatre and Music Control Section), PWD/SHAEF, 22 June 1945 to Wm. Kennedy, Film Officer, PWB, 7th Army; copies had to be sent from 25 June 1945, of course, beginning with issue no.7.

14. OMGUS 5/243–2/1. Patterson to Lt.Col. Murphy, 6 November 1945, p.2, point 6.

15. The following files have been used for this report:
(a) OMGUS ISD Reports office: 5/242 – 1/4 . . . 5/243 – 1/18;
(b) OMGUS ISD C/F: 5/260 – 1/14 . . . 5/265 – 1/19;
(c) OMGUS ISD DIR OFF: 5/267 – 3/4 . . . 5/270 – 2/3;
(d) OMGUS ISD MPB: 10/11 – 1/29 . . . 10/18 – 1/1.

5/242 – 1/4: 1945/5 – 1947/12: History.
5/242 – 1/5: 1945/9: Information Control Committee of Political Directorate.
5/242 – 2/36: 1945/5 – 1946/2: Psychological warfare and control of German information services.
5/243 – 2/1: 1945 – 1948: Newsreel 1945: Instructions.
5/243 – 1/18: 1945/10 – 1945/12: 6871 DISCC Weekly.
5/260 – 1/14: 1945 [/6 – 1945/10]: Psychological warfare activities for propaganda to Germany from British PID.
5/260 – 2/4: 1944/10 – 1947/12: Broadcasts.
5/260 – 2/5: 1945 – 1949: Broadcast secret.
5/260 – 3/32–33: 1944 – 1949: Films.
5/261 – 2/8: 1944/11 – 1945/12: PWD guidance.
5/261 – 3/2: 1945/5 – 1945/12: Guidance (OWI central directives, guidelines for ICD and PWD propaganda).
5/261 – 3/8: 1945/6 – 1949/6: Public opinion surveys.

Welt im Film: *Origins and Message*

5/264 – 3/19: 1944/12 – 1948/3: Minutes for tripartite meetings.
5/265 – 1/2: 1945/7 – 1947/2: Amusements and recreation.
5/265 – 1/19: 1944 – 1945: Intelligence — miscellaneous.
5/267 – 3/4: 1945/5 – 1949/3: Film, theatre and music control.
5/270 – 2/3: 1946/9 – 1947/1: Staff study file no.4.
10/11 – 1/29: 1945/11 – 1946/1: Newsreel productions.
10/11 – 2/8: 1946/5 – 1947/11: Documentary film production.
10/17 – 1/9: 1946/1 – 1948/8: Newsreel general.
10/17 – 3/12: 1945/4 – 1946/2: Film — Newsreels OWI and PID.
10/17 – 3/13: 1944/2 – 1945/3: History of newsreel (Germany): Planning.
10/18 – 1/1: 1945/9 – 1947/10: Quadripartite meetings.

16. Smither, 'Welt im Film', in Pronay and Wilson (eds), *The political re-education of Germany*, p.153: OWI's proposals in April and July 1945 'represented an idealist approach to news film usage', because the authors had wanted to produce a three or four reel issue every week.

17. Smither, ibid, p.164, has used the following files from OMGUS:
(a) 10/17 – 1/9: Newsreel general (Smither, 'NA RG 260/1') and
(b) 10/17 – 3/12: Film — newsreels OWI and PID (Smither, 'NA RG 260/2').

18. See note 9.

19. OMGUS 10/17 – 3/13. William H. Kennedy to W.D. Patterson, 'Rough draft', 6 February 1945.

20. OMGUS 10/17 – 3/13. W.D. Patterson, 3 March 1945, p.2: 'It is planned to show only documentaries and shorts in Germany. Perhaps, for reasons of morale, entertainment and feature films will be shown . . . into the theaters . . .'

21. OMGUS 10/17 – 3/13. W.D. Patterson to George Baker, OWI London, 16 February 1945, *re* informal contacts with Leonid Antonow, London; W.D. Patterson, OWI London, to Sidney L. Bernstein, MOI, 20 February, 1945; cf. note 6.

22. OMGUS 10/17 – 3/13. George Backer to Bernard Barnes, London, 6 March 1945: 'Notes for the American position of a policy directive to be issued to the Film Divisions in preparing for a multipartite newsreel'.

23. George Backer to Barnes, see note 22 — quotations here in a new order.

24. OMGUS 10/17 – 3/13. Bernard Barnes has used the arguments of George Backer as a measure to criticise three proof/specimen issues of the German newsreel: Barnes to W.D. Patterson and Montague, 10 March 1945.

25. OMGUS 10/17 – 3/13. For contacts: Sidney L. Bernstein, MOI, to Patterson, OWI, 26 March 1945.

26. OMGUS 10/17 – 3/13. Patterson's speech, 3 March 1945: 'United news', London edition in 12 languages for 21 countries; 'Free World' edited together with the governments in liberated Western Europe; see Patterson's answer to Heinz Roemheld, Chief of FTMC, ICD/USFET: 'The motion picture industry owns and operates the United Newsreel as a joint wartime enterprise under official United States supervision', letter from Roemheld to Lt.Col.Murphy, 22 October 1945.

Welt im Film: *Origins and Message*

27. OMGUS 10/17 – 3/13. Crossed through copy of a letter from Montague to W.D. Patterson, 27 March 1945; Bernstein, MOI, to Patterson, OWI, letter of 26 March 1945. Bernstein uttered his dissatisfaction with the specimen issues.

28. OMGUS 10/17 – 3/13. Copy without date, without title, without corrections: 6 pages.

29. Ibid., p.6, last chapter.

30. Ibid., p.1.

31. Ibid., p.2, point 3.

32. Ibid., p.1.

33. Ibid., p.2.

34. OMGUS 10/17 – 3/12. Montague to W.D. Patterson, 7 April 1945: 'Regarding the German news operation'.

35. OMGUS 10/17 – 3/12. The names of the last two countries are missing because p.2 is not in this file — of course Great Britain and the Soviet Union must have been mentioned, being the most important European Powers.

36. See *PWD Account* (note 4), pp.23f: 'Truth is the most important ingredient in psychological warfare. Such truth, to be sure, can, and sometimes must, be selective, for often the truth is not credible to the enemy. However, selective or not, use by overt propaganda of falsehood which can be proved false by the enemy is the same as killing the goose that might eventually lay golden eggs.' See Daniel Lerner, *Skewar*, pp.26–32: 'Strategy of truth'.

37. OMGUS 10/17 – 3/12. Davidson-Taylor, Chief of FTMC/USFET, to Gen. McClure, 2 June 1945 'German newsreel': Cmdr. D. McLachlan, PID, had reacted positively.

38. OMGUS 10/17 – 3/13. Several reports, e.g. 'Prisoner of war Special Projects Division', 20 February 1945 to MPB/OWI, New York; Patterson, OWI, London, to Robert Riskin, New York, 26 March 1945.

39. OMGUS 10/17 – 3/13. J.H. Lenauer to W.D. Patterson, 22 March 1945.

40. OMGUS 10/17 – 3/13. Elizabeth Stewart Roberts to W.D. Patterson, 14 February 1945: the Germans 'have no sense of humour or subtlety, therefore, it is important that we bang our ideas at them and do not leave anything to their imagination' — Patterson commented thus: 'Bravo!'

41. OMGUS 5/264 – 3/19. PWD/SHAEF: 'Minutes of staff meeting of Psychological Warfare held . . . on 1st May' (5 May 1945), p.2, point IV: 'Atrocities. Gen. McClure presented the fact . . .'; cf. OMGUS 10/17 – 3/13: Notice of Pete Davis, 23 February 1945, read before the German Committee in New York.

42. OMGUS 5/260 – 2/4. Daniel Lerner to Gen. McClure, see note 3; Lerner referred to the BBC monitoring service. The Foreign Broadcast Intelligence Service of the US Federal Communications Commission (FBIS) had its own monitoring service: Eric H. Boehm, 'The "Free Germans"' in Soviet psychological warfare', *Public Opinion Quarterly*, vol.14 (1950), p.287, note 3.

43. OMGUS 5/260 – 2/5. Reply 12th Army Group (Secret Priority) to PWD/SHAEF, 27 May 1945 *re* reports since 12 May 1945; Gen.

Welt im Film: *Origins and Message*

McClure to Lt.Col. Rosenbaum: 'Guidance on repeats and reporting of Berlin broadcasts by Radio Luxemburg. (Secret and personal)'; OMGUS 5/260 – 2/4. Crossman and Hale 'London Telecon', 29 May 1945, for PID, BBC and OWI.

44. OMGUS 5/261 – 3/2. OWI, Overseas Operations Branch, Washington: 'Central directive', 14 June 1945, p.3: 'American policy in Germany: 1. Political parties and trade unions in Germany': 'Treatment: without referring to Russian measures . . .' OMGUS 5/261 – 2/8. PWD/SHAEF: 'Guidance notes for week of July 9 to 16', (7 July 1945), p.2: 'Local political activities'; p.3: 'Allied Unity': Berlin Radio . . . 'It remains important to give good coverage to news of interallied activities . . . as treated in the APS newsfile. A small amount of unfavourable news, as provided through this channel, will be useful in maintaining a realistic note in output.'

45. OMGUS 5/260 – 1/14. PID, 'Central Directive, 20–27 June', (21 June 1945), p.4, first paragraph: 'Anniversary of Russia's invasion by Germany should not receive too much attention . . .'

46. OMGUS 5/265 – 1/19. Policy Adviser, US, William Harlan Hale, PWD/SHAEF, to Lt.Col. Gurfein, Intelligence Section PWD/SHAEF, 5 July 1945: 'preparations for the "build-up" campaign'. See OMGUS 5/261 – 2/8. PWD/SHAEF 'Guidance notes for week of July 9 to 16' (7 July 1945), p.1, point 2.

47. OMGUS 5/260 – 2/5. PWD/SHAEF: 'Radio propaganda to Allied Occupied Germany' (16 April 1945), p.2: 'Guidance for output', point 4c: '"atrocity propaganda" will be ineffective unless the atrocities are coldly treated within a frame-work of convincing and authoritative facts.'

48. OMGUS 5/261 – 2/8. PWD/SHAEF: 'Guidance notes for output in German for the week 30 April – 7 May 1945' (29 April 1945), p.1.

49. OMGUS 5/267 – 3/4. Gen. McClure to Philip Hamblet, Director OWI, Paris, 10 May 1945; Testing: Gen. McClure to 12th Army Group, 12 May 1945; see C.R. Powell to Gen. McClure, 24 May 1945.

50. OMGUS 5/242 – 2/36. Text of press release, 25 May 1945, pp.5f.

51. FRUS: Potsdam Papers, vol.I, doc.no.344, pp.487f.

52. OMGUS 5/242 – 2/36. Statement . . . 2 August 1945, p.1.

53. Ibid., p.3.

54. Ibid., p.2.

55. Ibid., p.4.

56. OMGUS 5/267 – 3/4. 'The variety and extent of devastation in German cities must be seen to be believed. City dwellers are so stunned by the terrors they have undergone that it may prove difficult to move them by showing them the miseries of the concentration camps . . . The relative priorities of our propaganda lines change radically when one has an opportunity to see the people and view the conditions under which they exist', Davidson-Taylor to Gen. McClure: 'Report on trip to Munich . . .', 27 June 1945, p.4, last sentences of point 3.

57. OMGUS 5/243 – 2/1. ICD/USFET: 'Approved film list no.1', 25 July 1945, contains only issues nos. 1–4 of *Welt im Film*. Since 30 July 1945 issue no.10 was shown in Frankfurt on Main (*Frankfurter Rundschau*, no.1, 1 August 1945, p.3, column 5).

58. OMGUS 5/267 – 3/4. Testing obviously had been precipitated,

because the War Department had invited renowned representatives of Hollywood to make a trip through Germany, beginning 22 June 1945: Letter, Gen. McClure to Davidson-Taylor, 5 June 1945, p.1.

59. OMGUS 5/267 – 3/4. C.R. Powell to Gen. McClure, 24 May 1945: 'Erlangen . . . has suffered comparatively little damage and is rather thoroughly Nazi.'

60. OMGUS 5/242 – 1/4. HQ 12th Army Group, Publicity and Psychological Warfare: 'Activities report for the month of June 1945', 3 July 1945, Appendix p.8: 'Entertainment control. A. Film, 1.'

61. OMGUS 5/260 – 3/32. ICD/USFET, Intelligence Section: 'Reactions of German civilians to a program of short films (Program no.1)', 20 July 1945, p.1.

62. OMGUS 5/267 – 3/4. Davidson-Taylor to Gen. McClure, 27 June 1945: 'Report on trip to Munich . . .', p.6.

63. OMGUS 5/260 – 3/32-3. ICD/USFET Intelligence Section: 'Reactions . . . (program no.1)', 20 July 1945, p.2.

64. OMGUS 5/267 – 3/4. Davidson-Taylor to Gen. McClure, 27 June 1945, 'Report on trip to Munich . . .', p.6.

65. OMGUS 5/267 – 3/4. Copy of letter from Brigadier A.G. Neville to Gen. McClure, 19 June 1945.

66. OMGUS 5/267 – 3/4. Davidson-Taylor to Gen. McClure, 28 June 1945.

67. OMGUS 5/265 – 1/2. 'Short . . . notes on a meeting held . . . on the 12th July 1945', point 4: Films, p.3.

68. OMGUS 10/17 – 3/12. W.D. Patterson, OWI, to Davidson-Taylor, FTMC/USFET, 13 July 1945.

69. OMGUS 10/17 – 3/12. Copy of the draft 'German newsreel operation', 1 August 1945 as a letter of W.D. Patterson, OWI, London to D. MacLachlan, PID.

70. In October 1945 this was the hint: 'Films . . . It had been the original PWD/SHAEF plan to proceed slowly with the reopening of the theaters, but as time went on, under pressure of demand and in view of the more liberal policy of the other Allies . . .', p.103 in *PWD Account*.

71. E.g. Richard Crossman, PID/PWE, author of 'Standing Directive . . . ' (see note 4).

72. Criticism regarding the 'unconditional surrender' formula.

73. McClure's criticism with regard to initiatives of OWI, London, Gen. McClure to Davidson-Taylor, 5 June 1945 (OMGUS 5/267 – 3/4) and to the proposals of Marion Dix, OWI, London, 22 September 1945; Gen. McClure to Ambassador Murphy, US Political Advisor, 29 September 1945 (OMGUS 10/17 – 3/12).

74. OMGUS 10/18 – 1/1. Nicholas Nabokof, Deputy Chief FTMC to Col. Powell, 24 October 1945, p.5, with regard to the study of Daniel Lerner, Deputy Chief of Intelligence, ICD, 'Present American–Soviet relations' (13 October 1945).

75. OMGUS 5/242 – 1/5. ICD/USFET: 'Information control policies in the light of JCS 1067 . . . and the Potsdam Agreement. Draft', 29 September 1945, to Gen. McClure, point 7: 'Educational task of information control', pp.6–8; Film and 'positive reeducation': completed by hand, p.8.

Welt im Film: *Origins and Message*

76. *Frankfurter Rundschau* no.32, 16 November 1945, p.3, columns 4–5: 'Die Todesmühlen'.

77. Joint Chief-of-Staff Directive, JCS 1067/6, 26 April 1945, published 17 October 1945. OMGUS 5/261 – 3/2. Among others, Alfred Toombs, ICD Chief of Intelligence, protested against these alterations — OMGUS 5/242 – 1/4. Directive ICD, OMGUS/USFET 'Special guidance German guilt' (17 January 1946) was the decision of Gen. McClure. Draft of 'History PWD': 'Instead of the "collective guilt" of the German nation, and "there are no good Germans", which had until recently been the *leitmotiv*, the German people's guilt in the Nazi regime and the war was to be presented in terms of cause and consequence, a workable means of creating the new Germany.' (Policy/German guilt).

78. OMGUS 10/17 – 3/12. Heinz Roemheld, Chief of FTMC Section, ICD/USFET to Lt.Col. Murphy, 22 October 1945. OMGUS 10/11 – 1/29, OMGUS 5/243 – 2/1. W.D. Patterson, OWI, during PID–OWI meeting at Bush House, London, 29 November 1945, *re*: joint newsreel OWI–PID, p.1.

79. OMGUS 10/18 – 1/1. William P. Montague to Col. J.H. Hills, 15 November 1945, p.2.

80. OMGUS 10/18 – 1/1. W.D. Patterson to H. Roemheld, 19 November 1945, point IV, p.7. Because of this pressure the British supported the plan of a 'Quadripartite News Reel', see 'Unofficial meeting of Information Services Group', 15 November 1945, Berlin, Record, points nos. 16–23, pp.2/3.

81. OMGUS 5/243 – 2/1, Patterson to Murphy, 6 November 1945, p.2, point 6, or OMGUS 10/18 – 1/1, Patterson to Roemheld, 19 November 1945, point IV, p.6.

82. See OMGUS 10/17 – 3/12, W.D. Patterson, Chief of Film Production, to Heinz Roemheld, 20 October 1945: 'One-reel newsreel'; Eric T. Clarke to Heinz Roemheld: 'Preservation of joint newsreel' 23 October 1945, points 3, 6 and 8.

83. OMGUS 10/18 – 1/1. W.P. Montague to Col. J.H. Hills, ICD/USFET, 15 November 1945, p.3(*e*) and (*i*).

84. OMGUS 5/243 – 2/1 — OMGUS 10/11 – 1/29, W.D. Patterson during PID–OWI meeting, Bush House, London, 29 November 1945, Record p.2.

9
Welt im Film 1945 and the Re-education of Occupied Germany[1]
Stephan Dolezel

A detailed analysis of the 33 newsreels *Welt im Film* issued in 1945[2] reveals a more or less clear break after August, marked by several events of that month: the capitulation of Japan, the East–West tensions following the Potsdam Conference and the fact that the British definitely entered the production team.

Up to the issue of 12 October, showing Tokyo's final capitulation on 2 September, *Welt im Film* had been a wartime newsreel, its front reports showing almost exclusively US victories in the Pacific. Beside this, *Welt im Film* was extremely dominated by political events in general during this first period. In the atmosphere of the first five months after the Allied victory in Europe, there was no place for a newsreel with its 'normal' mixture of politics, curiosities, sports and entertainment.[3] This was not so much the problem of German post-war reality, as that of a precise political message. Berlin had been Tokyo's ally. It was important to keep this recently defeated ally in check. Following the principles established by OWI in April 1945,[4] the consequent presentation of the United States invasion of Japan was part of the psychological warfare programme showing the Germans the effectiveness of 'Allied', i.e. mainly US, troops and weapons, for example *Die Macht der alliierten Luftwaffe* (*The power of Allied Air Force*), especially significant in a story of the same title in *Welt im Film* of 10 August, combining pictures of heavy damage from Allied bombing in Germany and Italy with those of Okinawa with the comment: 'and now: Japan!'

Although *Welt im Film* had been up to August 1945 produced provisionally by the United States element, beside the US front reports the OWI principle of a joint newsreel of the 'Big Three' was maintained *de facto* in this first period, considering not only the British partner, but also the Soviet Union. Without any official agreement with the Soviet partner, the Russians were represented by the newsreel in a fair way: Soviet footage was even accepted. Indeed, this originally 'American' newsreel starts in its first issue of 18 May with a report based on the official Russian record film from the Yalta Conference, *Krimskaya Konferentsia*. In the beginning of *Welt im Film*, the absolute harmony between Roosevelt, Churchill and Stalin is stressed. In the following issues, showing the German surrender, the Russians and the Western allies are in complete unity as well. It is not by chance that the second issue of 25 May describes a story about the world security conference in San Francisco like this: 'Mr. Eden, Foreign Secretary of Great Britain, Molotov, the Soviet Foreign Minister, Lord Halifax, the British Ambassador to the United States, ... in friendly conversation before taking their seats at the conference table.' The producers of *Welt im Film* were too aware of the National Socialist hopes for an East–West conflict in the last moments of the war, which would have destroyed the Alliance. They were most concerned to refute this idea. May Day ceremonies in 1945 were another chance to demonstrate East–West partnership on the screen. In *Welt im Film* on 8 June, displaced persons from Russia offer US soldiers flowers during a May Day ceremony in Neustadt; in Kaiserslautern, US officers join a Russian May Day parade. *Welt im Film* of 13 July showed the Moscow May Day parade with 'the attachés of the United States, Britain and France as guests of the Russians ... for the first time, the Soviet Union celebrates May Day together with those who were fighting with her shoulder to shoulder: the Americans, the British and the French.' Soviet footage on the Battle of Berlin followed in *Welt im Film* of 3 August, combined with pictures showing the Western presence in Berlin after its fall.

However, the reports on the Potsdam Conference in the issues of 17 and 24 August can hardly gloss over the increasing East–West tensions by the declaration, that 'the conference was dominated by the will that the unity and fellowship lasting all the long years of the war must serve the aims of peace ... In these hopes, in this friendship, lies the future of the world.' In spite of the fact that the weekly reports of Information Control, OMGUS, booked all visits of Soviet film officers as a success for a joint newsreel policy, during the second half of 1945 hopes for such a policy dwindled more and more. Once again, on 5 October, in a story on the first session of the Allied Control

Commission in Berlin, the 'clear example of Allied co-operation' is being demanded. Then, after a long break, on 19 November and 11 December two last Soviet stories (28th anniversary of the October Revolution, celebrated in Vienna; the golden cupola of Leningrad Admiralty shining again) were accepted by *Welt im Film*, but without any further political comment. Contrary to the May Day celebrations, no Soviet footage on the 1945 Moscow commemoration of the October Revolution appeared. From now on in *Welt im Film* the Soviet Union was totally misrepresented. Thus, all the increasing problems of the Cold War were glossed over up to the issue of 19 December 1947, blaming *expressis verbis* the Russians for the lack of progress over German economic questions at the London conference of the 'Big Four' foreign ministers. The Cold War chapter of *Welt im Film* now began.[5]

News of the Germans' 'unconditional surrender' was doubtless the common central message of the Allies for Occupied Germany in the 'zero hour'. The first three issues of *Welt im Film*, produced between 18 May and 1 June, bring this news in variations repeatedly and pointedly. The fact is hammered into the defeated people: in the 'unconditional surrender' story of the second issue called *Germany is beaten*, for example, the Germans surrendered 'unconditionally', 'absolutely', there was a 'complete and final defeat of Germany', 'Germany is defeated'. The National Socialist propaganda was known to have successfully distorted the end of the First World War in 1918, claiming that the Imperial army was not beaten in the field, but was forced to make peace by left-wing 'defeatists and pacifists' in a so-called political 'stab in the back'. In 1945 the German cinema public was made to see on the screen that the outstanding Wehrmacht officers, film stars so familiar to the public — Keitel, Jodl, von Friedeburg — had to sign the capitulation personally. Certainly the behaviour of the Allies during the capitulation ceremonies (Eisenhower, Montgomery, Zhukov, etc.) was 'icy'; and so is the commentator's voice and the depressing music in the *Welt im Film* versions of the same subject, compared with the cheerful soundtrack in British and US newsreels covering the same stories for their domestic audiences.

As 'icy' in their manner of expression are *Welt im Film* reports from spring and summer 1945 dealing with the restoration of law and order by the Allied Powers of Occupation, for example in the issue of 25 May. The story '*Military Government in Germany*' shows Germans looting a goods train, US troops combating chaotic conditions in West Germany, the surrender of Nazi party insignia and weapons, the registration of all civilians, the centralisation of all food supplies and restoration of public services, with the execution of a German civilian by an American firing squad at the end. The subject 'Germans looting' was a favourite film cliché, used in British and US domestic newsreels as well, in this case heightened by shots of clearly tipsy German youths. The first year of *Welt im Film* took no account of the material needs of the millions of German air-raid victims and refugees who were forced to get hold of basic essentials — by illegal means if necessary. In the beginning of the re-education newsreel, this theme was taboo, perhaps not least because Germany had meted out the same misery to other countries for years. Characteristically, in *Welt im Film* on 22 June, a story about Dutch children receiving Allied gifts of food is commented upon as follows: 'Those who have hungered longest shall be fed first. Germany will have to wait.' Whereas stories on persons displaced during the war by Germans appeared rather frequently after 1 June, the first report on Sudeten Germans from Czechoslovakia, forced to leave their country after the war, had been published no earlier than 28 December.

Drastic means to show Allied power being the power of order were execution sequences like that of 25 May, with its commentary: 'The laws of the Allied Military Government have to be obeyed.' They appeared not infrequently in the first half-year, up until the end of July 1945.[6] In all legal steps taken by the Allied military forces against the Germans the newsreel commentator stresses, as in this case, that the delinquents have been 'questioned and sentenced by the Allied Military Court' in an orderly fashion. Nevertheless, these references were not able to prevent hefty protests on the part of the cinema-goers, who merely saw the execution of a fellow countryman, but not his guilt.[7] With the British joining the *Welt im Film* staff, the newsreel avoided this kind of story.

Making the German cinema public aware of German atrocities was one of the major tasks of the re-education newsreel. Here, film reports from concentration camps play the most important role. The fifth issue of *Welt im Film*, that of 15 June, dealt exclusively, for a full 20 minutes, with 13 different concentration camps, among them Bergen-Belsen and Buchenwald, depicting their situation immediately after the liberation by British and US troops. Recent research from British and American archives has established that films of this sort were created according to precise instructions. Summoning prominent Germans (doctors, lawyers, etc.) from neighbouring towns to the scene of crime, where they had to give evidence in front of the camera for the benefit of their fellow citizens, was just as much a part of the planning as the instructions to the cameramen to provide a document of the camp in its surroundings, with its railway connections, approach roads, electricity supply for the barbed wire, in such a way as to identify it for the residents, removing any possible room for suspicion of a fake.[8] The correctness of the investigations was to be emphasised. In the first story of this issue, on the concentration camp of Ohrdruf near Leipzig, General Eisenhower (accompanied by General Patton) 'headed the investigations himself'; the camp officials 'are handed over to the appropriate courts for sentence'. Particular care was taken here in the choice of words: the dead of Ohrdruf were honoured as 'the first German fighters against National Socialism'. A general anti-German wording was carefully suppressed; the Germans had to be educated by the newsreel, not shocked. As we know from Eisenhower's memoirs, he had visited Ohrdruf on 12 April.[9] In the US and British domestic newsreels this news was presented immediately after the event, in the Universal Newsreel, for example, on 26 April (together with four other reports on German concentration camps). *Welt im Film* offered the report after nearly two months' delay. Perhaps the producers had serious problems in finding a form that would meet the Germans' acceptance. As we know from the history of the parallel US documentary on German concentration camps *Die Todesmühlen* (*The Death Mills*), finished not earlier than in autumn 1945, the Allies themselves were in doubt whether a film on a subject like this would not be counterproductive. Regarding the OMGUS files, we may hesitate to say that it was a success; the cinemagoers felt no connection between themselves and the KZ murderers.[10]

For the basic change in the voice of *Welt im Film* after August 1945, the clearest signal is the fact that Germans themselves had a chance to speak before Allied cameras, and it is significant that for the first time this chance was given by the British. In the story of September 1945 on the *Beginning of term in a Hamburg elementary school*, the new Hamburg School Senator Landahl (a man with the rank of regional minister), a Social-Democratic member of parliament before 1933 and thereafter pursued by Nazis, 'teaches' democracy in an address to parents and members of staff:

> We no longer live under the dictatorship of National Socialism which knew nothing but blind obedience. We all have a public responsibility again. That is what living democracy is all about . . . Let us bring our children up to be good, honest and tolerant human beings, peace-loving people rejecting violence, people who can think for themselves and are able to express what they think and defend it before everybody. People who are willing and able to serve the society they live in without thought for themselves.

Once more, on 19 October, a German has the opportunity to speak before British cameras. Following the handover by a British officer of the traditional Hamburg Trade Union House to the newly formed democratic trade unions, the insignia of the National Socialist Union is symbolically removed with hammer and chisel by one of the old union members, himself a victim of the Nazis. In his words, he removes with the insignia 'the poison of National Socialism from the intellectual armoury of Hamburg workers' and wishes 'to contribute to the realisation that the poison of Nazi propaganda must be completely eradicated from the German people, for it is the only way to ensure that Germany develops into a truly free and democratic society.'

For the British, their contact with like-minded German political partners (German Social Democrats or trade union members as partners of the ruling Labour Party in London) seemed to be easier than for the Americans, who found no parties in their zone of occupation corresponding with those at home. Significant for this might be a *Welt im Film* story of 26 October, depicting the foundation of the *Süddeutsche Zeitung* in Munich (the first US-licensed German newspaper in Bavaria).[11] In Munich's city hall Colonel McMahon of the United States hands over the licence to the three publishers of the *Süddeutsche Zeitung*, all of them victims of persecution under the Nazi regime. On this occasion, McMahon himself pontificates: 'Teach the citizens of this land that human dignity is a precious commodity. Tell them that freedom . . . can only be achieved through decent behaviour and an upright state of mind.' Afterwards, in front of the newspaper offices, he and other American officers are welcomed by the *Münchner Kindl* (the figure of a monk, emblem of Munich).

Then, 'an act of symbolic importance takes place in the casting shop': the casting die of Hitler's *Mein Kampf* is thrown into the smelting furnace; 'from the lead that once produced Hitler's book the printing plate for the first independent newspaper in Bavaria is made.' McMahon operates the smelting furnace and sets the rotary printing machine in motion. As the first reader of the freshly printed newspaper, the chief burgomaster of Munich is shown.

This is a perfect story: like early German post-war democracy, the newspaper licence is a gift of the occupying forces. The charming actress playing the *Münchner Kindl* and the US officer laughing as he receives from her his jug of beer both signal the already established relaxation of tension. The melting down of the plate of *Mein Kampf* symbolises the end of Hitler's ideas. From the festive article of the *Süddeutsche Zeitung*, however other decisive details can be learned. Like the Hamburg Social Democrat and his trade union colleague in Munich, two of the three publishers propagated their democratic ideals during the city hall ceremony themselves. In spite of the fact that the *Welt im Film* commentator has confidence in these men, 'persecuted by the National Socialists', they are shown for less than five seconds, mute. In the newsreel none of the prominent German guests of the ceremony is mentioned, not even Bavaria's Prime Minister Högner (a Social Democrat as well); excepting the *Münchner Kindl* and the burgomaster, the Americans are shown as the only active element of the story. Whereas after August 1945 the British had encouraged German democrats to offer their own political message in *Welt im Film*, no parallel can be found for the US zone up to the end of the year. The British were also the first to introduce stories on German sports as well, starting on October 1945 with a report on the opening of the football season in Hamburg.[12]

Beginning with 7 December, *Welt im Film* started its series of reports from the Nuremberg Trials. Carefully avoiding any suggestion of '*Siegerjustiz*' (Victor's justice) these reports attach great importance to presenting the correctness of the proceedings. The accused leading National Socialist war criminals are never prejudged, either by the use of the camera, or by the commentator, who quotes the charges in a quite dispassionate manner. These stories are a sort of sheer exercise in 'formal procedure': positions of the court and the accused, simultaneous translation equipment, objections by the defence, indictment by the prosecution. It is certainly not by chance that the camera even shows the accused talking among themselves for consultation during the pause. In the second Nuremberg report, after excerpts of the indictment, the US chief prosecutor Robert Jackson is quoted: 'We would like to point out that we do not intend to accuse the whole of the German nation.' As in the reports on German concentration camps, here also the idea of a collective guilt is categorically rejected, doubtless without any conflict between the British and the US elements of the newsreel staff.

Germans as equal partners in a democratic society — this was the ultimate goal of Anglo-American re-education policy. *Welt im Film* had to pursue this goal not obviously but subconsciously. An excellent example of how a message like this could be 'wrapped up' is a two-part story presented by the British on 14 December under the title: *1939–1945: Aircraft factories work for peace in 1946.* First, an English armaments factory is shown which had up to then been manufacturing the plywood Mosquito bombers and was now producing furniture. A report immediately follows on a North German armaments factory, which had made parts for the Focke Wolf 190 airplane and 'now' turns to peace production and supplies kitchen appliances and medical equipment, with the commentator's pacifistic conclusion: 'The arms workshops of the world are no longer producing the things mankind fears, but the things it needs.'

The Allied example as mentor and guide is presented. Ultimately, not only stories constructed like this (encouraging the Germans to follow the British in peacetime production), but more or less all *Welt im Film* reports of events in Britain or the United States had to act as examples for the Germans to integrate, and all the more so since the 'world' presented in its issues was largely Anglo-American. Reports on the election defeat of Churchill and the ensuing natural shift of power to Attlee and his Labour Party, on American charity projects, on stories from the Anglo-American cultural scene, the private life of the Royal Family and of Hollywood film stars, reports on racing at Ascot and American baseball games, on English fashions and American New Year pranks doubtless made a lasting impression on Germans in the British and American zones where this re-education newsreel had a monopoly status until September 1949 and the creation of the German Federal Republic. And *Welt im Film* maintained its influence even after this last point of its compulsory screening, being produced by the British and Americans until the end of May 1950, by Americans alone until June 1952.[13]

Similarly, the inhabitants of the French zone — through the occupation newsreel *Blick in die Welt (Look at the World)* — and the inhabitants of the Soviet zone — through the East German newsreel *Augenzeuge (Eyewitness)* — were tuned in to the civilisation, and with it the political ideas, of their respective occupation forces. Not only the 'world', but also the newsreels' Germany, was divided. British and Americans scarcely mentioned the French zone in their newsreel and likewise the French tended to ignore the British and Americans in theirs. Similarities between the newsreels of the Western occupying forces and those of the Russian-influenced *Augenzeuge* vanished rather early in 1946–7 due to the increasing pressures of the Cold War.[14]

Notes

1. This contribution, describing not more than the phenomena, is understood as a supplement to the previous chapter by Heinrich Bodensieck: For methodological questions of newsreel analysis see the introduction by Stephan Dolezel and Heinrich Bodensieck, 'Zur historisch-kritischen Analyse von Kinowochenschauen am Beispiel ausgewählter Berichte der anglo-amerikanischen Besatzungswochenschau WELT IM FILM,' in: *Rapports I, Comité International des Sciences Historiques*, XVIe Congrès International des Sciences Historiques (Stuttgart 1985), p.189–205. Short survey of the subject by Stephan Dolezel, 'The Anglo-American occupation newsreel *Welt im Film* as an instrument of "re-education" in 1945' in his *German Newsreels 1933–1947* (Munich 1984), p.38ff.

2. Clive Coultass and Roger B.N. Smither, *Welt im Film 1945–1950*, Microfiche Film Catalogues no.1, Imperial War Museum (London 1981), p.2–13. Unfortunately, some of the first issues of *Welt im Film* are missing. Some survived only incomplete, and none of the archives holding the *Welt im Film* series (London: Imperial War Museum; Washington: National Archives; Hamburg: Deutsche Wochenschau GmbH; Koblenz: Bundesarchiv-Filmarchiv) has absolutely identical versions. In this case, international exchange of film material is more than necessary. The following is based on the collections held in Hamburg and Koblenz.

3. Allied sports events (Swedish athletes in London, 31 August, US forces athletic meeting in Nuremberg, 14 September) are the first sports news in *Welt im Film*. Reports on German sports events do not appear earlier than 12 October, see below, note 13.

4. See Bodensieck, Chapter 8.

5. Nevertheless, the Communist take-over of Prague 1948 was still announced in a very vague manner in *Welt im Film* of 19 March 1948: the 'tragical suicide' of Foreign Minister Jan Masaryk (and nothing else!) 'leaves the world in new sorrow and consternation'. It is not until the

issues of 7 May, dealing with the Communist suppression of academic freedom in the Soviet zone, and especially on 9 July, depicting the beginning of the Berlin Blockade, that anti-communism is subsequently introduced.

6. Examples of executions of Germans in *Welt im Film* 1945: 25 May (1 person), 29 June (2 persons), 20 July (5 persons).

7. See Smither's 'Introduction' to the *Welt im Film* catalogue.

8. See Brewster S. Chamberlain: 'Todesmühlen. Ein Versuch zur "Umerziehung" 1945–1946', *Vierteljahreshefte für Zeitgeschichte* vol.29, no.3 (1981), 420–36.

9. Analysis by Dolezel in *Rapports I*, p.191ff.

10. Chamberlain, 'Todesmühlen. Ein Versuch zur "Umerziehung" 1945–1946'.

11. Analysis by Dolezel in *Rapports I*, p.194ff.

12. In fact, even the first story of Allied sporting events in *Welt im Film* on 31 August was a British one; see above, note 3.

13. See Smither's 'Introduction' to the *Welt im Film* catalogue.

14. The 'world' being Anglo-American: see the analysis of the original year's end issues of *Welt im Film* for the years 1946, 1947 and 1948 by Christine Held and Ursula Lorenz in *Filmdokumente zur Zeitgeschichte*, film editions by the Institut für den Wissenschaftlichen Film nos. G155, G156, G141 (Göttingen, 1974).

10

The Problem of 'Authenticity' in the German Wartime Newsreels[1]

Karl Stamm

Motto: 'Pictures can't lie!'[2]

The question of the 'authenticity' of the German wartime newsreels is somewhat confused: on the one hand the veracity and documentary character of the newsreels was always emphasized during the period of the 'Third Reich' itself,[3] but on the other hand since the end of the war the same newsreels have been considered as a deception used by Propaganda Minister Goebbels. There have even been specific accusations that, for example, pictures of the Russian campaign were filmed on the Oberwiesenfeld in Munich.[4]

As the source of material necessary to discuss this question is extremely diffuse, it is perhaps useful, before going into details, to ask what exactly the term 'authenticity' means in this context, for whom and for what purposes particular film material was authentic and whether authenticity itself cannot have different forms.

A categorical formulation may be made at the outset: propaganda films are authentic as propaganda rather than in terms of the facts by which the propaganda is disseminated — in the same way that advertising films are authentic as publicity rather than in terms of the actual features of the products being advertised. Unfortunately this analogy cannot be taken any further because, in contrast to the fictive and illusionary nature of advertising films, however well it is disguised, newsreels deal with reality documented in other media — photography, radio, military reports, special reports by the Armed Forces High Command (OKW), not to mention eyewitnesses. In view of this it would seem appropriate to compare these different types of sources, as Peter Bucher did, most interestingly in my opinion, for the Ufa-Tonwoche (451/1939).[5]

In a totalitarian state where the information media are extensively co-ordinated there is, however, a limit to such a media comparison. For this reason it is important in the case of the newsreels, consisting as they do of separate components such as image and sound (noise, music, commentary), to determine whether all these components are equally authentic from the point of view of the event shown or 'depicted', or whether they can be classified by degrees. This method of approach is not uncontroversial. In terms of philosophical or scientific methodology, it can be argued that a film document must be either authentic or not authentic.[6] By the same token, however, the term 'authenticity' has already established itself in the context of discussion of the information and/or propaganda content of the German war newsreels in such a way that it would seem more practical to retain this term as it is, rather than to continue discussing terminology which might not be generally known or understood, particularly as the problems arising out of an investigation of the war newsreels tend to be of an interdisciplinary nature and are by no means restricted to the scientific sphere. As a proviso, however, it should be added that the term 'authentic' in this sense is used as a general expression meaning factually correct as opposed to 'falsified', 'manipulated' or 'simulated' ('posed'). The term can only be modified by examining the individual elements of the wartime newsreels in greater detail. It would be preferable, however, to proceed chronologically, i.e. in the sequence in which the newsreels originated.[7]

The *image* is a very authentic element of the newsreel, at least potentially. The large network of cameramen in the propaganda companies and the great technical and personnel involvement[8] meant that, for most of the war at least, exemplary material filmed on the spot in the various 'theatres of war' was at all events available. The short reports sent in most cases by the film-reporters to accompany the shipments generally permitted very precise identification and classification of the material received.[9] A high degree of authenticity may be attributed to this material, often filmed under hazardous circumstances, as typified by the uncut colour material of Hans Bastanier from the summer of 1942, filmed near Kharkov in the Ukraine.[10]

In this context it is worth noting the following extracts from instructions to film-reporters issued in September 1943:

> 1. Always remember that through your personal effort millions can participate in world events and that in your work you must give this and coming generations a *truthful* and vivid presentation of the gigantic struggle for Germany's greatness ...
> 4. *Avoid posed battle pictures* as they do not look genuine and endanger the reputation of the film reporter ...
> 10. Send in a detailed report with the film material (date, exact location, *faithful* description of course of events).[11]

All kinds of qualifications have also to be made, however, with regard to the picture:

> 1. Pictures were sometimes 'touched up', i.e. adapted a little to the prevailing photo and film aesthetics through the artificial addition of 'scenery', such as the inclusion of branches in the picture to make it more 'graphic'. From our point of view, however, this hardly affects the question of authenticity, particularly as it is highly unlikely, for example, that palm trees will have been included in footage from East Prussia.
> 2. It was not usually possible to take pictures during the actual battles and for this reason it was generally the preparations for battle or the situation following it that was filmed (although in comparison to the newsreel material from the First World War the footage was often very vivid and close to the action, and not only with film shot from cameras fixed into aeroplanes, etc). As this was considered to be a shortcoming, many films were shot and later edited in such a way that they appeared to have been filmed in actual battle situations.

From the vast array of possible subjects the U-boat stories are selected here. These usually had a fixed 'iconography': life on board, emotive images (sunsets, etc.), then alarm, hatch down, dive, torpedoes away, surface, etc. The attack in a real alarm situation could not be filmed in the necessary visual quality and was thus simulated, as if there had been an actual alarm — not to mention the fact that U-boat attacks frequently took place at dawn and could not be filmed because of the poor light.

When processing U-boat material in the newsreel company other aids were often used: film supposedly shot through a periscope was often simulated with the aid of superimposed masks (with cross hairs and scales) and one editor specialising in U-boat stories admits having ready a few rolls of film with convoys (from earlier films) which could be included at appropriate points.

An extreme example of a U-boat story of this type is provided in the 5th sequence from DW 753/8/1945 which was probably fabricated completely at the cutting desk.[12]

Makers of the newsreels did not regard these 'as if' representations as falsifications, arguing rather that this type of action could have taken place except that under real conditions it would not have been possible to film adequately, if at all. The desire (or compulsion?) to show this type of film to the public provided the justification for the specific style.

Another variation of the 'as if' category is provided by certain newsreel reports in which minor military engagements were more or less staged, e.g. with the numerous shock troop engagements during the Russian campaign.

3. There were also cases in which specific situations were filmed deliberately in a specific manner for use as film evidence of completely different situations. In one instance, described by an eyewitness cameraman, reporters filmed shots of passing merchant vessels in the Baltic with the most powerful wide-angle lens available. These shots gave the impression that the ships were just visible on the horizon and were included in corresponding U-boat films to depict enemy convoys (or at least commissioned with this purpose in mind).

4. There were also cases of obvious manipulation of external film material in the war newsreels (known examples include speeded-up shots during the Western campaign intended to suggest the impetuous and hectic behaviour of politicians in 'so-called democracies'). These should be distinguished from falsifications such as the use of American newsreel material from 1937 at the start of DW 754/9/1945 to illustrate a contemporary situation.[13]

It is, however, significant that, as far as the author is aware, this type of manipulation and faking in film took place not at the shooting but rather at the editing stage.

5. In this context mention must be made of *non-existent material*, i.e. that which, because of military censorship,[14] although relevant from the point of view of authenticity, was eliminated and stored in the archives from the very beginning. Involved here in particular were new weapons and means of transport, etc., details

of which were to be kept from the enemy.[15]

Apart from the official censorship one can also talk, at least retrospectively, of 'unofficial' censorship in the form of self-censoring in a way which the film-reporters of the time might not have been completely aware of: although they were basically at liberty to film what they considered of importance, there was some consensus between the newsreel company and the cameramen as to what ought to be filmed and what not (because it would not have been included in the newsreel in any case, such as pictures of dead German soldiers). It is not, however, easy to determine the date and extent of this consensus.

To give a concrete example: during the battle for the Crimea a reporter shot film, at great personal risk, of Soviet positions directly after a German flame-thrower attack — until he was informed from Berlin that he had filmed sufficient material of this nature, (either because the pictures were too gruesome or because the avoidance of international discussion of the use of flame-throwers was sought).

The *sound* in German war newsreels was seldom authentic because very little film was shot with an original soundtrack, as was the case, for example, with the 'Führer's speeches' where a lead camera with combined sound recording was used while other silent cameras supplied the cut-ins. The other sounds were dubbed on later, although great importance was attached to their correctness. Following complaints by the military censors, an extensive archive of the noises of all types of weapons had been established so that the silent films could be dubbed in an analogous (although not strictly authentic on-the-spot) manner.

The *music* which played such an important part in the inspirational quality and hence the propaganda effect of the newsreels is not of significance in considering the authenticity of what was shown, because it was applied later and usually without real connection with the theatre. (Along with the commentary, however, it is a very good indication of how the material was meant to be interpreted).

During the entire war the *commentary* gave the newsreels the meaning desired by the Ministry of Propaganda and the army propaganda. It is only authentic in terms of the material shown when it gives objective explanations of the images, based on the reports by the cameramen (which front, which type of weapons, etc.), although such comments were limited. Its achievement was in the way it impressed the watcher through pathos or specific intonation, and not in the way it conveyed authentic information.

Apart from this brief *cross-sectional* analysis which examines, albeit summarily and generally, the authenticity of the individual elements, it is also interesting to look at the same problem from the point of view of *longitudinal-section* analysis. If the newsreels are looked at chronologically it can be seen that the truth content of the commentaries gradually collapses: during periods of military success there was little need for falsification (except for racist comments and verbal descriptions of the enemy which were written into the text by the Ministry of Propaganda), whereas at times of military stagnation or defeat and retreat the pictures were unscrupulously falsified with speeches enjoining to hold on for the final victory. The same applies to the music: the victory music is comparatively appropriate for the initial military successes, whereas towards the end of the war even film of retreat (particularly from Russia) was dubbed, at the instigation of the Ministry of Propaganda, with 'advance music'.

Oddly enough, the opposite is true of the images: the less material available and the more it was necessary to use relatively fewer shots more extensively, the greater the authenticity conveyed and the more the watcher has the feeling of 'being there', as now, instead of large montages of heterogeneous material, more intensive and coherent film reports of militarily meaningless retreats were produced. As the single fighter comes to the fore, he loses his anonymity as 'the German soldier', as portrayed at the start of the war. Furthermore, the film became more realistic and verifiable and in greater contrast, at least from our point of view today, with the music and commentary — thus contributing in no small measure to the 'perverse honesty'[16] of the 1945 newsreels which, as a medium, failed as the military operation collapsed, being designed from the eagle symbol onwards as victory newsreel.

Returning, after these brief comments, to considering for whom and what purpose the newsreels were and are (more or less) authentic, in other words what the term 'authenticity' actually means, we should perhaps ask ourselves the following questions:

Do we really want to know whether tank A, number B, fired the shot seen in the newsreel at time C on date D in location E, whether it belonged to company F, operating to strategic plan G? Apart from the question of whether the military history reports are structured finely enough to be able to make something of such detailed information (if we had it), we are more concerned today with deciding whether we can have any idea whatsoever of how the advance on and retreat from the Russian front, for example, actually took place.

Again, is it really so important to know whether the celebrations on Hitler's return to Berlin in the final sequences of DW 514/29/1940 come from an original sound recording or from a preserved celebration recording on Hitler's return after the Munich Pact or after the entry into Sudetenland?[17] Didn't the people in the street cheer wildly, sometimes hysterically, on all these occasions? Would a new and original sound recording in some way improve the state of our knowledge today (or that of the cinema-goers of the time) — not to mention the fact that, because of technology available at the time, the sound recordings in any case were only partially authentic, and were adapted by means of a sound controller — or falsified — when being synchronised with the pictures? Is it not more important that a sequence such as this is capable of fictionally recreating 50 years later the situation and mood of the time? There was no necessity, from a propaganda point of view, to falsify the overall impression — on the contrary. In addition, the film-makers would surely have been aware that many people had seen the event with their own eyes and would have reacted negatively to any falsification — a further criterion for the authenticity of the newsreels, whose true and documentary character was not questioned at the time.

Authenticity cannot have been a matter of details: even when the length of the newsreels was tripled, the events of the week could only be summarised briefly because of the number of different theatres of war (not to mention domestic events), and for this reason topographically heterogeneous film material had to be combined and provided with a relatively general commentary.[18] The intention was to convey a 'picture of the whole', while the public at the time wanted to '*see* how it was' and 'be there'. Given the established newsreel format and the amount of material received it was completely feasible to present a new show every week — and it is here that these newsreels are of value to us today as a pictorial chronicle of the Second World War whose 'picture', then as now, was and is characterised by the newsreels).[19]

Because of its propaganda nature, however, this pictorial chronicle must be regarded critically, which normally means that we should penetrate through the secondary and obscuring propaganda effect of the soundtrack to the primary and potentially authentic pictures or, in other words, read the pictures 'against the grain'. To do this it is necessary firstly to confront these pictures with other material, such as the war diaries of the Armed Forces High Command and the results of post-war historical research — a further example of media variety, albeit with diachronic material. Secondly, efforts must be made to increase our knowledge of how the newsreels were made in general, and the way in which specific commissions were dealt with (in the form of case studies) so as to obtain further criteria by which to judge the extent to which the film material is authentic.

This, in turn, presupposes that the evidence (including oral history) is safeguarded, that documentary and photographic material in the hands of former members of the propaganda companies and employees of the Deutsche Wochenschau GmbH is saved from destruction, and that the existing and complete newsreel footage is researched intensively from an 'iconographic' angle, in other words that the 'topoi' — specific film language platitudes and the specific propaganda (which are almost inseparably linked) — are listed and evaluated.[20] Art historians would talk of a distinction between type, motif and (period and individual) style.

This might sound like a complicated process and prompt the question as to whether such efforts can be justified. In response it may be said that the opportunity of separating pictures of the past from the propaganda is worth taking, both to 'redeem the physical reality' as S. Kracauer has put it and, in particular, with regard to future generations, who would otherwise be completely at a loss if we were unable to develop criteria and to make plausible standards by which the authenticity of the existing audio-visual material can be measured.

To avoid any misconceptions it should be stated that it is not the intention, as part of some 'change of heart', to state now that the newsreels of the Second World War are authentic, any more than the Nazi newspaper reporting in the *Völkischer Beobachter* can be called objective historical writing. The aim is rather to make proper scientific use of the material, including oral reports, in a discriminating manner made possible by the distance in time now separating us from the events, and to pass on the findings to a wider and, as has been shown, inquisitive audience (a feat which will require even more effort). This has to be done before it is too late — and, given the age of the eyewitnesses still living, the time is running out. The authentic experiences in their former activities are an essential prerequisite for judging the authenticity of the German war newsreels.

Notes

1. This is a revised version of a paper delivered at the 11th IAMHIST Congress '1945 – From War to Peace' at the Institute for Scientific Film, Göttingen, 21–24 August 1985. This paper has benefited from the critical comments of Hermann Kalkofen, Göttingen, and Ernst Opgenoorth, Bonn.
I would like to thank all former employees of the Deutsche Wochenschau, whose information was instrumental in the preparation of this paper.
My thanks also to Stephan Dolezel, Hans Barkhausen and Heinrich Bodensieck for reading the manuscript and offering suggestions for improving it. The author is responsible, however, for all possible errors.
2. This is the unanimous feeling of former film-reporters of the Second World War, as expressed at a conference at the Munich College of Television and Film at the Academy for Political Education in Tutzing (17–21 March 1980) (Zweimal Deutschland seit 1945 im Film und Fernsehen. I: Von der Kino-Wochenschau zum aktuellen Fernsehen — the corresponding publication is by Karl Friedrich Reimers, Monika Lerch-Stumpf and Rüdiger Steinmetz, published in the series 'kommunikation audiovisuell — Beiträge aus der Hochschule für Fernsehen und Film München', vol.3, Ölschläger-Verlag, Munich, 1983). In this paper an attempt is made to describe conditions by which this slogan can be measured.
3. See collection of quotations by the author in his article 'Das "Erlebnis" des Krieges in der Deutschen Wochenschau' in *Die Dekoration der Gewalt: Kunst und Medien im Faschismus*, published by Hiuz/Mittig/Schäche/Schönberger (Giessen, 1979), pp.116–18.
4. According to Jost van Rennings, 'Die gefilmte Zeitung', Phil. diss., Munich 1956 (typed copy). Unfortunately no source is mentioned for this quotation.
In such cases insufficient attention is often paid today to the army film department (*Heeresfilmstelle*) which in its films frequently used captured weapons such as Anglo-Saxon or Soviet tanks.
5. Peter Bucher, 'Hitlers 50. Geburtstag. Zur Quellenvielfalt im Bundesarchiv', in *Aus der Arbeit des Bundesarchivs*, published by Heinz Boberach and Hans Booms (Papers of the Federal Archive 25) (Boppard am Rhein, 1977), pp.423–46.
6. Herman Kalkofen argued in the discussion following the Göttingen paper that the term 'authenticity' should not be falsified and that 'semi-authentic' would be better termed 'veridical' (a term from perceptual psychology).
7. See Stamm, 'Das "Erlebnis" des Krieges in der Deutschen Wochenschau' (see note 3), pp.118–19. In the discussion following the

Göttingen paper Ernst Opgenoorth expressed his misgivings with regard to a 'genetic' classification of the term authenticity and opined that the final audio-visual version of the newsreel should be regarded as a unit which is either authentic in terms of itself, or not, although he was well aware that pragmatically there are grey or black areas of authenticity.

The distinction used by Opgenoorth between 'specific' and 'unspecific' film (e.g. the barrel of a gun to represent a threat, irrespective of which type of weapon it is, as in this context it is unspecific) is claimed by the author to be a particularly fortunate choice of terms which he would like to make use of when classifying (film) shots. The question remains, however, of the grey area between 'specific' and 'authentic' footage, dependent on the definition in a particular case.

8. See most recently Hans Barkhausen, *Filmpropaganda für Deutschland im Ersten und Zweiten Weltkrieg* (Hildesheim/Zürich/New York, 1982), pp.205–43.

9. Copies of such reports have survived in some cases, e.g. those of Navy film-reporter Horst Grund in the Federal Archive in Koblenz.

10. The film material is in the Federal Archive, Koblenz. There is an interesting television film about these pictures and Hans Bastanier himself made by Dieter Zimmer (broadcast on ZDF on 23 June 1981).

11. '12 Gebote für den Filmberichter' with dateline 'Berlin, September 1943', without sender (probably OKW/WFSt/WPr(F) = Armed Forces High Command, Armed Forces Operational Staff, Army Propaganda (Film Department), as is the case with comparable documents), hectographed copy in the possession of Horst Grund at the Federal Archive, Koblenz. Author's italics.

12. See the IWF publication to accompany DW 753/8/1945 (G152), Göttingen 1979, pp.20–1 and 36.

13. See the IWF publication by the author to accompany DW 754/9/1945 (G153) by Martin Friedel, Göttingen 1979, p.34.

14. See Barkhausen, *Filmpropaganda*, pp.222–3 (see note 8) and Stamm, IWF edition G152, 1979, p.8, note 17 (see note 12).

15. A good estimate of the extent of military censorship is obtained by looking at random at the 'black list' kept by the Federal Archive in Koblenz, which makes reference to the footage taken by the Navy film-reporter Horst Grund between June 1941 and December 1943 and can be compared with the copies of his short reports on these films (see note 9).

16. Ulrich Kurowski, *Lexikon Film* (Munich, 1976), p.196.

17. The author has information of corresponding remarks by former employees of the Deutsche Wochenschau.

18. Here the newsreel is distinguished as a type from scientific film documentaries, for example, in which experiments are filmed simultaneously at a single location and are therefore authentic in another sense.

19. Despite a series of newsreels ('Messter-Woche' and 'Eiko-Woche') available, the picture of the First World War is more influenced by early sound films such as *All Quiet on the Western Front* and *Western Front 1918*. As far as the Second World War is concerned, however, feature films (such as Karl Ritter's *Stukas*) played and continue to play an insignificant role.

20. Presumably the model for this is not so much Hans Magnus Enzenberger's 'Scherbenwelt. Die Anatomie einer Wochenschau' in *Einzelheiten I., Bewusstseins-Industrie*, edition suhrkamp 63, 8th edition (Frankfurt on Main, 1973), pp.106–33 as Helmut Regel's 'Zur Topographie des NS-Films', *Filmkritik*, vol.1 (1966), pp.5–18).

11
Film as a Source of Historical Authenticity

Peter Bucher

Sources of reference are a testimony of human life. All historical research is based upon them, whether they are studied from a purely historical point of view or are understood as critical social science, whether they simply and individually consider personalities or more generally and systematically pursue the study of structural history. Sources reflect man, as well as the time and place in which he lives as a social creature and upon which his actions, aspirations and sufferings depend. They are always fragmentary, though they are not confined to individual sections only, but actually embrace the whole of human existence.[1]

This generally recognised principle is part of the elements which make up classical as well as modern history. It is not narrowly biased towards 'literary sources of reference' in the interest of historicism as has been the case in recent times.[2] Admittedly its leading exponents themselves have done much to encourage the prejudice about the limitations of some references valuable for the study of history. In spite of their knowledge of 'popular trends' (*'Massenströmungen'*), of economical and social connections, they exclusively and one-sidedly preferred writing political history.[3] The central point of discussions was the state, its prevailing ideas and outstanding personalities, the endeavour to probe and understand the character of things historical, and their unique features, while neglecting, even ignoring, economic and sociological areas to a large extent.[4] It is a well-known fact that closer investigation of these areas was left to only a very few 'outsiders'.[5]

Historicism judged the very basis of history, the sources of reference, in as narrow-minded a way as the actual object of its study. Historians believed they could gather knowledge mainly from documents and official records close to government sources; they would only recognise non-official documents from private papers as an acceptable source if they contained state-political references. All other sources, especially non-written statements, were considered worthless for historical purposes, even when they gave rise to further claims, albeit unsubstantiated.[6] Such development was moreover encouraged by record offices, claiming authoritative status[7] and in this capacity stressing the state-political sector of their collections, placing special emphasis on written records. Systematic recording of non-official or non-written statements was never under consideration.[8] This equally applies to film. Certainly there existed at the beginning of the twentieth century a belief that film, according to its basic purpose, was capable of reflecting a sequence of historical events in full-scale pictures,[9] and registrars, too, detected in film the true model of a 'modern German state'.[10] Such opinions, however, were held by only a few.

Resolutely continuing to use the recognised and much-preferred source material, history generally rejected film as a source of reference;[11] so too did the German Ikonographische Ausschuss, founded in 1930 to develop methods for the inclusion of non-written evidence in historical investigation.[12] And textbooks agree with this point of view. As far as they mentioned film and pictures at all they were only interested in paying lip-service to the basically distasteful principle according to which references were to consider the whole of humanity and thus ought to include visual means. They were not prepared to argue the intellectual power nor did they wish to quote the source if both were coloured by historical interpretation. Introductions into history of a different hue were in those days a rare exception.[13] Since the understanding of history in Germany had remained almost unchanged after the Second World War, and as the historical exploration took up and continued from the questions and methods of the twenties and thirties, it seemed unnecessary to redefine the basic principles of sources of reference for the subject.[14]

The continued predominance of state-political recording of history became clear when the Bundesarchiv was founded in 1950.[15] At first its only function was to record and keep civilian and military documents which had accrued and would in future develop from central German government and administrative authorities; non-official documents, however, received little

Film and Historical Authenticity

attention as did non-written evidence, and this also included film. And when historians like Walther Hubatsch and Percy Ernst chramm founded a special film archive[16] in order to be able to include and place film under the jurisdiction of the Bundesarchiv, it did not mean a departure from a traditional concept of history; it rather meant that they considered it logical, in view of the success the National Socialist State had undoubtedly achieved in influencing the masses (large masses) of people, that the Bundesarchiv should look after the propaganda material produced or controlled by above all Goebbels' Reichsministerium für Volksaufklärung (education of the people) und Propaganda, or the Reichspropagandaleitung of the NSDAP respectively. They regarded newsreel and documentary film as part of this material, but not feature films.

Archivists endorsed the following opinion: when the Filmarchiv was set up at the beginning of 1954 as a subsidiary of the Bundesarchiv, it first of all limited its collections to newsreel and documentary films, showing no interest in feature films. Only from the mid-1960s did archivists also concern themselves with preservation, the determining factors being not so much historical but media-political and film-artistic reasons.[17]

At the same time, though independently from the development in the archives, historians slowly began to question their orthodox (hitherto accepted) ideas about the responsibility of history. Examination of the state and the individual, recognition and understanding of their respective importance, which had been if not the sole, certainly the favourite object and aim of history for more than a century, could no longer do justice to the needs of recording modern history, especially since the basic requirements which had led to the education of historical understanding no longer existed. Historians became aware that they simply could not disregard the change in human thought and deed which had taken place in the twentieth century in all walks of life. 'In the era of democracy anonymous man becomes more capable of action than he has ever been before', claimed Theodor Schieder in 1965, 'he is a participant in the historical education of the mind, nay its creator.'[18] And what applied to human existence equally applied to the community. The state more and more lost its predominantly politically orientated law-and-order image, which had been generally accepted in the nineteenth and early twentieth centuries and which had been honoured accordingly by historians; instead it became instrumental in the realisation of social concepts and needs. And although they included the political spectrum they were aimed at all areas of life from their very beginning.[19]

The change has touched all sciences concerned with the study of man, albeit in different ways. As far as history is concerned it meant a greater concern with social and economical problems; the exploration of these had always been regarded as useful but nevertheless had to a large extent been neglected. Although it was acknowledged as an indisputable fact that the sources remain the starting point and basis of any further historical work, it has been shown that traditional historical information is only of limited value for the extended topic areas:[20] they are too closely tied to individuality and the character of man's deeds and suffering. When transferred to historical research the methods employed in the related sciences too, like sociology, anthropology, psychology or economics, only lead to new knowledge if adequate sources of reference are available. To create such a basis is the most important task of modern historical source study.

Its starting point must be that records of historical personalities have been kept in the traditional written manner, namely in official records and documents.[21] Furthermore it must be remembered that the person living in a community has only created and handed on a small part of written work: the great mass dispenses with written evidence.[22] All information about those people mentioned in written documents is on the whole not the work of history itself but the judgement of a literate minority. The historian certainly cannot ignore such testimony. But he must first of all find evidence which shows the actions and suffering of the 'masses' in an unadulterated fashion, so to speak. There are of course such references even in the realm of written documentation: materials of a statistical nature like address books and marriage registers, population and professional censuses, documents of the registration and employment offices and finally the press. For this purpose the audio-visual media must be taken into consideration above all, and film in particular. Methods for its use and significance are detailed as follows.

Whether feature film, newsreel or documentary, the film is a mass media. Right from its beginning it was to address countless unknown individuals by entertaining, instructing, informing, or influencing through advertisements — and it is impossible to separate these criteria clearly.[23] How to consider the characteristics of film for historical purposes will now be examined. To elucidate further, the complete film-making process must be taken into account, from its planning stages right through to the completed film.

Starting with political, economical and social factors during the making of a film, the historian must first of all determine the intended audience, i.e. he must establish the social structure of the audience at which an intended filmic statement was aimed.[24] References can be found in contemporary publications, either in trade journals or the general press. In the autumn of 1930, for instance, Béla Balázc stated in the *Weltbühne* that in the 'interest of profitability' film has to be aimed at the 'lower classes', by which he meant the petty bourgeoisie.[25] Considered in the light of the social structure of the relevant permanent readers, the volume and frequency of contributions which daily papers allocate to film events also provide certain clues. But it is true to say that information gathered in this way is too much subject to an element of pure chance to be able seriously to claim general validity from the start. This may however be balanced by consulting the records of the numerous statistics gathered by state departments, organisations of the film industry and others. They are published on a more or less regular basis and taken as a whole, together with the above-mentioned sources, yield more reliable indications of the social structure of the cinema audience. Also useful might be existing figures of census or professional statistics, unemployment figures from government sources and production statistics from the film industry, film distribution and sales, number of cinemas and available seats, number of visitors, price categories and others.

Only when the historian has clarified these basic requirements can be turn his attention to the film production. Every film has an employer and a producer. He may be — and occasionally is — one and the same person. The employer, mostly a film company, a political party, an administrative body or an organisation in the field of economics determines the leading idea. By its nature this idea is frequently politically or economically and sometimes quite simply lucratively orientated. His tasks and aims should be traced, his dependence on political, economical, social, cultural or other factors must be examined in order to gain information about the intentions associated with the production of a film. It is the producer's task to translate a given theme which follows a basic idea into filmic language. The success of a film thus also depends on the choice of the script-writer, the vocation of the director, and in feature films the actors as well as the combination of artistic and technical personnel. They too must be subject to examination by the historian. In this context attention should also be paid to background conditions which existed at the beginning of the production: film-technical possibilities, censorship and other limitations.

The next point concerns the production work, from the first day when shooting begins through to the first night performance of the completed film.[26] The historian must track down the locations where actions took place or were reported. Above all he must re-effect the joining to a harmonious whole of individual parts which were filmed in studios or on original locations and which determine the final form of a film. The film industry has never left any doubt about the significance of cutting and editing.[27] After all, they afford both a final and an effective opportunity to influence decisively the content and character of a film. This poses the following questions for the historian: Which criteria did the director use for recutting and editing? Can an outsider's influences be detected? If so, who has initiated the actions? Why did they happen? Which alterations of the total concept did they produce? The last part of the theme 'production' is the first performance of the film: preparations, sequel, participants, etc.

The common denominator of all this information is the fact that it could all be discovered with the help of recorded sources, mainly through the records of the production firms. Unfortunately these have mostly been destroyed or are unobtainable for various other reasons; it is sad to say that the remainder of the UFA (Universum-Film-Aktiengesellschaft) records in the Bundesarchiv is a rare exception.[28] Scripts or private papers, memoirs, diaries, and correspondence belonging to individuals who were engaged in the production, are only available in modest amounts. It is even more difficult to prove interference by third persons. Even the attempts of party offices and government ministries during the time of National Socialism have only yielded incomplete references if at all[29] in the records of the authorities, departments or governments. And even Goebbels' diaries,[30] in part very detailed and usually rich sources of information about the inordinate ambitions of National Socialism, only give tangible evidence of interference in rare cases; yet this has been frequently testified to by those involved in films during the time of the Third Reich.[31] As far as that goes, the historian cannot help but gather

Film and Historical Authenticity

at least part of the information directly from the film itself; he has to examine each individual scene for its content and dramatic character and in doing so reconstruct the script as well as the direction. Even then, when the records do not necessitate the use of film as a replacement source, the historian may not dispense with a precise and detailed analysis. Its function is to identify the shape and content of the 'end result' which is to convey a film statement to the cinema audience.

For this purpose several patterns have been developed in the past which gather information from filmic and sociological aspects.[32] Even if occasionally they make attempts to take into account historical issues, they are on the whole useless to history. It is essential to use a method which readily lends itself to the transfer of elementary critical principles of history to the modern audio-visual media. More suited to this end are the fundamental elements which have been formulated in archives for use of audio-visual resources and which embrace both the content as well as the optical–acoustic form.[33] They make sure that firstly the content of each scene in a film is interpreted by tracing the persons, i.e. their actors, by finding the locations and the action, or rather the circumstances in which the action takes place and in which the actions are described by means of explanation of the pictures, and for sound film through reconstruction of sounds and spoken text.

As for the optical representation reference must be made to camera settings (like close-ups, close-range, etc.) camera angle (i.e. worm's-eye view, bird's-eye view and others), camera movement (pan shots, speed etc.), assembly (cutting and editing, shutter setting), trick shots, etc. All these must be considered within the framework of individual scenes. The analysis of acoustics requires once again statements about language, music and noise, again within the framework of individual scenes. In this way the historian can determine the specific goal which the production of a film has — even without consultation of written documents. What is more he can also recognise the form in which the film was presented to the public. Exactly how the public accepted the film will now be discussed.

It happens rarely that central offices, for example the police authorities, are instructed to gather information regarding the reasons for rejection or support of a film by an audience. When such intelligence, however, is available — as is the case for the Third Reich during the Second World War — it is a unique source for the historian.³⁴ At this point critical reference problems shall be ignored for the time being, as must be statistics about the success or failure of a film, since attendance figures relating to individual film titles are — with a few exceptions — not available or non-existent at least for the time before 1950.³⁵ But at this point there may be available substitute references for the historian. As far as the local area is concerned, information may be gathered from the length of run of a film in local cinemas. This can be ascertained from advertisements in the daily press. For the regional areas figures about takings may be of interest. These may be gathered from sales and distribution and are easily obtainable, especially when they are the basis of certain promotional measures either on the part of the state or other organisations. Assuming that the requirements of awards are to be considered, predicates, awards and film trophies are also useful reference points for the reactions of the public to a film. And finally there is the evaluation of discussions which are published for most films in the general and technical press. Certainly they present considerable critical problems since their interpretation must always be judged in connection with and in relation to publisher, editor and the readers of the newspaper.

As far as the significance of film as a historic source is concerned, it will no doubt continue to enjoy the recognition accredited to it.³⁶ And film does serve to recognise and reconstruct historical events, newsreel and documentaries being particularly suitable for this purpose. Thus Goebbels' introduction and Hitler's speech in the *Berliner Sportspalast* on 10 February 1933, for example, can only be fully documented with the help of remaining film, because the printed and taped versions merely represent fragments.³⁷ If in these circumstances film can lead to new understanding in only a few cases, it is quite another matter when portraying the life and work of historic personalities. Film can reflect the looks, behaviour, appearance, gestures, mimicry and speech of the figures of contemporary history more truly than any description could ever do.

This leads us to a further possibility of identification which is not limited to the biographical sector. In evaluating films as images of optical and acoustic reality, and because of the vividness which is their characteristic as well as that of graphic pictures,³⁸ they are suitable to convey the 'historical atmosphere' and to illustrate the milieu and environment of a historic event. But in this evaluation the aim of such a film must necessarily come under special scrutiny. The account of the Deulig-Tonwoche newsreel about Hitler's seizing of power certainly reflects the mood of 30 January 1933 on the streets of Berlin, and yet it is also obvious how much the makers of the newsreel — who depended much on Alfred Hugenberg — endeavoured to stress to excess the participation of the Deutschnationalen Volkspartei and of the Stahlhelm in the so-called *'Nationalen Revolution'*.[39] When a state like the National Socialist State deliberately stages events like these, either because they are part of its self-esteem or because it wants to link certain aims to them, film can show up these links all the better for being closely drawn to the course of events, or because it is designed to effect relative responses in the population. This clearly was the objective of Leni Riefenstahl's film about the Reichsparteitag of the NSDAP in 1934, *Triumph des Willens*. The shape and form of its content — especially the selectivity and emphasis of focal points — reveal to historians the relationship of party and state during the early days of the Third Reich.[40]

These examples show that the reference value in those circumstances is solely judged by the contribution a film can make to the exploration of historically significant events and personalities. If it is to fulfil this role certain provisos must be made: the shots concerned must reflect the actual reality at the time they were taken and must be closely linked to the object of investigation. This means it must be guaranteed they are not falsifications but correspond with real events.[41] For this reason only those parts of newsreel and documentaries dealing with personalities and mainly political events are of use. As far as the feature film is concerned, it is, in this respect only, of limited use as a historical source, although it constitutes the biggest part of film production by far.[42] It was only included as a source of reference when the study of history extended the range of questions.[43]

The knowledge of its production, its content and dramatic creation, and finally the effect of a film, enable historians to turn to questions which could only be inadequately answered with the help of written references alone. Research along those lines must also include the social structure of cinema audiences as mentioned earlier, and which can be pinpointed more accurately by means of reception theory rather than with the help of written references alone.[44] The starting point must be the fact that a film addresses the senses of its audience before the intellect. As motion pictures act upon the senses the viewer subconsciously identifies with them, expressing agreement, disapproval or indifference. When a large number of feature films were made in Germany in the 1920s, making no demands on the intellect of the audience, it does not only show that these films enjoyed a certain popularity, but it must also be concluded that cinema audiences apparently lacked intellectual curiosity. This in turn throws light upon the audiences' social strata. Furthermore, the historian can also use film as a reference when the attitude of the 'anonymous mass' or 'faceless masses' with regard to individual problems is to be interpreted. Thus an examination of if and to what extent the German nation was a slave to anti-semitism must rely mainly on documentary films, newsreel and feature films,[45] and less on written evidence. Research has shown that the more readily the spectator in the cinema identifies with film images the more he feels personally spoken to. This is because he believes he recognises his own actions and aspirations on the screen. If then a film is intended to influence the masses, in political, economic or military spheres in particular, the producer must endeavour to forge as close a link as possible between the audience and the film events. This object he achieves by aligning the content and form of a film with the expected, or rather previously researched actions and aspirations of the public. And in this way he manages to hide the real aim of the film. Taking this frequently employed principle in propaganda and advertising as a starting point, the historian should be able to recognise the aim of a film and to retrace its translation into film language. By studying content, and visual as well as acoustic form, and with the help of the above mentioned questions, historians should be able to reach some conclusion as to the actions and aspirations of the audience. This point can be illustrated with the newsreel about Hitler's 50th birthday on 20 April 1939. It focuses on and brings to the fore the cheering crowds on the one hand and the military parade on the other.[46] It is therefore assumed that Hitler did indeed enjoy enormous popularity with the great majority of the German people in the spring of 1939; but since the film report at the same time tries to link the parade to the general jubilation it has to be further deduced that military rearmament, as symbolised by the march past, did not have widespread support. This has been confirmed — in some cases by sources other than film. At any rate it seemed prudent to those employed by the Reichsministerium responsible for the education of the people as well as propaganda measures to extend the trust shown to Hitler to the army as well.[47]

On the whole the historian must not overlook that statements about the social behaviour of the 'masses' cannot be based only on one single piece of evidence, whether written or film — if he does not wish to enter the field of pure speculation. The diversity of human life manifests itself in all the testimonies man, as the indisputable representative of history, has left behind. To record it in its entirety and to verify its testimony is a demand which historians can and must satisfy. The methods of critical analysis of historical sources are still valid today and apply equally to written and non-written references. In a great variety of sources film has a significance equal to all others, be it as a feature film, newsreel or documentary. The difference between written and non-written evidence is not so much its inner knowledge but its outer form, but this is not an issue for the historian's evaluation.

Notes

1. Johann Gustav Droysen, *Historik* (Darmstadt 4. Aufl. 1960), s.37f.; Ernst Bernheim, *Einleitung in die Geschichtswissenschaft* (Berlin und Leipzig 3. und 4. Aufl. 1926), s.99; Erich Keyser, *Die Geschichtswissenschaft. Aufbau und Aufgaben* (München und Berlin 1931), s.32, 46ff. u.ö.; Paul Kirn, *Einführung in die Geschichtswissenschaft* (Berlin 1952), s.30; Karl-Georg Faber, *Theorie der Geschichtswissenschaft* (München 3. Aufl. 1974), s.30; Rudolf Vierhaus, 'Was ist Geschichte' in *Probleme der Geschichtswissenschaft* (Düsseldorf 1973), s.7–19, hier s.8; Hans-Walter Hedinger, *Subjektivität und Geschichtswissenschaft. Grundzüge einer Historik* (Berlin 1969), s.276, 431 u.ö.; Joachim Radkau, 'Aufgaben für die Praxis der Geschichtswissenschaft', in *Ansichten einer künftigen Geschichtswissenschaft* (München 1974), s.173–189, hier s.174.

2. Beispielsweise Wolfgang J. Mommsen, 'Die Geschichtswissenschaft in der modernen Industriegesellschaft in *Vierteljahrshefte für Zeitgeschichte* 22 (1974) s.1–17, hier s.2f.

3. Droysen (Anm.1) s.166 u.ö.; Brief Droysen an Dahlmann vom 26.5.1844 in Johann Gustav Droysen, *Briefwechsel. 1.* Bd. (Berlin und Leipzig 1929), s.280f., an Wilhelm Arendt vom 20.3.1857 in ebda. Bd. 2 s.442, vom 10.3.1858 in ebda. s.534 u.ö.; Friedrich Meinecke, 'Persönlichkeit und geschichtliche Welt' in *Zur Theorie und Philosophie der Geschichte* (Stuttgart 1969 (= Werke Bd. 4)), s.32 u.ö.; ders., 'Geleitwort zum 150. Bande der Historischen Zeitschrift', abgedruckt in *Zur Geschichte der Geschichtsschreibung* (München 1968 (= Werke Bd. 7)), hier s.21; ders.: Zur Beurteilung Rankes. In ebda. s.54ff. u.ö.

4. Wolfgang J. Mommsen, *Die Geschichtswissenschaft jenseits des Historismus* (Düsseldorf 1972), s.15f.; Faber (Anm. 1) s.30ff.; Theodor

Schieder, *Geschichte als Wissenschaft* (München und Wien 1965), s.17.

5. Gerhard Oestreich, 'Die Fachhistorie und die Anfänge der sozialgeschichtlichen Forschung in Deutschland', in *HZ 208* (1969) s.320–363; Georg G. Iggers, *Deutsche Geschichtswissenschaft. Vom Historismus zur Historischen Sozialwissenschaft* (München 1971), s.34ff.

6. Vgl. besonders Droysen (Anm. 1) s.127; Brief Droysen an Ludwig Moser vom 17.12.1846 in Droysen (Anm. 3) s.343, an Sybel vom 3./6.12.1853 in ebda. Bd. 2 s.195f., vom 31.12.1853 in ebda. s.213f., vom 26.9.1856 in ebda. s.477; an Gustav Freytag vom 14.12.1853 in ebda. s.205f., an Treitschke vom 22.3.1873 in ebda s.907, an Gustav Droysen vom 8.3.1884 in ebda s.977; Friedrich Meinecke, *Erlebtes 1862–1901* (Stuttgart 1969 (= Werke Bd. VIII)), s.134 u.ö.; ders., 'Geschichtswissenschaft und moderne Bedürfnisse' in *Zur Theorie und Philosophie der Geschichte* (Anm. 3), s.177f.

7. Eckhart G. Franz, *Einführung in die Archivkunde* (Darmstadt 1974), s.11ff.

8. Hierzu z.B. Helmuth Rogge, 'Nachlässe und private Archive im Reichsarchiv' in *Korrespondenzblatt des Gesamtvereins der deutschen Geschichts- und Altertumsvereine 72* (1924), Sp. 96–104; Ludwig Dehio, 'Politische Nachlässe des 19. Jahrhunderts im Besitz der preussischen Staatsarchive' in: Ebda. 75 (1925), Sp. 53–61.

9. Paul F. Liesegang, *Entwicklung, Wesen und Bedeutung des Kinematographen* (Düsseldorf 1910), s.49f.; Dr. Beuscfh *Der Film als Geschichtsquelle. Bild und Film I*, 2 (1912), s.35f. Zur Geschichte des Films vgl. Friedrich von Zglinicki, *Der Weg des Films* (Berlin 1956); Georges Sadoul, *Geschichte der Filmkunst* (Frankfurt/M 1982); Ulrich Gregor und Enno Patalas, *Geschichte des Films* (Reinbek bei Hamburg 1976); Jerzy Toeplitz, *Geschichte des Films*, 4 Bde (München 1973–1983); für die Weimarer Republik Siegfried Kracauer, *Von Caligari zu Hitler* (Frankfurt/M 1974); für das 'Dritte Reich' Francis Courtade und Pierre Cadars, *Geschichte des Films im Dritten Reich* (München und Wien 1975); Gerd Albrecht, *Nationalsozialistische Filmpolitik*, (Stuttgart 1969).

10. Helmuth Rogge, 'Das Reichsarchiv' in *Archivalische Zeitschrift 35* (1925), s.119–133, hier s.129f.

11. Vgl. z.B. den Brief Meinecke an Steffens vom 12.11.1940: 'Und Molotow ist hier! Man erlebt alles das eigentlich nicht mehr als echte Weltgeschichte, sondern als Filmstreifen im Kientopp' (Friedrich Meinecke, *Ausgewählter Briefwechsel* (Stuttgart 1962), s.196).

12. Gegründet auf Veranlassung der auf dem Internationalen Historikertag in Oslo 1928 errichteten Internationalen Ikonographischen Kommission. Er setzte sich zusammen aus Karl Brandi, Percy Ernst Schramm und Walter Goetz mit Sigfrid H. Steinberg als Sekretär. Vgl. Sigfrid H. Steinberg, 'Die Internationale und die Deutsche Ikonographische Kommission', in HZ 144 (1931), s.287–196.

13. Erich Keyser, *Das Bild als Geschichtsquelle* (Berlin 1935).

14. Ausführlich Iggers (Anm. 5); dazu Werner Conze, 'Die deutsche Geschichtswissenschaft seit 1945', in HZ 225 (1977), s.1–27, hier s.12; Hans Mommsen, 'Betrachtungen zur Entwicklung der neuzeitlichen Historiographie in der Bundesrepublik' in *Probleme der Geschichtswissenschaft* (Düsseldorf 1973), s.124–155, hier s.125f.; Wolfgang J. Mommsen,

Geschichtswissenschaft (Anm. 4) s.23; Ernst Schulin, *Traditionskritik und Rekonstruktionsversuch* (Düsseldorf 1979), s.136f.; u.a.

15. Peter Bucher, *Das Bundesarchiv. Geschichte, Aufgaben, Probleme* (Koblenz 1982), s.3f.

16. Auszüge aus dem Schriftwechsel bei Hans Barkhausen, 'Probleme der Filmarchivierung', in *Der Archivar 20* (1967), Sp. 361-368; vgl. auch Walther Hubatsch, 'Probleme des geschichtswissenschaftlichen Films', in *Geschichte in Wissenschaft und Unterricht 4* (1953), s.476-479; Fritz Terveen, 'Der Film als historisches Dokument', in *VfZG 3* (1955), s.57-66, hier s.59.

17. Peter Bucher, *Wochenschauen und Dokumentarfilme 1895-1950 im Bundesarchiv-Filmarchiv* (Koblenz 1984 (= Findbücher zu Beständen des Bundesarchivs Bd. 8)), s.XIIIff.

18. Schieder, *Geschichte als Wissenschaft* (Anm. 4), s.102.

19. Ders., *Staat und Gesellschaft im Wandel unserer Zeit* (München 1958), s.203.

20. Thomas Nipperdey, 'Die anthropologische Dimension der Geschichtswissenschaft', in *Geschichte heute* (Göttingen 1973), s.225-255, hier s.247f.; Faber (Anm. 1) s.115; Jürgen Kocka, 'Theorien in der Sozialund Gesellschaftsgeschichte' in *GG 1* (1975), s.9-42, hier s.11; Hans-Ulrich Wehler, *Geschichte als Sozialwissenschaft* (Frankfurt/M 1973), s.27f; Vierhaus (Anm. 1), s.15; Wolfgang Benz und Martin Müller, *Geschichtswissenschaft* (Darmstadt 1973), s.38.

21. Faber (Anm. 1), s.148; Schieder, *Geschichte als Wissenschaft* (Anm. 4), s.100.

22. Schieder, *Geschichte als Wissenschaft* (Anm. 4), s.101; Radkau (Anm. 1), s.174; Jürgen Kocka, *Sozialgeschichte* (Göttingen 1977), s.89.

23. Walter Hagemann, *Der Film. Wesen und Gestalt* (Heidelberg 1952), s.169ff.

24. Walter Dadek, *Die Filmwirtschaft. Grundriss einer Theorie der Filmökonomik* (Freiburg/Brsg. 1957), s.133ff.; Dieter Prokop, *Soziologie des Films* (Neuwied und Berlin 1970), s.35ff.

25. Belá Balázs, 'Der Film des Kleinbürgers' in *Weltbühne 26* (1930), Bd. 2, s.232.

26. Zum Folgenden Fritz Kempe, *Film. Technik, Gestaltung, Wirkung* (Braunschweig 1958); Werner van Appeldorn, *Der dokumentarische Film. Dramaturgie, Gestaltung, Technik* (Bonn 1970).

27. Siegfried Kracauer, *Theorie des Films* (Frankfurt 1973), s.106ff.; Rudolf Arnheim, *Film als Kunst* (München 1974), s.110ff.; Belá Balázs, *Der Film* (Wien 5. Aufl 1976), s.103ff.; Ernst Iros, *Wesen und Dramaturgie des Films* (Zürich 1962), s.108ff.

28. Bundesarchiv Koblenz, R 109.

29. Vgl. für einen Teilbereich Peter Bucher, 'Wochenschau und Staat 1895-1945' in *GWU 35* (1984) s.746-757.

30. Bundesarchiv Koblenz, NL 118; Louis P. Lochner (Hrsg.), *Goebbels Tagebücher aus den Jahren 1942-43* (Zürich 1948).

31. Vgl. z.B. den 'Text des Gerichtsurteils über Veit Harlan' vom 15.7.1950 in *Filmpress* vom 22.7.1950.

32. Etwa Werner und Ingeborg Faulstich, *Modelle der Filmanalyse* (München 1977); Thomas Kuchenbuch, *Filmanalyse* (Köln 1978);

Alphons Grubermann, Michael Schaaf und Gerhard Adam *Film-analyse* (München 1980); Gerd Albrecht 'Die Filmanalyse — Ziele und Methoden' in *Filmanalysen 2* (Düsseldorf 1964), s.233–270.

33. Zuletz Peter Bucher, 'Zur Erschliessung audiovisuellen Archivgutes' in *Nederlands Archievenblad 88* (1984), s.148–157.

34. Vgl. Heinz Boberach (Hrsg.), *Meldungen aus dem Reich* (Neuwied 1965).

35. *Akten des Reichsministeriums für Volksaufklärung und Propaganda, Frühjahr 1944*, Bundesarchiv Koblenz, R 55/663.

36. Günter Moltmann, 'Film- und Tondokumente als Quellen zeitgeschichtlicher Forschung' in ders. und Kar-Friedrich Reimers (Hrsg.), *Zeitgeschichte im Film- und Tondokument* (Göttingen, Zürich und Frankfurt 1970), s.17–23; Wilhelm Treue, *Das Filmdokument als Geschichtsquelle* in *HZ 186* (1958), s.308–327.

37. *Hitlers Aufruf an das deutsche Volk*, Bundesarchiv-Filmarchiv Mag. Nr. 924; vgl. dazu Karl-Friedrich Reimers (Hrsg.), *Hitlers Aufruf an das deutsche Volk vom 10. Februar 1933* (Göttingen 1971 (= Institut für den Wissenschaftlichen Film. Filmdokumente zur Zeitgeschichte Nr. 126).

38. Willy Stiewe, *Das Bilde als Nachricht* (Berlin 1933).

39. Deulig-Tonwoche Nr. 57/1933. Vgl. dazu Peter Bucher, 'Wochenschau und Machtergreifung. Die Deulig-Tonwoche 1932/33' in *Publizistik 30* (1985), im Druck.

40. *Triumph des Willens*, Bundesarchiv-Filmarchiv, Mag. Nr. 964. Vgl. Peter Nowottny, *Leni Riefenstahls 'Triumph des Wilens'* (München 1981); Karlheinz Schmeer, *Die Regie des öffentlichen Lebens im Dritten Reich* (München 1956).

41. Treue (Anm. 36), s.317ff.; Terveen (Anm. 16) s.64f.; Helmut Regel, 'Die Authentizität dokumentarischer Filmaufnahmen. Methoden einer kritischen Prüfung' in *Aus der Arbeit des Bundesarchivs* (Boppard 1977 (= Schriften des Bundesarchivs 25)), s.487–498.

42. Vgl. Bodo Scheurig, *Einführung in die Zeitgeschichte* (Berlin 2. Aufl. 1970), s.58ff.; Boris Schneider, *Einführung in die Neuere Geschichte* (Stuttgart, Berlin, Köln und Mainz 1974), s.56f.; Ernst Opgenoorth, *Einführung in das Studium der neueren Geschichte*. Brunschweig 2. (Aufl. 1974), s.56ff.; u.a.

43. Friedrich P. Kahlenberg, 'Zur Methodologie und Auswertung audiovisuellen Archivgutes als Geschichtsquelle' in *Der Archivar 28* (1975), sp.50ff.; ders., 'Spielfilm als historische Quelle? Das Beispiel "Andalusische Nächte"' in *Aus der Arbeit des Bundesarchivs* (Boppard 1977), s.511–532; Benz/Müller (Anm. 20), s.78f.

44. Vor allem Kracauer, Theorie (Anm. 27), s.216ff.; dazu Jochen Beyse, *Film und Widerspiegelung. Interpretation und Kritik der Theorie Siegfried Kracauers* (Diss.phil. Köln 1977) (masch.verv.); Herman Josef Berger, *Psychologische Untersuchungen des Zusammenhang von Wirkungen und Nachwirkungen bei Spielfilmen* (Diss.phil. Köln 1973)(masch.verv.); abweichend Prokop (Anm. 24) s.237ff.

45. Peter Bucher, 'Die Bedeutung des Films als historische Quelle — "Der ewig Jude" (1940)' in *Festschrift für Eberhard Kessel zum 75. Geburtstag* (München 1982), s.300–329; Friedrich Knilli, *Jud Süss* (Berlin 1983); Régine Mihal Friedman, *L'Image et son Juif. Le Juif dan le Cinéma Nazi*

(Paris 1983).

46. Ufa-Tonwoche Nr. 451/1939 und Tobis-Wochenschau Nr. 18/1939; Bundesarchiv-Filmarchiv.

47. Peter Bucher, 'Hitlers 50. Geburtstag am 20. April 1939. Zur Quellenvielfalt im Bundesarchiv' in *Aus der Arbeit des Bundesarchivs* (Boppard 1977), s.423–446.

Contributors

Heinrich Bodensieck is a Professor in the Faculty of History at the University of Dortmund.

Peter Bucher is director in the Film Archives of the Bundesarchiv at Koblenz.

Stephan Dolezel is Head of the Department for Humanities at the Institut für den Wissenschaftlichen Film, Göttingen.

Sergei Drobashenko is the Deputy Director of the All-Union Film Art Institute, Moscow, and a Professor of Documentary Cinema at Moscow University.

Peter Gerdes is Associate Professor in Media Studies, University of New South Wales, Australia, and former editor and editor-in-chief of *Ciné-Journal Suisse*.

Stanislaw Ozimek has been Head of the Film History Section and Deputy Director of the Institute of Arts PAN and is the co-author, along with Professor Jerzy Toeplitz, of the *History of the Polish Cinema*.

Nicholas Pronay is Senior Lecturer in Modern History at the School of History, Leeds University.

Richard C. Raack is Professor of History at the California State University, Hayward.

K.R.M. Short is Senior Lecturer in Modern History at Westminster College, Oxford and the Editor of the *Historical Journal of Film, Radio and Television*.

Karl Stamm is Curator at the Museum of Cologne and a lecturer at the University of Bonn.

David Welch is Lecturer in Modern History at the Central Polytechnic of London.

Index

Actualités Françaises 74
A Defeated People 46
Allied Four Power Control Commission 13
Allies Fight Nazi Counterblow 8
Ament, W. 3
Anders, General W. 71, 79
An End to Murder 44
A Night in Nuremberg 39
Archivio della Resistenza, Turin 72
Ardennes Offensive 6, 7
Army Pictorial Service Laboratories 2
Arnhem, Battle of 7
Assmann 91
Aviation in the News 9

Backer, G. 126
Baldwin, S. 34
Balfour, A. 33
Baptism by Fire 4
Bastanier, H. 159
Battle of Berlin 50, 57, 64
Battle of the Bulge 6, 12, 16
Battleship Potemkin 62
Belazc, B. 173
Belsen 41–3, 73, 151
Berchtesgaden 4–5, 13
Berlin 73
Berlin State Opera 37
Berling, General Z. 70
Berzarin, General N. 54, 55
Bierut, B. 78
Bismarck, O. 36, 37
Blomberg, General von 37, 38
Bormann, M. 92
Bossak, J. 72, 73, 77
Bradley, General O. 37, 38
Braun, E. 14
Brezhnev, L. 64
BBFC (British Board of Film Censors) 44
BBC 131
Bryan, J. 70

Buchenwald 113
Bucher, P. 159
Buhle, General 91

Cadogan, A. 35
Canadian Army Film and Photo Unit 2
Cass, L.S. 13
Central Red Banner Documentary Film Studio 59
Chamberlain, N. 31, 35
Chuikov, General 59
Churchill, W. 149
Communist Party 55
Communist Polish Workers Party 77
Confessions of a Nazi Spy 4
Crown Film Unit 46

D-Day 7, 11
Davidson, J.C.C. 34
Davis, E. 3, 132
Day, Professor 78
Desert Victory 6
Dietrich, General S. 8
Doenitz, K. 91
Douglas, Air Marshal Sir S. 78

Eden, A. 9, 149
Egorov, Lieutenant 61, 62, 64
Eisenhower, 6, 42, 78, 138, 150, 152
Eisenstein, S. 59, 62
Emmett, E.V. 42

Ford, Colonel A. 72, 73
Fox Movietone 1, 2
Friedeburg, H. von 150
Funk, W. 91

Gasser, B. 100, 112
Gaule, General de 111
Gaumont British 31, 32, 40, 42, 74
General Staff 8

185

Index

Germany asserts right to rearm 38
Germany in Ruins! 8, 12
Gestapo 5
Globocnik, Gruppenführer O. 72
Goebbels, J. xii, 5, 51, Ch. 6, 171, 174, 176
Goering, H. 13, 38, 91, 92
Grohe, Gauleiter 94
Grosz, General G. 79
Guderian, H. 92
Guisan, General 110, 117

Halifax, Lord 149
Hamilton Wright Organisation 13
Harcourt, Lord 34
Harlan, V. 73
Hauptmann, G. 56
Hearst Corporation 1
Heidelberg University 10–11, 16
Herzstein, R. 80
Himmler, H. 5, 92
Hindenburg, P. von 36
Hiroshima 79
Hitler, A. x, xi, 4, 5, 8, 12, 13, 30, 31, 36–9, 41, 44, 51, 75, 80, 91, 92, 93, 95, 155, 164, 176, 178, 179
Hitler Youth 5, 83, 89, 94
Hogner 155
Horror in our Time 42
Hubatsch, W. 171
Hugenberg, A. 177

Illakowicz, K. 70
Imperial War Museum xi
Inside Nazi Germany 4
IAMHIST (International Association for Audio-Visual Media in Historical Research and Education) xii
In the Wake of War in Germany 99
Institut für den Wissenschaftlichen und Film (IWF) xii

Jackson, R. 139, 154
Jodl, A. 92, 150
Johnson, Dr 78

Kantaria, Sergent 61, 62, 64
Karmen, R. 51, 61, 62, 63
Keitel, Field Marshal General von 53, 150
Kesselring, A. 13
Khrushchev, N.S. 59, 64
Koblenz 11
Kolberg 73
Kolberg, fall of 73
Korten, General 91
Kostring, General 94
Kracauer, S. 84, 165
Kruger, Field Marshal von 5

Lammers, H. 92
Lancaster, B. 62, 63
Lauterbacker 92
Lazarfeld 48
League of Nations 37, 39
Lend-Lease 12
Library of Congress Film Project 3, 5, 23–7
Life 17
Locarno, Treaties of 38
Look 17
Luce, C. Booth 42
Ludendorf, General E. 30
Luftwaffe 40, 82, 148

MacArthur, General D. 60
McClure, Brigade-General R.M. 131, 132, 133, 136, 138
Mackensen, Marshal von 38
McMahon, General 153
Madru, G. 13
Majdanek, Cemetery of Europe 72
Manteuffel, H. von 7
March of Time, The 2, 3, 4, 128
Marlene 52
Mein Kampf 155
Mejat, G. 15
MGM 1, 11, 13
Mikolajczyk, S. 74
Ministry of Information 2, 3, 34, 45, 132
Model's Army Group 3, 7
Molotov, V.M. 9, 149
Montague, W.P. 126, 127, 128, 129, 130, 137

Index

Montgomery, Field-Marshal B.L. 28, 136, 150
Movietone News 13, 30, 36, 42, 43
Mussolini, B. 5, 108, 116

Nagasaki, 79
National Archives 4
NBC Television 3
National Film Board of Canada 2
National Unity Government 78
Navy Department 2, 3
Nazi Atrocities 11
Nazi Counter Offensive, The 7
News of the Day 1, 2, 5, 7, 13
Niemoeller, M. 11
Nimitz, Admiral C. 14
Northcliffe, Lord 34
Novosti, D. 74
Nuremberg Rally (1935) 39
Nuremberg Trial 73

October 62
OWI (Office of War Information) 2, 3, 6, 122, 126, 130, 131, 132, 133, 136, 137, 138, 139, 148
Oradour massacre 41
Ozmanczyk, E.J. 59

Papen, F. von 36
Paramount News 1, 2, 32, 36
Paramount News (British) 43, 104
Paramount Pictures 11
Pathé News 1, 7, 13, 30, 36, 39, 42, 44
Patton, General G. 11, 152
Payot, R. 115
Pearl Harbour 12
Petitpierre, M. 109
Pick, W. 55
Polish Committee of National Liberation 74
Polish Socialist Party 75
Potsdam Conference 53, 56, 131, 138, 148
Proof Positive 43
Puttkammer, Admiral von 91

RKO 1
RKO Pathé 3
Raizman, I. 62, 73
Remer, Major O. 92
Reoccupation of Rhineland 38–9
Ribbentrop, J. von 5
Riefenstahl, L. 177
Robertson, Sir C.G. 49
Rockefeller Centre 15
Rockefeller Foundation 3
Rockefeller, J.D. Jnr 11
Rola-Zymierski, General 76, 78
Roosevelt, President F.D. 24, 79, 149
Rundstedt, K.R.G. von 7, 13

Sanders, G. 4
Sauckel, Gauleiter F. 91
Sauer, W. 92
Schell, M. 52
Schenck, N.M. 11
Scherk 91
Schieder, T. 171
Schleicher, General 36
Schoerner, Lieutenant Colonel 94
Schörner, General 92
Schramm, P.E. 171
Schussnig, Baroness 13
S.S. (Schutz Staffein) 4, 43, 45, 72, 92, 112, 116
Shneiderov, M. 63
Siegfried Line 29
Speer, A. 91
Stahlhelm 36
Stalin, J. 40, 58, 59, 60, 149
Starzynski, S. 71
State Department, US 8
Steevens, G.W. 33
Stettinius, E. 9
Svensk Film News 74

Taglische Rundschau 55
Tate, M. 42
Telpuchowski, B.S. 59
Tennessee Valley Authority 14, 123
The True Glory 6
Thyssen, F. 13
Torment of Berlin, The 73

Index

Triumph of the Will, 4, 177
Truman, President 9
Tunisian Victory 6
Tydén ve Filmu 74

UFA 174
Unio News 74
United Nations Relief and Rehabilitation Administration 78, 125
United States Army Signal Corps 2
Universal 1, 2, 4, 7, 8, 12, 13, 14, 16, 152
Unknown War, The 51, 62

Vansittart, Lord 35, 40, 42
Veit, C. 4
Vergeltung (V1 and V2 missiles) 90
Versailles, Treaty of 38
Victory in the West 4

Vorobev, F. 59

War Department 3, 5
Warner Bros 4, 11
Warner, H.M. 11
Warsaw Fights 71
Warsaw Rising (1944) 74, 75, 77
Wehrmacht 4, 51
Welt im Film 74, Chs. 8, 9
Werner, Dr 55
Wilkinson, E. 45
Wittmann, SS Sturmfuhrer 92
Wlassow, General 94
WNBT 3
Wohl, S. 72
Wortmann 91

Yalta Conference (1945) 24, 78, 119, 124, 126, 131, 149

Zhukov, Marshal G. 50, 52, 53, 54, 61, 150
Zukor, A. 11

For Product Safety Concerns and Information please contact our EU representative GPSR@taylorandfrancis.com
Taylor & Francis Verlag GmbH, Kaufingerstraße 24, 80331 München, Germany

www.ingramcontent.com/pod-product-compliance
Lightning Source LLC
Chambersburg PA
CBHW070610300426
44113CB00010B/1482